Northrop Frye:
Eastern and Western Perspectives

Northrop Frye: Eastern and Western Perspectives

Edited by
Jean O'Grady
and Wang Ning

UNIVERSITY OF TORONTO PRESS
Toronto Buffalo London

© University of Toronto Press Incorporated 2003
Toronto Buffalo London
Printed in Canada

ISBN 0-8020-3720-8

Frye Studies

Printed on acid-free paper

National Library of Canada Cataloguing in Publication

Northrop Frye : eastern and western perspectives / edited by
Jean O'Grady and Wang Ning.

(Frye studies)
Includes bibliographical references and index.
ISBN 0-8020-3720-8

1. Frye, Northrop, 1912–1991 – Criticism and interpretation.
2. Frye, Northrop, 1912–1991 – Appreciation – China.   I. O'Grady,
Jean, 1943–   II. Ning, Wang   III. Series.

PN75 F7 N67 2003   801'.95'092   C2002-903274-1

This book has been published with the help of a grant from the
Michael G. DeGroote family.

University of Toronto Press acknowledges the financial assistance
to its publishing program of the Canada Council for the Arts and the
Ontario Arts Council.

University of Toronto Press acknowledges the financial support for
its publishing activities of the Government of Canada through the
Book Publishing Industry Development Program (BPIDP).

Contents

Foreword

I first visited China in July 1976, two months before the end of the Cultural Revolution. The country's universities were in a state of almost complete disarray, with faculty members sent into exile in the country or otherwise prevented from doing their academic work. For most students, sloganeering and rampaging had replaced study. The physical conditions of the campuses were squalid or worse. A generation of Chinese intellectual life had been largely squandered and an enormous task of reconstruction lay before those willing to take up the challenge. Critical consciousness, and the expression of real thought and creative imagining, had been stifled by political propaganda. It had become clear to thoughtful people that only after the obsessive ideological commitments of the Cultural Revolution were silenced would a genuine cultural revolution become possible.

In the almost quarter century since the fanaticism and upheavals of the 1960s and '70s, China has opened itself to the rest of the world. Again it is possible for those of us in other countries to become familiar with Chinese culture and society, even as China itself seeks access to other cultures. Once more the universities of China are becoming centres of genuine learning, not only playing vital roles in the reconstruction of a great country but exercising positive cultural influences in the wider world. Perhaps understandably, it was Western technology, capital investment, and business management expertise that China first looked for from the West. As president of McMaster University in Canada from 1980 to 1990, I was privileged to help facilitate part of that interchange. Funded by the Canadian International Development Agency, my university was host to several hundred junior faculty members, each one selected to spend two years in intensive training in our laboratories and then return to build or strengthen key programs in their home universities. Most of those visitors were involved in scientific and technological disciplines, especially in matters like iron and steel making, but there were a handful in the health sciences and a few, a very few, in the humanities and social sciences. At the same time, our Faculty of Business was responding energetically to requests from China to establish programs in business administration in that country. A decade later, China is vigorously working towards membership in the World Trade Organization. As a professor of English literature interacting with Chinese colleagues both in Canada and China, I often wished that China and the government of Canada would show a comparable zeal in helping the two countries become acquainted with each other in the ways made possible only through the humanities and social sciences. That now appears to be happening, as students and faculty members in these disciplines, in significant numbers, move back and forth between China and other countries, partially hampered by linguistic, social, and financial obstacles, but persisting nevertheless and making progress.

In October 1993, at the invitation of Peking University, I made my sixth trip to China, to lecture and give a graduate seminar on Northrop Frye. It was my first visit there as a scholar and professor of the humanities rather than a senior administrative officer of a university. Given the eminence and importance of Frye and the stature of Peking University, the invitation was an honour and provided a fascinating opportunity. I found the twenty-one graduate students admitted to the seminar keen and alert, and they delved deeply into the assigned text, *The Modern Century*. I learned that a growing number of faculty members in China were genuinely interested in Frye and his work. One of those individuals was Wang Ning, editor with Jean O'Grady of this extraordinary cross-cultural volume. Professor Wang was busy at the time helping to organize the first international conference in China about Frye, held the following year. That conference was succeeded by a second, organized by Wu Chizhe, in 1999, out of which have come Dr O'Grady's paper and several of the other contributions to this volume. A third Frye conference is in the early planning stages. These animated meetings of thinkers from several countries are the internationally visible manifestations of an intense ongoing program in China of reading, translating, teaching, publishing, and writing about this major thinker and student of the human imagination. Why is Northrop Frye the intellectual figure from the West who, perhaps after Marx, is attracting such attention? Readers of the papers in this volume will probably find themselves formulating their own answers to the question. As a long-time Frye scholar and general editor of his Collected Works, I think, and hope, that his attractiveness in China arises, at least in part, from what he says about myth and concern, about the ways in which the imaginative or hypothetical possibilities articulated in the human arts and sciences can become the charter of our freedoms, even while making possible concerned, responsible citizenship in the world.

ALVIN A. LEE
Professor and President Emeritus, McMaster University
General Editor, Collected Works of Northrop Frye

Acknowledgments

A somewhat different version of this collection has been published in China as *New Directions in N. Frye Studies* (Shanghai: Foreign Language Education Press, 2001). We thank editor-in-chief Wang Tongfu for his generous permission to produce a revised North American edition. For aid in its publication, we gratefully acknowledge financial support, through McMaster University, from the Michael G. DeGroote family. We are also indebted to the two anonymous readers of the manuscript for the University of Toronto Press, who provided useful suggestions for its improvement, and to Allyson May, who copy-edited the manuscript for the Press. Marc Plamondon checked some of the notes with his usual efficiency. For permission to reproduce the covers of Chinese translations of Frye, we are indebted to the China Social Sciences Publishing House, Peking University Press, Liaoning Educational Press, and Hundred-Flower Literary and Art Press. Robert D. Denham kindly provided copies of these designs from his extensive collection of Frye material. Finally, we thank Alvin A. Lee, general editor of the Collected Works, and Ron Schoeffel of the University of Toronto Press, for their support and encouragement.

Contributors

ROBERT D. DENHAM is John P. Fishwick Professor of English at Roanoke College in Virginia, and bibliographer and editor of Frye.

SANDRA DJWA is professor of English at Simon Fraser University, Burnaby, British Columbia.

MICHAEL DOLZANI is professor of English at Baldwin-Wallace College, Berea, Ohio, and an editor of Frye's unpublished works.

GRAHAM NICOL FORST is professor of English at Capilano College, British Columbia.

GLEN ROBERT GILL is a graduate student in English at McMaster University, Hamilton, Ontario.

JAN GORAK is professor of English at the University of Denver.

GU MINGDONG is assistant professor in the Department of Foreign Languages and Literatures, Rhodes College, Tennessee.

ALVIN LEE is general editor of The Collected Works of Northrop Frye at Victoria University, Toronto, and professor and president emeritus of McMaster University, Hamilton, Ontario.

JEAN O'GRADY is associate editor of The Collected Works of Northrop Frye at Victoria University, Toronto.

JAMES STEELE is adjunct professor of English at Carleton University, Ottawa.

WANG NING is professor of English and Comparative Literature, and director of the Centre for Comparative Literature and Cultural Studies, at Tsinghua University.

THOMAS WILLARD is professor of English at the University of Arizona.

WU CHIZHE is professor of English and former director of the Center for Canadian Studies at Inner Mongolia University.

YE SHUXIAN is a research fellow at the Institute of Literature under the Chinese Academy of Social Sciences.

Abbreviations of Frye's Works

AC	*Anatomy of Criticism*. Princeton: Princeton University Press, 1957
BG	*The Bush Garden: Essays on the Canadian Imagination*. Toronto: Anansi, 1971
CP	*The Critical Path: An Essay on the Social Context of Literary Criticism*. Bloomington: Indiana University Press, 1971
CW	The Collected Works of Northrop Frye. Toronto: University of Toronto Press, 1996–
DG	*Divisions on a Ground: Essays on Canadian Culture*. Ed. James Polk. Toronto: Anansi, 1982
Diaries	*The Diaries of Northrop Frye, 1942–1955*. Ed. Robert D. Denham. Vol. 8 of CW. Toronto: University of Toronto Press, 2001
EI	*The Educated Imagination*. Toronto: CBC, 1963
FI	*Fables of Identity: Studies in Poetic Mythology*. New York: Harcourt, Brace & World, 1963
FS	*Fearful Symmetry: A Study of William Blake*. Princeton: Princeton University Press, 1947
GC	*The Great Code: The Bible and Literature*. New York: Harcourt Brace Jovanovich, 1982
LN	*Northrop Frye's Late Notebooks, 1982–1990; Architecture of the Spiritual World*. Ed. Robert D. Denham. Vols. 5–6 of CW. Toronto: University of Toronto Press, 2000
MC	*The Modern Century*. Toronto: Oxford University Press, 1967
MM	*Myth and Metaphor: Selected Essays, 1974–1988*. Ed. Robert D. Denham. Charlottesville: University of Virginia Press, 1990

NFC   *Northrop Frye in Conversation*. Ed. David Cayley. Concord, Ont.: Anansi, 1992

NFCL   *Northrop Frye on Culture and Literature: A Collection of Review Essays*. Ed. Robert D. Denham. Chicago: University of Chicago Press, 1978

NFF   Northrop Frye Fonds, Victoria University Library

NFR   *Northrop Frye on Religion*. Ed. Alvin A. Lee and Jean O'Grady. Vol. 7 of CW. Toronto: University of Toronto Press, 2000

RW   *Reading the World: Selected Writings, 1935–1976*. Ed. Robert D. Denham. New York: Peter Lang Publishing, 1990

SE   *Northrop Frye's Student Essays, 1932–1938*. Ed. Robert D. Denham. Vol. 3 of CW. Toronto: University of Toronto Press, 1997

SM   *Spiritus Mundi: Essays on Literature, Myth, and Society*. Bloomington: Indiana University Press, 1976

SR   *A Study of English Romanticism*. Chicago: University of Chicago Press, 1968

TBN   *The "Third Book" Notebooks of Northrop Frye, 1964–1972: The Critical Comedy*. Ed. Michael Dolzani. Vol. 9 of CW. University of Toronto Press, 2002

WE   *Northrop Frye's Writings on Education*. Ed. Jean O'Grady and Goldwin French. Vol. 7 of CW. Toronto: University of Toronto Press, 2000

WP   *Words with Power: Being a Second Study of "The Bible and Literature."* New York: Harcourt Brace Jovanovich, 1990

WTC   *The Well-Tempered Critic*. Bloomington: Indiana University Press, 1963

WANG NING

Introduction

Many of the essays included in this volume were selected from among papers delivered at the International Symposium on Northrop Frye Studies held on 15–17 July 1999 at the Inner Mongolia University in Hoh-Hot, China. The other sponsors of this significant event, the second international conference on Northrop Frye held in China, were Victoria University in the University of Toronto, Beijing Language and Culture University, and Shanghai Foreign Language Education Press. Without their support, the conference would not have been the success it was. Although this book brings together papers selected at the invitation of Wang Tongfu, then editor-in-chief of Shanghai Foreign Language Education Press, it is not merely a collection of conference proceedings. The remainder of the essays were solicited by the editors exclusively for the volume. The essays are divided into three parts. The first deals with Frye's theories in general, the second focuses on his thoughts on Canadian literature, and the third contains essays by Chinese scholars reflecting the assimilation of his thought in Chinese scholarship.

The first essay, by Robert D. Denham, is a revision of a paper given at a conference on Frye held in Beijing in 1994. Denham's essay provides a useful introduction to the present volume in that it establishes Frye's knowledge of and appreciation for Eastern thought in general. It also provides a foretaste of the third section, specifically on China. Denham's essay indicates as well an important new direction in Frye studies in its use of Frye's notebooks. Now being published as part of the Collected Works, the notebooks reveal hitherto little-known aspects of Frye's intellectual and spiritual life.

Graham Nicol Forst contributes to the growing study of the origins of Frye's thought, maintaining that Frye's emphasis on the aesthetic function of literary works is greatly influenced by the Kantian tradition. His essay explores the way in which Frye draws out "the most productive and fruitful implications of the transcendental philosophy," maps out for us "the crucial milestones on the critical path," and emphasizes and clarifies "the social and moral implications of Kant's centralization of the aesthetic function."

Jean O'Grady's essay focuses on the question of liberal education and the role of literary studies. The paper was originally given at the Hoh-Hot conference, in the hope that it would be relevant to Chinese educators who want to popularize elementary education and allow higher education to flourish, working towards the building of one or two world famous universities in China in the near future. O'Grady presents Frye as an upholder of the autonomy of the university: for Frye liberal education involves truth that is pursued for its own sake, as opposed to being "pressed into the service of an immediate social aim." The essay then explores the way in which that disinterested truth, as discussed in Forst's essay, is theorized by Frye as serving society.

The next two essays focus on the way in which, in his later work, Frye developed and expanded the notion of the hypothetical in literature that is the basis of its social vision. Glen Robert Gill's essay was delivered in Hoh-Hot to introduce Chinese scholars to *Words with Power*, which has not yet been translated. Gill shows how Frye's reconfiguration of myth criticism in terms of kerygma answers some of the objections made to the *Anatomy* by materialist critics. Far from being "collective utopian dreaming," literature addresses and in some way fulfils primary concerns, material and non-material, through the power of ecstatic metaphor. Gill argues that kerygma is "both the medium and the message of a collective humanistic epiphany."

Michael Dolzani's essay also deals with the revelatory or kerygmatic qualities of literature, as it studies the problem of wish-fulfilment in Frye's criticism from the point of view of "how the patterns of myth and literature inform life as we experience it outside of books." In elaborating a way of understanding comedy in which the happy ending may be seen not as idle wish-fulfilment but as spiritual insight, Dolzani utilizes two perspectives that will be increasingly important in future Frye studies. As an editor, along with Robert Denham, of Frye's unpublished notebooks, he introduces some of Frye's far-reaching speculations that did not achieve final published form. Dolzani's discussion also suggests that the focus in Frye studies is moving from his literary criticism to his interest in levels of consciousness beyond the egocentric—a yogalike interest which, as the essay demonstrates, is shared with Eastern thinkers.

Jan Gorak's essay studies the genesis of Frye's early theory of comedy, as expressed in "The Argument of Comedy" (1949); like Forst, he is interested in establishing an intellectual context. Gorak's discussion of the ideas current among early twentieth-century theorists of comedy such as Bergson, Freud, Edmund Wilson, and H.L. Mencken not only indicates lines of intellectual descent but also highlights the originality of Frye's contribution. Alone among these theorists, who stress in different ways the repressive weight of society, Frye celebrates the comic vision as demonstrating society's capacity to renew itself. Finally, however, Gorak contends, "Frye steps back from the vision of freedom embodied in festive comedy," stressing Prospero's imaginary world over Falstaff's subversive one, and in so doing is typical of immediately post-war criticism.

In the last essay in this section, Wang Ning explores Frye's connection (conscious or unconscious) with, and potential significance to, the current debate on postmodernism and postcolonialism in the broader context of cultural studies. To Wang, Frye was a pioneering figure who addressed many issues which are heatedly discussed among contemporary practitioners of cultural studies. Frye's research on Canadian literature as part of "Commonwealth" or "postcolonial" literature rather than as part of world literature is just one example. As an Oriental scholar standing outside of Canada, Wang offers one reason why Frye's ideas have a continuing relevance. To scholars in China, the legacy of Northrop Frye does not belong only to the Canadian nation or more generally to the West, but should be appreciated by scholars in the West and East alike. Thus, since 1994, two international conferences on Frye studies have been held in a country to which Frye had never been and about which he knew very little, and an ambitious series on Frye studies has been published by two leading Chinese publishers, including not only four of Frye's own books but also a collection of essays about him.

The volume's second section on Frye and Canada opens with Sandra Djwa's essay, which reveals the important role Frye played in the writing of the *Literary History of Canada*. While Frye's two conclusions to the *History* are widely read and celebrated, it is less generally recognized that he was a major collaborator in the whole project and that his writings on Canadian literature provided the rationale and guiding principles of the work. Klinck as general editor adopted the stance of the anthologist in Frye's "Preface to an Uncollected Anthology," somewhere between the ordinary literary critic and the social scientist and constantly aware of the cultural context. Avoiding value judgments, the *Literary History* aimed to provide an inductive survey of all that had been written in Canada. Thus Frye's sense of the importance of the verbal imagination throughout a culture informed this pioneering work of literary scholarship.

Thomas Willard studies the influence of two major works, Frazer's *The Golden Bough* and Spengler's *The Decline of the West*, on Frye's archetypal theory and particularly on his understanding of primitivism in Canadian literature. Frye integrated a number of traditions in forming his own critical theory; hence he is still studied by different schools of criticism today. Williard looks at the way in which Frye employs insights from Spengler and Frazer, along with his own sense of Canada's natural environment and history, to arrive at his persuasive and influential view of Canadian literature.

Concluding the second section, James Steele's essay illustrates the way in which Frye's archetypal theory and theory of modes may be used to illuminate particular works of art, in this case Margaret Atwood's novel *Cat's Eye*. As will be seen in the next section, the practical application of Frye's theory from the *Anatomy* period has been a major preoccupation of Chinese critics.

Issues raised in the third section of this volume may be new to the Western audience, many of whom might well question whether Frye, deeply educated in Western culture, had any connections to China or Chinese culture. If not, then to what extent is Frye's critical theory applicable to studies of Chinese literature? Why are Chinese critics and scholars so interested in Frye's myth-archetypal critical theory? Ye Shuxian's tracing of the origin and development of archetypal critical theory in China may partly answer these questions. First, ancient Chinese literary works are almost all connected to mythology or even derive from mythologies, making it easy to trace the "archetype" of these literary works in accordance with Frye's theory. Second, Frye's theory enables Chinese scholars to re-code those ambiguous old texts from a new perspective, although many scholars of classic Chinese literature resist this procedure. Third, Frye's way of approaching literary works provides Chinese scholars with a broad horizon on which they may scrutinize and compare numerous literary works, both Western and Eastern, in order to reach new conclusions. In this sense, Ye's approach, known as influence study in comparative literature, is useful and valuable to Frye scholarship, especially in Western countries.

Wu Chizhe's discussion points out not only that Frye himself mentions Chinese language and culture in his writings but also that his theory allows Chinese scholars to deal with some old problems in history from a new perspective. Frye was interested in Oriental culture and literature, including Chinese culture and literature, and frequently mentioned Chinese philosophical and literary thinking. However, not knowing the language, he was unable to make a careful study of Chinese literature. If he had, his archetypal critical theory would have been more comprehensive and applicable to literary phenomena in the East as well as the West.

Gu Mingdong's study of Frye's relations with psychoanalysis presents other revelations. Frye was an astute reader of Freud and demonstrates knowledge of him in numerous places in his writings. Gu's analysis of the parallel between Frye's archetypal theory and Freud's psychoanalysis provides the reader with a Chinese perspective on these two theories with regard to their possible application to Chinese literature.

Frye studies have become an international topic of research, extending well beyond Western discourse. Scholars from the West and the East can now discuss common issues in literature and art in general, and the possible application of Frye's critical theory to non-Western literature and culture. If a theory were to be universally applicable, it would illuminate not only literary phenomena in the West, but world literature more generally. I am sure that through the fruitful collaboration and effective dialogue between North American and Chinese Frye scholars, the universal value of Frye's theories will be "rediscovered" in the broader context of East-West comparative studies. As the bibliography of Chinese publications on Frye at the end of the third section shows, this process is already under way. The continuing publication of the Collected Works of Northrop Frye by the University of Toronto Press will enable international Frye scholarship to broaden immeasurably its field of work.

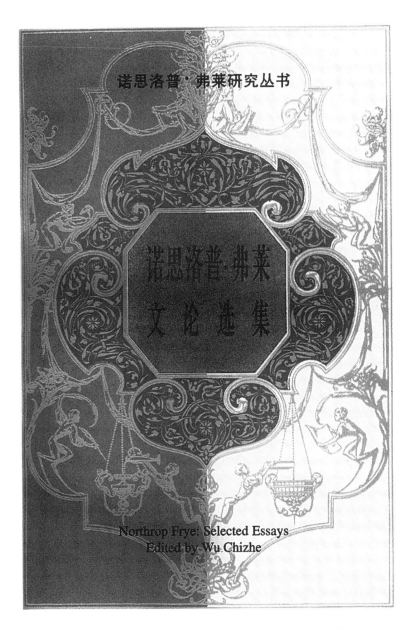

Northrop Frye: Selected Essays. Edited by Wu Chizhe; prefaced by Robert D. Denham, William H. New, and Richard King. Beijing: China Social Sciences Publishing House, 1997.

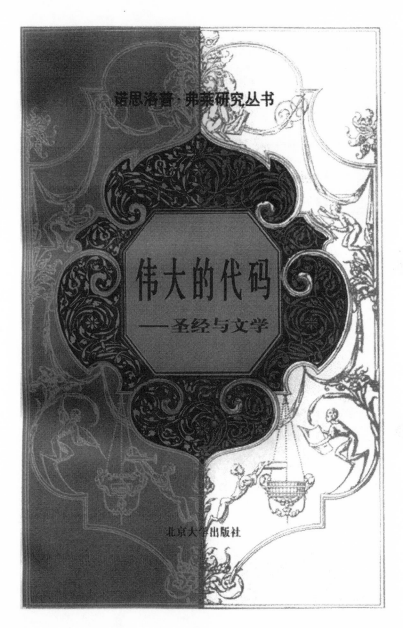

Weidade Daima: Shengjing yu Wenxue [The Great Code: The Bible and Literature].
Translated by Hao Zhenyi, Fan Zhenguo, and He Chengzhou. Beijing: Peking
University Press, 1998.

牛津精选
Oxford

NORTHROP
FRYE

NEW EDITION
The
Modern
Century

〔加〕诺斯洛普·弗莱著

盛 宁译

现代百年

辽宁教育出版社
牛津大学出版社

Xiandai bainian. Tranlated by Sheng Ning. Shenyang: Liaoning Educational
Press; Hong Kong: Oxford University Press, 1998.

Northrop Frye:

批 评 的 解 剖
ANATOMY OF CRITICISM

[加]诺恩洛普·弗莱

2000 年 7 月

Piping de Jiepou. Translated by Chen Hui, Yuan Xianjun, and Wu Weiren; revised by Wu Chizhe and annotated by Wu Chizhe and Robert D. Denham. Tianjin: Hundred-Flower Literary and Art Press, 2000.

Frye as Theorist

ROBERT D. DENHAM

Frye and the East: Buddhist and Hindu Translations

Frye was always forthright in acknowledging the significance of the "mythological framework" he inherited. He was inescapably conditioned, he says, by the "cultural envelope" of the Classical and Christian traditions of Western culture, the Methodist heritage of his upbringing, and his white, male, middle-class identity. The antifoundationalists, along with others more interested in difference than identity, refer fashionably to this conditioning as a "social construction." The implication has often been that Frye is unable to step outside his Western heritage to take a broader and more inclusive view of the world, rendering the structure of his thought insular, ethnocentric, and outmoded. Thus Jonathan Culler attacks Frye for being a dogmatic religious ideologue and Terry Eagleton berates him for being a middle-class liberal and Christian humanist.[1] While there can be no doubt that Frye is rooted in the tradition of Western liberal humanism in its Classical and Christian forms, I want to suggest that he was more influenced by the East than is commonly imagined and thus able not only to engage worlds outside his particular cultural envelope but also to assimilate their religious principles into his own world-view.

While Frye's readers will be aware of passing references to the religion and culture of the East—from comments on Zen Buddhism in *Fearful Symmetry* at the beginning of his career to those on Eastern techniques of meditation in the posthumously published *Double Vision*—no one would take such occasional comments to be significant features of Frye's grand vision.[2] In a 1989 interview Frye remarked that he thought the vogue for Oriental religions was at its peak about twenty years ago, when the students were desperately looking for something but were not in the mood to be sent back to Sunday school. I remember around that time one of my colleagues was listening to me lecture, when a hippie who had come in off the street and who was sitting beside her, squirming and fidgeting, said, "When is he going to get to Eastern symbolism?" My colleague said, "I don't know that he's going to. This is advertised as a course in the Bible." So he just signed off at that point. But you often get a very cleaned-up interest in Eastern religions. You get hippies going to India looking for yogic ecstasies and ignoring the poverty, the illiteracy, the violence, the things the Indians themselves have to struggle with. These cleaned-up versions, extracting religion from the culture from which it is embedded, strike me as a bit phony. That's not to say, of course, that we cannot learn infinitely and indefinitely from Oriental religions. Of course we can. But we have to remember the rock from which we were hewn, which is something else again. (*NFC*, 194–5)

The message here is twofold: first, one can learn from Eastern religions but the process requires total immersion in Eastern culture; and, second, total immersion is very difficult for Westerners. Again, Frye's published work reveals clearly that he was the product of Western culture. The references in Frye to things Eastern are, we might imagine, only to be expected from someone with his breadth of interests. But although Frye never experienced total immersion, he did, I believe, wade more deeply into Eastern waters than his public writings suggest. His knowledge of Eastern culture, especially Eastern religions, is not inconsequential, and his interest in Buddhism and yoga was at times an intense preoccupation. We see this most clearly in his notebooks, currently making their way into print, and his diaries.

It has become increasingly clear that the narrative pattern of Frye's grand imaginative journey is that of a quest romance. Its goal, spiritual vision, draws upon a number of traditions: some are mystical and esoteric, others are decidedly Christian; some are imaginatively visionary, others are conceptual; some are rooted in the Everlasting Gospel, others in the *philosophia perennis*. Frye spent his whole life trying to find the right verbal formulas for representing the quest, searching for a proper rhetoric to say what he felt compelled to say. His interest in things Eastern is a significant part of this effort.

It is difficult to say precisely when Frye first began reading Eastern religious texts. A few references to Buddhism appear in several of the twenty or so papers Frye wrote as a student at Emmanuel College, but his knowledge of Eastern religions at this time came primarily from *The Golden Bough* and Spengler's *Decline of the West*, which, along with the Bible, were his sacred texts in theology school. The first Eastern text Frye seriously contemplated seems to have been the *Lankavatara Sutra*, which he came to in the mid-1940s by way of Peter Fisher, one of his students. Frye remarks that he had earlier been misled in his reading of Oriental philosophy by bad translations, but that thereafter his and Fisher's conversations "took the form of a kind of symbolic shorthand in which terms from Blake and from Mahayana Buddhism were apt to be used interchangeably."[3] These dialogues were frequent: in the 1940s Frye and Fisher met every Monday to drink beer and talk about litera- ture, philosophy, and religion, and Frye often recorded the essence of their conversations in his diaries, especially in his 1949 diary.[4] In any event, sometime during the 1940s Frye first encountered the *Lankavat- ara Sutra*, a copy of which Fisher gave him, as well as the *Avatamsaka Sutra*, which he came to by way of D.T. Suzuki's *Essays in Zen Buddhism* and *Studies in the Lankavatara Sutra*.[5] It was during this decade as well that Frye first read *The Tibetan Book of the Dead* and Patanjali's *Yoga-Sutra*. Frye's interest in the sacred texts of the East is recorded primarily in Notebook 3, which dates from 1946 to 1948.[6] On the flyleaf of this notebook Frye wrote *Paravritti*, Sanskrit for "the highest wave of thought," but for Frye "a turning around" or "reversal."[7] What was it about these Eastern texts that appealed to Frye? We can perhaps begin to formulate an answer to this question by surveying his diary and notebook references to the sutras of Mahayana Buddhism, the Bud- dhist conception of bardo in *The Tibetan Book of the Dead*, and certain practices of Hindu yoga.

The Mahayana Sutras

The *Lankavatara Sutra*, which means literally "Sutra on the Descent to Sri Lanka," is a Mahayana Buddhist text, translated from Sanskrit into Chinese in the fifth century, which stresses inner enlightenment, the erasing of all dualities, the concept of emptiness, and the truth of *Cit- tamatra* or "mind only." The *Avatamsaka Sutra*, an extravagant and often ponderous text, provided the foundation for the Chinese Hua- yen school of Buddhism initiated by Tu-shun (or Fashun) in the sixth century. In India the *Avatamsaka* (Sanskrit for "flower ornament") was the central sacred book of the Yogacharins and eventually of the sect known as Kegon in Japan. This sutra stresses the identity of all things or the interpenetration of all elements in the world. The doctrine of interpenetration was, as we shall see, compelling for Frye. While the *Avatamsaka* is the only Mahayana text he mentions in his published work—there is a single reference in *The Great Code* to D.T. Suzuki's commentary on interpenetration (168)—Frye recorded his observations on one or the other of the two sutras in forty-eight entries in his diaries and notebooks. For all their complexity[8] the *Lankavatara* and the *Avatamsaka Sutras* became for Frye, as he says in one notebook, "vade mecums of practical meditation" (*LN*, 714). Both sutras advance a form of absolute idealism, which has a Western analogue in Hegel's *Phenomenology of Spirit*, but the *Avatamsaka* presents it in a mode that is often concrete and metaphoric, whereas the *Lankavatara* favours the abstract (Hegelian) mode over the symbolic.

Sometimes Frye seems to find in the sacred texts of the East analogies of Western ideas. For instance, he observes that the Protestant conception of conversion, which differs from the straight line of Dante's *Commedia* or the parabola of rise and descent in tragedy, is like the vortex of transformation in the *Lankavatara*: they "point in the same direction" (3.45). At other times Eastern and Western conceptions seem to be virtually identical for Frye. In the Buddhist conception of *maya* (the illusion of the phenomenal world which the unenlightened mind takes as the only reality) Frye finds both an affirmation and a denial of the law of noncontradiction, and he remarks that the "Christian conception of evil as the product of original sin & a fallen world is really exactly the same: the same combination of something that exists & yet cannot exist" (3.105). When identity rather than similarity underlies the East-West conjunction, the result is an insight that helps to define Frye's own position. In such cases Eastern ideas are constitutive.

Frye is wary of framing the East-West connections in philosophical terms. He is attracted to the *Lankavatara* idea of *Cittamatra* (mind-only), but he finds that it "suggests pantheism to a Western mind" and that the doctrine of *Vijñaptimatra*, put forth by the rival Yogacara school of Buddhism, is "very like Platonic idealism" (3.111).[9] What draws Frye towards the *Lankavatara* is the presentation of its message in a kind of primary-phase language based on identity. The *Lankavatara*, he says, "does not teach a doctrine but inculcates a mental attitude" (ibid.). Thus, it stresses not simply hearing or understanding the word but "actually possessing it" (3.112), possession being one of the common metaphors in Frye for metaphor itself, the complete identity achieved when A internalizes B and becomes one with it. The ultimate Christian metaphor for Frye is the Incarnation, and the *Lankavatara Sutra* is "based on a conception of a divine man" (3.111). "I can take no religion seriously, for reasons I don't need to go into here, that doesn't radiate from a God-Man, & so Christ & Buddha seem to me the only possible starting points for a religious experience I don't feel I can see over the top of ... I'm just beginning to wonder if Protestantism & Zen—not as churches but as approaches to God-Man—aren't the same thing, possessed by the same Saviour" (3.110). This, again, is not a matter of doctrine but of mental attitude:

> When we read the history of Western philosophy we pass Aristotle & Plotinus & then find ourselves suddenly reading about "Christian" philosophers. Where did these Christians come from? Well, from Jesus. And what was his philosophical position? Well, he didn't exactly have one. Philosophy disappears into a vortex at that point. So with the Buddha here, who stigmatizes every attempt to make him define his "position" as "materialism," who answers all Mahamati's 108 questions by ignoring them all completely & then trying to make him grasp the mental attitude that will make answering them unnecessary. Buddha is not Mephistopheles, promising esoteric knowledge in exchange for your soul, & you can't talk to him in those terms. The Buddha is very subtle in analyzing the unconscious motive of panic in the desire to understand. Knowledge grasped at out of fear & bewilderment of ignorance remains grasped knowledge, that is, imperfect & inadequate knowledge. (3.113)

Frye writes in the 1940s that he wishes he could find a good translation of "the Avatamsaka, or enough of it, & one of another Sutra, perhaps the one on the void [the *Diamond Sutra*], [so that he] might do a series of three essays called 'certain wise men'" (3.162). What so intrigued Frye about the *Avatamsaka* was the idea of interpenetration, an idea that he called on repeatedly over the years, usually in an effort to explain the concrete universal or the unity of the one and the many. The concept of interpenetration takes many forms in Frye's published and unpublished writings—philosophical, social, metaphorical—but its primary context is spiritual vision. Frye associates the paradox of interpenetration, as I have attempted to show in another essay, "with anagogy, kerygma, apocalypse, spiritual intercourse, the vision of plenitude, the everlasting gospel, the union of Word and Spirit, the new Jerusalem, and atonement."[10] In four different notebooks, spanning almost a decade, Frye refers to his "Avatamsaka hunch" (*TBN*, 30, 231; 13.92; 18.123), which is a hunch about the universal decentralized vision and identity of interpenetration.

The sole reference to the *Avatamsaka* in Frye's published work has to do with interpenetration. It appears in the context of Frye's explaining what he means by "the expanding of vision through language" and what Blake means by seeing the world in a grain of sand. This, Frye writes,

> would lead us to something like the notion of interpenetration in Buddhism, a type of visionary experience studied more systematically in Oriental than in Western traditions. The great Buddhist philosopher D.T. Suzuki gives an account of it in his study of the Avatamsaka or Gandavyuha Sutra, the Buddhist scripture that is most fully devoted to it. Suzuki speaks of it as "an infinite mutual fusion or penetration of all things, each with its individuality yet with something universal in it." As he goes on to speak of the "transparent and luminous" quality of this kind of vision, of its annihilating of space and time as we know them, of the disappearance of shadows (see Song of Songs 2:17) in a world where everything shines by its own light, I find myself reminded more and more strongly of the Book of Revelation and of similar forms of vision in the prophets and the gospels. (GC, 167–8)

Frye is uncertain about his first encounter with the idea of interpenetration. The poetic counterpart of propositional language, he writes in a late notebook, "is what I've been calling interpenetration, the concrete order in which everything is everywhere at once. Whitehead's SMW [*Science and the Modern World*] says this in so many words: I must have got it from there originally, though I thought I got it from Suzuki's remarks about the Avatamsaka Sutra" (LN, 616).[11] Whitehead may have been the primary philosophical source (Frye also encountered the idea in Coleridge and Plotinus),[12] but the *Avatamsaka* was clearly his primary spiritual source: practically all of the nineteen references to this sutra in the notebooks relate to interpenetration.

As for the essays on "certain wise men," Frye goes on to say that "The Preface would explain that I know nothing first-hand about oriental culture, & that experts who do don't need to read me. I'm just trying an experiment in the translation of ideas. That today we find both a lot of false antitheses about Eastern vs. Western thought & a general vague hunch that these antitheses *are* false" (3.162). Perhaps the phrase "an experiment in the translation of ideas" best describes what Frye is doing in Notebook 3. He is trying to translate rather than reconcile. A year after he wrote this notebook Frye reviewed F.S.C. Northrop's *The Meeting of East and West* in the *Canadian Forum*. Northrop's goal was somehow to unify the Eastern "immediate apprehension of experience," which he called "aesthetic," with the Western "theoretical construction made from experience." Frye thought that such a synthesizing project was doomed to fail, and he concluded the review by say-ing, "I imagine that whatever an Oriental philosopher tries to tell us about his Tao, his Citta, his Nirvana, his Brahman, he is also telling us, in Eastern language, that an intellectual and cultural synthesis that gets everything in and reconciles everyone with everyone else is an attempt to build a Tower of Babel, and will lead to confusion of utter-ance" (*NFCL*, 110).

But we must consider the gift of tongues as well as their confusion, as we see in Frye's final "translation" from the *Sutra on the Descent to Sri Lanka*:

> The Lankavatara says there are three levels of understanding: imaginary or materialistic, interpenetrative, & detached. Learning a language by labori-ously boning it up is knowledge on the first stage; getting a swift intuitive knack or flair for languages belongs to Paratantra [literally, beyond the con-tinuum]: the gift of tongues is on the third level.
>
> One thing I didn't have too clearly in mind when I wrote the Blake book is that the total imaginative power we feel in a language or a religion is, like the Bible, sifted by tradition so that it is a cultural product, & a cultural product suggests imaginative totality as no one man can ever do. The indi-vidual's powers are limited & predictable, or if they aren't he soon passes out of range. But a big library really has the gift of tongues & vast potencies of telepathic communication. You can't "substitute art for religion" without making art include religion, & so recovering it from the individual or ego-centric sphere. That's really what I'm trying to do.
>
> The 18th c. English philosophers, reflecting a mercantile civilization, thought of ideas as possessed things; Plato, reflecting a community, thought of them as an order to be entered. We have to disentangle ourselves from such subjects & objects. (3.127–9)

Commentary on these entries would require a small book: the detached vision, the gift of tongues, imaginative totality, escaping the ego-centric sphere, moving beyond subject-object distinctions, interpenetration, the three levels of understanding—these are themes Frye circled around for the next forty-five years, and in order to find the right verbal formulas he continually translated in his notebooks between East and West.

Bardo

In Mahayana Buddhism, bardo, a concept that dates back to the second century, is the in-between state—that period that connects the death of individuals with their subsequent rebirth. The *Bardo Thödol*, literally "Liberation through Hearing in the In-Between State," distinguishes six bardos, the first three connected with the suspended states of birth, dream, and meditation and the last three with the forty-nine-day process of death and rebirth. In *The Tibetan Book of the Dead*, the principal source for Frye's speculations on bardo,[13] the focus is on the second three states: the bardo of the moment of death, when a dazzling white manifests itself; the bardo of supreme reality, in which five colourful lights appear in the form of mandalas; and the bardo of becoming, characterized by less brilliant light. The first of these, Chikhai bardo, is the period of ego-loss; the second, Chonyid bardo, is the period of hallucinations; the third period, Sidpa bardo, is the period of re-entry.

In recounting one of his Monday sessions with Peter Fisher in 1949, Frye writes, "we went on to discuss the life-Bardo cycle. Normally we are dragged backwards through life & pushed forwards through Bardo, & attempt to find some anastasis at the crucial points, or else go through a vortex or Paravritti which leads us, not to escape, but to implement charity by going forwards through life, as Jesus did, & withdraw in retreat from Bardo" (*Diaries*, 118). Here we have the fundamental dialectic so often encountered in Frye: the raising up or removal to another level, represented by bardo, or the vortical descent, or turning away from what bardo represents. Bardo is a subject Frye frequently returns to in his diaries (eighteen entries) and notebooks (sixty-five entries), although he seldom mentions it in his published work.[14] But what exactly does bardo mean for Frye?

In the 1940s Frye entertained the notion of writing a bardo novel, the point of view being that of a dead narrator looking at the world—a supernatural novel, but one based on intellectual paradox and without morbidity (30m.20). By 1949 he had begun to find some models: Robert Nathan's *Portrait of Jennie*, a romantic fantasy about a young girl who, defying time, mysteriously vanishes and reappears, and Henry James's *A Sense of the Past*, an unfinished ghost story in which characters disappear from one century and resurface in another. But when Frye discovers Charles Williams's *All Hallows' Eve*, a supernatural tale that explores a parallel world, with its characters, some dead and some alive, interacting with our own, he temporarily loses his ambition to write a bardo novel: Williams has already done it. In 1962, however, the idea is resurrected. "How the hell would one write a good Bardo novel?" Frye asks, and he proceeds to outline in some detail the narrative of a character who prepares for death, dies, and wakes up in bardo not knowing that he had died but living in some vision of a liberated world. But just as *All Hallows' Eve* had earlier dissuaded Frye from pursuing his fiction-writing project, so now the appearance of Katherine Anne Porter's *Ship of Fools* (1962) makes him realize that he has again been pre-empted. Thus he concludes, "my Bardo novel is not something to write, but a *koan* to think about and exercise the mind" (2.18).[15] And exercise his mind he does: once he has abandoned the novel project, Frye engages in a series of "translations."

Two aspects of bardo proved to be enigmas for Frye: its relation of Purgatory, which he worries about in a dozen or so notebook and diary entries,[16] and what he refers to as chess-in-Bardo, a "will-o-wisp I've been chasing for thirty years." The in-between state of Purgatory is the obvious Christian link: "Purgatory was invented by the R.C.Ch. [Roman Catholic Church] to bring Bardo into Xy [Christianity]" (*Diaries*, 131). Frye appears to see Purgatory finally not as a translation but as an analogy. It turns out to be too Catholic, and Catholicism always raises a red flag for Frye. He says, in any event, that Purgatory is "an illegitimate adaptation of Bardo" (*Diaries*, 142) and that bardo as a "hyperphysical form of the Church" leaps over Purgatory by virtue of the vortex-creed of Protestantism (31.52).[17] As for the cryptic phrase "chess-in-Bardo," Frye associates chess throughout the notebooks and diaries with the theme of ascent and the world of romance—what he calls the Eros archetype.[18] Solving the "chess-in-Bardo problem," he writes, "will give some indication of what it feels like to live in a totally mythical universe" (*TBN*, 56). Frye circles around the "problem" throughout his notebooks, associating chess-in-bardo with the *agon* or contest, with the recognition scenes in *Alice in Wonderland*, *The Tempest*, and *Finnegans Wake*, and with a vision opposite from that of the dice-throw in Mallarmé (the Adonis archetype). By the time he came to write *The Secular Scripture* (1976) Frye had caught up with the *ignis fatuus* he had been tracking since the 1940s. In that book he clarifies the phrase "chess-in-bardo" in a brief commentary on *Alice in Wonderland*:

> Alice passing through the looking-glass into a reversed world of dream language is also going through a descent. ... Before long however we realize that the journey is turning upwards, in a direction symbolized by the eighth square of a chessboard, where Alice becomes a Psyche figure, a virginal queen flanked by two older queens, one red and one white, who bully her and set her impossible tasks in the form of nonsensical questions. Cards and dice ... have a natural connection with themes of descent into a world of fatality; chess and other board games, despite *The Waste Land*, appear more frequently in romance and in Eros contexts, as *The Tempest* again reminds us.

As Alice begins to move upward out of her submarine mirror world she
notes that all the poems she had heard have to do with fish, and as she
wakes she reviews the metamorphoses that the figures around her had
turned into. (155–6)

Twice Frye writes that completing *Anatomy of Criticism* left him free
to engage in free-wheeling speculations about bardo (*TBN*, 190; 20.10),
to move from structure to spirit and vision. What then is bardo? It is a
link, to use one of Frye's favourite words, to a number of features in
what he calls his "metaphysical cosmology" (*TBN*, 21). It is a link with
the reconciliation that emerges from the *agon* (*TBN*, 150; 14.40), with
"the opportunity for the inspired act" (*Diaries*, 131), with the timeless
moment (14.31), with a "plunge into another order of being" (2.19),
with the point of epiphany (*TBN*, 150; 31.85), with "the archetypal
dream-state achieved after death" (33.20), and with Blake's Beulah.
Frye almost always refers to bardo in a telic sense. Bardo does not
mark the end of the quest, as the dozen linkages with Beulah indicate,
but it is a stage towards that end. Frye ordinarily speaks of bardo as the
stage before Eden or apocalypse (*Diaries*, 561; 11f.90). But if it is a stage
in the universal story, it was also a stage in Frye's own life. Here is the
way he puts it in one of his early notebook entries on the bardo insight
born of negative capability:

The Tibetans say that when you die you get a flash of reality (Chih-kai
[Chik-hai] Bardo) that for everyone except a yogi saint is bewildering &
unrecognizable, whereupon you pass into a plane of hallucination (Chonyid Bardo) & then seek a womb of rebirth (Sidpa Bardo). I don't know about
after death, but it's an excellent account of all other crises of the spirit, & so
may be true of that one. So often it happens in meeting someone who needs
help & can be helped (or encouraged) there comes a sudden flash of the
right thing to do, the courteous & beautiful act, instantly smothered under a
swarm of spawning Selfhood illusions of timidity, laziness, selfishness & the
rest, whereupon the moment of what we rightly call inspiration passes, and
we return to the ordinary level of existence. It's only rarely that we even
recall having such a moment, & perhaps the capacity for having them could
be destroyed. One of the major efforts of all discipline is to unbury the consciousness of the moment that Satan can't find, as Blake calls it. Hence the
importance of achieving spontaneity, Butler's unconsidered control. In
social relationships we always admire the person who acts, to quote Blake
again, from impulse & not from rules, and we assume, however unconsciously, that such impulses can be trained to achieve adequate & accurate

expression. That is perhaps why Jesus stresses the unconsidered life—I'm not thinking of the lily passage so much as the instructions to the apostles not to rehearse their speeches. It is true, however, that the way of achieving such development is to concentrate on the present moment, which implies that all idealization or brooding over the past, and all idealization or worry over the future, are diseases of the soul—hence the lily passage. (3.15)

Yoga

One of the forms of yoga that figures importantly in the notebooks, especially Notebook 3, is that of Patanjali, the founder of the Hindu yoga philosophy in the second century B.C.[19] Patanjali was interested not in metaphysics but in spiritual freedom through physical practices. In the 1940s Frye set out to follow Patanjali's eightfold path, devoting a number of pages of Notebook 3 "to codify[ing] a program of spiritual life" for himself (3.78). He does not get beyond the fourth stage— *pranayama*, the control of breathing—but he outlines in some detail what he proposes to do in the first three stages—*yama* (withdrawal from negative habits), *niyama* (concentration and proper timing), and *asana* (meditative exercises and postures) (3.78–88). Frye yearns for moments of withdrawal and concentrated attention, times when he can turn off what he later calls the incessant babble of the drunken monkey in his mind (*LN*, 161, 326, 481). He looks to Patanjali for almost purely personal reasons, feeling that the *Yoga-Sutra* provides sound advice on how to cleanse the temple of his own psyche, to overcome the timidity and irritability of his cerebrotontic self, to repair the weakness of his body, to defeat inertia, to establish a proper, relaxed rhythm in his life. Although Frye makes his way through only half of the eight stages ("genuine withdrawal, the pratyahara or fifth stage, is away out of my reach as yet" [3.81]), Patanjali nevertheless provides him with an occasion to engage in serious self-reflection and critique. Here the East-to-West translation has to do with his own physical, moral, and mental habits. Frye finds analogues between certain Western ethical principles and Patanjali's *sattva*, the ideal of harmoniousness, uprightness, and composure—the noblest of the three *gunas* or fundamental qualities: "Patanjali says Sattva, Castiglione (or Hoby) grace and recklessness, Aristotle the mean. All three mean what Samuel Butler means when he speaks of complete knowledge as unconscious knowledge. The first stage of awareness is a 'morbid' self-consciousness of which schizophrenia is the opposite, as lunacy is the opposite of creating forms & conditions of existence & atheism the opposite of secular mysticism.

Then comes, with practice and a continuous relentless analysis, a gradual overcoming of the rigidity begotten by this self-consciousness"
(3.7).

But there is a speculative side to Frye's interest in yoga that goes
beyond Patanjali's *raja* or royal yoga, and his less personal speculations provide another example of the East-to-West recreation. "I seem
to be trying," Frye writes, "to interpret as much of the Gospels as possible in Yoga terms" (3.29). Here is one such interpretation:

> The Christian Gospel and Indian Buddhist systems associated with the
> word yoga seem to me to make sense of this process [of liberation from a
> fallen world], & perhaps the same sense. The advantage of using the latter is
> that Hindu Buddhist conceptions have for us fewer misleading associations
> of ideas left over from childhood, and the thunder of their false doctrines is
> less oppressive in our ears than the thunder of ours ... When Jesus speaks of
> "righteousness" the word is an English word ... which in turn translates an
> Aramaic word I don't know translating a concept with a Hebrew back-
> ground. I have to recreate it into something more like "rightness," but think
> how clear such a word as Tathagatca is![20] (3.4)

Frye is speaking here of Bhakti yoga, the path to the devout love of
God.[21] He associates Bhakti with both militant monasticism in Christianity and with Western mysticism, and finds Bhakti to be wanting
because it is too partial and fragmentary, too much removed from the
world (3.29–33). It is "the expanded secular monastery I want," Frye
announces, adding that "there isn't much for me in high Bhakti, &
Jnana if not Mantra ... is my road" (3.34, 40). He says little about Jnana
yoga, but unlike Bhakti, which relies on intuition and which for Frye
remains on the Beulah level of existence, Jnana is the yoga of the intellect, in a Platonic or Shelleyan sense. "Jnana" in Sanskrit means "to
know," and it has to do with both general knowledge and spiritual
wisdom or illumination. Mantra is the form of yoga that aims to
achieve union with God through the repetition of God's name. Given
the stress Frye places upon the repetitive rhythm of practice and habit,
one can understand how he would be drawn to the principle, at least,
underlying Mantra yoga. "Yoga," he says, "attaches great importance
to "muttering" ritual forms (dharani) and to the working word, the
mantra or verbum mirificum." He finds a Western analogue in the discipline of listening to music without any sense of "panic & laziness"
(3.9).

Frye's ultimate problem with the yogas of any school is that they have no place for art and no real theory of creation. He thus proposes to develop one, which he calls, reversing Patanjali's terms, Sutra-Yoga. Such a yoga, Frye says, "is identical with what I have been calling anagogy" (3.47), a unifying principle that spiritualizes the law (3.63). He explains the growing interest in poets such as Rilke and Rimbaud as stemming from their having made "a yoga out of art"; they "have employed art as a discipline of the spirit that takes one all the way. Rimbaud is the great denier & Rilke the great affirmer of this aspect of art" (3.49).

Towards the end of Notebook 3 Frye returns to the sense of calm watchfulness he finds in Patanjali, combining it, in a rare third-person reference to his own approach to the life of the spirit, with the change in consciousness that is always for Frye the end of the universal quest:

> The wind bloweth where it listeth, and the unconscious will is not on the same time clock as the conscious one, the S of U [Spectre of Urthona] which is always getting into a dither every time the clock strikes. We must not *do* things, but let them happen. This is the Chinese *wu wei*, Keats' negative capability, which imitates Milton's God in withdrawing from the causation sequence and simply watching with prescience. In Frye's thought this faithful watching is the literal apprehension of art, the willing suspension of disbelief which is the prelude to all understanding (at least all *detached* understanding). What the consciousness *can* do, perhaps, is take out the obstacles hindering the union of life & consciousness, the Indian yoga, the Chinese Tao (which means "head-going"). (3.151)

In a time when criticism in the Anglo-American world shows signs of collapsing in upon itself, Frye's work more and more moves centrifugally out into the larger world. A substantial part of this global movement is towards the East. The Japanese, Koreans, and Chinese have now translated twenty-six of Frye's books,[22] and there have been three conferences on his work in Korea and China. Just as readers in the East have sought to assimilate Frye's world, so Frye for more than fifty years sought to assimilate the East into his grand encyclopedic vision. My intuition is that this assimilation—what I have called the translation process and what Frye called variously interpretation and recreation—did not merely enrich his thought but helped to shape it as well. We will be in a better position to test this hypothesis once all of Frye's previously unpublished work makes its way into print. My preliminary study by no means exhausts the attraction that Eastern thought had for Frye. His considerable interest in Taoism, for example, remains to be explored. There are scores of speculations in the notebooks about the *I Ching* and the *Tao-te Ching*, and at one point Frye speaks of a projected book on the *I Ching* (*TBN*, 192). In the 1980s we find Frye reading contemporary physicists, such as Fritjof Capra and Ken Wilber, who had an interest in Taoism—"the Tao of physics people," he calls them. But that and other of Frye's Eastern interests, such as Zen, will have to wait for another day: the Ken hexagram is staring me in the face, and that means, the *I Ching* tells me, that it is time to stop.

ACKNOWLEDGMENT

This essay is a revision of an earlier paper on Frye's Eastern connection that appeared in *Foreign Literatures* 1 (1955): 12–15, trans. into Chinese by Shi An Bin.

NOTES

1 Jonathan Culler, "A Critic against the Christians," *TLS*, 23 Nov. 1984, 1327; Terry Eagleton, *Literary Theory: An Introduction* (Minneapolis: University of Minnesota Press, 1983), 199–200.

2 I have listed the major references to Eastern religious and literary texts in Frye's published work in my essay "Interpenetration as a Key Concept in Frye's Vision," in *Rereading Frye: The Published and the Unpublished Works*, ed. David V. Boyd and Imre Salusinszky (Toronto: University of Toronto Press, 1999), 156.

3 Frye, preface to Peter Fisher, *The Valley of Vision: Blake as Prophet and Revolutionary*, ed. Northrop Frye (Toronto: University of Toronto Press, 1961), v. After Fisher graduated from college, he had come to Frye saying that he wanted to do an MA thesis on Blake. As Frye reports, Fisher "nearly walked out again when he discovered that I had not read the *Bhagavadgita* in Sanskrit, which he took for granted that any serious student of Blake would have done as a matter of course" (ibid.).

4 For the Frye-Fisher sessions see *Diaries*, 12, 23, 30 (Buddhist wisdom), 43 (the Rajas-Tamas opposition), 58, 73, 86–7, 97, 98 (Agni Yoga), 108, 109, 114, 117–8 (bardo), 124, 133–5 (Tibetan Buddhism's fear of Bön, Parabrahman, Japanese No drama), 143, 144, 149, 153–4, 157, 172 (Pratyekabuddha), 177, 183, 187, 198, 203–4, 206–7 (Isa Upanishad), 209, 212, 345, and 388.

5 Frye apparently did not have access to the *Avatamsaka Sutra* until forty

years after his initial encounter with it in Suzuki's two volumes. We do know from *LN*, 153, that he was reading the *Avatamsaka* in the late 1980s. His text was almost certainly *The Flower Ornament Scripture: A Translation of the Avatamsaka Sutra*, vol. 1 (1984), trans. Thomas Cleary, an annotated copy of which is in NFF. Cleary's three-volume edition was not published until 1993.

6 References to Frye's unpublished Notebooks, all of which may be found in NFF, will hereafter be made in the form "Notebook number.paragraph number." Thus the reference in the following note to 3.50 denotes Notebook 3, paragraph 50.

7 Frye also translates the word as a return through the vortex, a conversion, and an "epistemological apocalypse." See 3.50, 3.115, 21.82, 21.474, and *Diaries*, 322. Suzuki translates *paravritti* as "revulsion." See D.T. Suzuki, *Studies in the Lankavatara Sutra* (London: Routledge & Kegan Paul, 1930), 72, 105.

8 Frye struggled with these dense texts. "I can't make any sense out of these infernal Sutras," he laments: "they seem designed for people who really can't read" (*LN*, 616). "The initial impression the [*Lankavatara*] Sutra makes on the candid reader [is] of an almost intolerable prolixity & obscurantism" (3.112).

9 Frye draws his account of the similarities and differences between *Cittamatra* and *Vijñaptimatra* from Suzuki's *Studies*, 278–82.

10 Denham, "Interpenetration as a Key Concept," 154–5.

11 The passage from Whitehead: "In a certain sense everything is everywhere at all times. For every location involves an aspect of itself in every other location. Thus every spatio-temporal standpoint mirrors the world." See Alfred North Whitehead, *Science and the Modern World* (New York: New American Library, 1948), 93. Suzuki remarks, in the passage Frye is referring to, that "in the world of the *Gandavyuha* [book 39 of the *Avatamsaka Sutra*] ... individual realities are folded into one great Reality, and this great Reality is found participated in by each individual one. Not only this, but each individual existence contains in itself all other individual existences as such. Thus there is universal interpenetration ... This is not philosophical penetration of existence reached by cold logical reasoning, nor is it a symbolical representation of the imagination. It is a world of real spiritual experience (D.T. Suzuki, *Essays in Zen Buddhism* [New York: Grove Press, 1949], 96).

12 See Denham, "Interpenetration as a Key Concept," 147, 159.

13 Frye had two editions of the *Bardol thödol*, both of which he annotated: *The Tibetan Book of the Dead, or, The After-death Experiences on the Bardo Plane*, 2nd ed., ed. W.Y. Evans-Wentz, trans. Kazi Dawa-Samdup (London: Oxford University Press, 1949); and *The Tibetan Book of the Great Liberation, or, The*

Method of Realizing Nirvana through Knowing the Mind, ed. W.Y. Evans-Wentz (London: Oxford University Press, 1954).

14 I find only three references to bardo in Frye's books and essays: *GC*, 137, *SR*, 63–4, and *MM*, 220–1.

15 On Frye's bardo-novel fantasies, see 2.13–19, and *Diaries*, 129–34.

16 See *Diaries*, 131, 132, 134, 142, and Notebook entries 2.15, 2.16, 3.136, 31.48, 31.52, 31.97, and 35.118.

17 The context of this point is Yeats's view of Purgatory—what Yeats "dimly felt" about Protestantism. But it appears to be Frye's view as well.

18 In the notebooks and diaries there are more than fifty references to chess, most of which speculate on the game as an archetype.

19 Little is known of Patanjali. Whether or not he is the same Patanjali who wrote a celebrated commentary on Panini's grammar is uncertain. He appears not to have authored the sutras but to have compiled them. Scholars date the compilation as occurring sometime between the second century B.C. to the fourth century A.D.

20 Taghagata = "the thus-gone one," i.e., the one who has attained supreme enlightenment.

21 I am uncertain about the source of Frye's knowledge of Bhakti and Jnana yoga. The annotated books in his library on yoga, which I have not yet been able to consult, are *Tibetan Yoga and Secret Doctrines, or, Seven Books of Wisdom of the Great Path*; Chao Pi Ch'en, *Taoist Yoga: Alchemy and Immortality*; Gopi Krishna, *Kundalini: The Evolutionary Energy in Man*; and Patanjali, *The Yoga-Sutra*.

22 There are even three editions of his work in English that have been published especially for Eastern readers: editions of *AC* for Korean and Taiwanese students and an edition of *MC* for Japanese readers.

GRAHAM NICOL FORST

Kant and Frye on the Critical Path

Immanuel Kant and Northrop Frye shared the same over-arching desire to transform their respective disciplines of philosophy and criticism, which they regarded as contaminated by scepticism and subjectivity, into "sciences"—a word Frye used exactly as Kant did, to denote a structured body of knowledge. As a result, the most characteristic work of both thinkers is propaedeutic, both in the common sense of referring to principles that establish the grounds for a procedure or program, and in the etymological sense, from the Greek *paideutikos*, pertaining to teaching. In other words, Kant was writing "metaphilosophy" and Frye "metacriticism" (or "meta-theory" as Hayden White calls it),[1] in that they both believed they were consciously establishing an objective basis upon which philosophy and criticism could proceed, rather than (or, in the case of Frye, along with) practising the disciplines themselves. As Frye said in his 1951 essay "The Archetypes of Literature," "What is at present missing from literary criticism is a coordinating principle, a central hypothesis which, like the theory of evolution in biology, will see the phenomena it deals with as parts of a whole" (*FI*, 9). Six years later, he would repeat this conviction at the beginning of the *Anatomy of Criticism*: "It is time for criticism to leap to a new ground from which it can discover what the organizing or containing forms of its conceptual framework are" (16), which criticism can do only by following, and here Frye quotes Kant directly, a "critical path."[2]

A shared interest in the conditions rather than the consequences of a procedure provides the first "topological" link between these two great thinkers, but the similarities only begin there. Using internal evidence in Frye's writings, my personal conversations with Frye, and my recent examination of annotations in the books of his private library,[3] it is my intention in this paper to reveal how Kant's critical principles, especially those in his *Critique of Judgment*, were adopted and reshaped by Frye in his most characteristic writings. I see my task as that identified by Imre Salusinszky, who suggests that it is less relevant now in Frye studies to defend his "idealism" and "historical transcendence" than to "[find] out where they come from"—to ascertain "their context" and determine "where they can be found in their least diluted version." This project, as Salusinszky correctly adds, "surely leads us straight into Romanticism."[4] As I plan to demonstrate, the path will lead us not only to Blake, Frye's most seminal teacher, but also to the thinker without whom Romanticism "is unthinkable":[5] Immanuel Kant.

In one of his early student compositions, a forty-thousand word essay ambitiously entitled "Romanticism," Northrop Frye concluded that the "matrix" of Romanticism lay in the writings of Immanuel Kant, which "gave Romanticism its *raison d'être*" (*SE*, 35). Frye's particular concern with the connections between Kantianism and English Romanticism is of special interest for the history of literary criticism, for in Frye's oeuvre we see some of the most vital practical ramifications of Kant's aesthetic theory, as they relate to humanism generally and to critical theory specifically. Frye's devolution of Kant's aesthetic theories into a humanist criticism is important for two reasons. First, Kant himself had no particular interest in literary criticism per se: his taste in literature was notoriously shallow (he was fond, for example, of the didactic poetry of Frederick the Great). More to the point, Kant's aesthetic theory served for him a formal rather than a practical purpose, that is, it provided a formal completion to his critical philosophy. So it is to Kant's followers, especially Frye—a practising literary critic with a strong tendency towards idealism and a good knowledge of Kant—that we look to see the critical potential of Kantian aesthetics, allowing us to discover that what is demanded by the necessity of philosophical thought in one can be presented as achievement and act in the other.

One of the most dramatic and recurring images in Blake is that of the blacksmith god Los at the smithy, forging a body for Urizen—that is, fixing in space and time the limits of reason— thereby "Giving a body to Falsehood that it may be cast off for ever."[6] It takes no great stretch of the imagination to see the enormous labour of Blake's near contemporary, Immanuel Kant, as serving in his *Critique of Pure Reason* exactly the same purpose: to limit reason's boundaries in order to assert and

demonstrate the vanity of its invasions into metaphysics. Reason, confined as it is to the "scanty plot and ground" of linear time and three-
dimensional space, clearly cannot broach the concepts of freedom, and
of infinity and eternity, the major terms of moral philosophy and metaphysics. But reason cannot rule out freedom and immortality either,
thus leaving a loophole for the pursuit of a "metaphysics of morals."
As Kant put it, "reason" had to be "abolished" not for the sake of a
sceptical philosophy, but "to make room for faith" (*CPR*, 29). Freedom
had similarly to be rescued from Hume's scepticism to permit the
investigation of reason in practice, or moral philosophy, the subject of
Kant's second critique, the *Critique of Practical Reason*.

The price Kant paid for this (he thought) indispensable separation of
epistemology and ethics is that there appears to be no "link" between
the two. In Kant's own words, philosophy had no way to "provide a
transition" between fact and freedom, between "is" and "ought"—a
subject I will return to later. Kant resolved this problem by claiming in
his third critique, the *Critique of Judgment*, that art can "mediate"
between nature and freedom, a claim which is both bold and historically unique. As Ernst Cassirer says, this claim "touched the nerve of
the entire spiritual and intellectual culture of his [Kant's] time."[7]

Since the late nineteenth and early twentieth centuries, Kantian aesthetics, because of its emphasis on the uniqueness of the aesthetic
object, has often been regarded as a forerunner of aestheticism and the
New Criticism, especially as it was articulated by Allen Tate and
Cleanth Brooks and their mentor, John Crowe Ransom. Ransom
believed Kant to be "the most radical and ultimate spokesman for
poetry that we have had."[8] Northrop Frye's attraction to Kantian aesthetics, however, owed less to its determination of the uniqueness of
the aesthetic object, which Frye thought led to arid rhetorical analysis,
than to Kant's philosophical emphasis on the aesthetic sphere, and its
consequent implications for the creative imagination. It is therefore not
surprising to find the following two passages from Marcuse's *Eros and
Civilization* heavily underlined in Frye's copy: "In the *Critique of Judgement*, the aesthetic dimension and the corresponding feeling of pleasure emerge not merely as a third dimension and faculty of the mind,
but as its *centre*, the medium through which nature becomes suscepti-
ble to freedom, necessity to autonomy"; "The aesthetic 'conformity to
law' links Nature and Freedom, Pleasure and Morality."[9] Or, as Frye
would put it himself in one of his last essays, "Literature as Critique of
Pure Reason," "as soon as we enter the world of design, beauty, play,
and the assimilating of nature and art, we begin to wonder whether

creation itself, rather than the exercising of consciousness within it, is not the primary human activity. The Romantics who followed Kant developed a conception of imagination, designed to express this. Imagination is a constructive, unifying, and fully conscious faculty that excludes no aspect of consciousness, whether rational or emotional" (*MM*, 179).

Essentially, Frye is proposing the same kind of case against Locke as was Kant, or for that matter, Blake and Coleridge, implying, as he does, that only by acknowledging the presence of a creative sensibility at the centre of the aesthetic experience, of positing "an oracular mind 'underneath' the conscious one" (*AC*, 353), can we experience, individually and collectively, "genuine" freedom—that is, "a freedom of the will which is informed by a vision" that "can only come to us through the intellect and the imagination, and through the arts and sciences which embody them, the analogies of whatever truth and beauty we can reach" (*CP*, 133). As Susanne Langer said, in a passage heavily marked and bracketed in Frye's copy of her *Freedom and Form*, "The function of artistic illusion is not 'make-believe,' as many philosophers and psychologists assume, but the very opposite, disengagement from belief—the contemplation of sensory qualities without their usual meanings of 'Here's that chair,' 'That's my telephone,' 'These figures ought to add up to the bank's statement,' etc. The knowledge that what is before us has no practical significance in the world is what enables us to give attention to its appearance as such."[10]

As mentioned earlier, in his first two Critiques Kant had rescued some knowledge of the world and of our moral nature from sceptical philosophy, but at the enormous cost of isolating that knowledge in two apparently irreconcilable realms: the "realm of the concept of nature" and the "supersensible realm of the concept of freedom." Between the two lies, says Kant, a "gulf" which might never be bridged, since "the concept of freedom as little disturbs the legislation of nature as the natural concept influences the legislation through the former."[11] Yet clearly, as Kant stresses, the concept of freedom is "meant" to "actualize" in the world of sense; otherwise, freedom would only be a theoretical, not a practical function (*CJ*, 11, 12). Thus it seems in Kant that man's inexorable destiny is that of Byron's Childe Harold: to stand perpetually on the "Bridge of Sighs" with "a palace and a prison on each hand." That is, man is free, and knows that he is free, from his ability to follow the dictates of duty *à contre coeur*, as Kant demonstrated in the *Critique of Practical Reason*. But at the same time, he can perceive no theoretical possibility of finding in this world a theatre for his ideals; no theoretical hope of transforming what *ought to be* into what *can be* (*CJ*, 12).

Kant's position on this dilemma, as it is defined in the introduction to the *Critique of Judgment*, essentially constitutes what Frye called "The Romantic Myth," or "Kant's riddle" (*SR*, 84).[12] For corresponding to Kant's concept of the theoretical estrangement of man and nature is, in Romanticism, a vision of man as "fallen," fallen not into sin, but into "self-consciousness," into "his present subject-object relation to nature, where, because his consciousness is what separates him from nature, the primary conscious feeling is one of separation" (*SR*, 17–18). And the function of art in this context is, as Frye often said, no less than the "recovery of Paradise" or "the reforging [of] the broken links between creation and knowledge, art and science, myth and concept" (*AC*, 354). As Blake put it, "Poetry, Painting & Music [are] the three Powers in Man of conversing with Paradise, which the flood did not Sweep away."[13] Thus, for Kant, for Romanticism in general, and later for Frye in particular, the uniqueness of art does not isolate it; rather, it is precisely this uniqueness that enables the aesthetic realm to join the sensible with the moral. Frye expressed this concept most eloquently in *The Educated Imagination*: "Literature keeps presenting the most vicious things to us as entertainment, but what it appeals to is not any pleasure in these things, but the exhilaration of standing apart from them and being able to see them for what they are because they aren't really happening. The more exposed we are to this, the less likely we are to find an unthinking pleasure in cruel or evil things" (42). For Kant, the uniqueness of the capacity of the aesthetic judgment to "bridge" the gap between nature and freedom is expressed in two ways. First, such judgments are "disinterested," and second, the objects of such judgments reveal a "purposiveness without purpose." For disinterestedness and obliviousness to purpose guarantee the "purity" of aesthetic judgments; thus, for example, non-Christians can respond positively to a painting of the holy family, or to *Paradise Lost*—or, of course, to the Bible itself.[14]

These concepts are no less crucial in Frye's critical writings than they are in Kant's philosophical works. In fact, the latter formula is often referred to literally by Frye, especially in his late notebooks (e.g., *LN*, 94, 192), and Stephan Körner's definition of "interest" in Kant is one of the very few passages marked off in Frye's copy of Körner's commentary on Kant.[15] To Frye, poetry was above all else "a *disinterested* use of words" (*AC*, 4) and the myths poems articulate are similarly "disinterested" (*CP*, 169), in so far as they "tell stories" rather than advocate behaviour. Thus, "in reading a work of literature, no process of belief ... is involved. What is involved is a continuous process of acceptance" (*MM*, 96). Therefore, criticism is "a disinterested response to a work of literature in which all one's beliefs, engagements, commitments, prejudices, stampeding of pity and terror, are ordered to be quiet. We are now dealing with the imaginative, not the existential, with 'let this be,' not with 'this is'" (*WTC*, 140). In a similar vein, Frye speaks in the *Anatomy of Criticism* of how "the contemplation of a detached [i.e. disinterested] pattern, whether of words or not, is clearly a major source of the sense of the beautiful, and of the pleasure that accompanies it" (74). As he put it in *The Critical Path*, "the critic *qua* critic is not himself concerned but detached. His criteria are those of the myth of freedom, depending on evidence and verification wherever they come into the picture" (99).

Kant's description of art as appearing to us as "purposive without purpose" is equally central to Frye's thinking,[16] as the following observation from "Literature as Critique of Pure Reason" makes clear: "Man's imitation of the sabbatical aspect of creation is the subject of Kant's third critique, the *Critique of Judgment* (*Urteilskraft*). Here the mind is neither reflecting on itself nor motivated by desire, but is studying that curious assimilation of nature and art that seems to underlie so much of what we call beauty, design for its own sake, purposiveness without purpose, as Kant says" (*MM*, 179). This essentially Kantian strategy of isolating "purpose" from "purposiveness" leads directly to one of the most central doctrines in Frye: the doctrine of *free play*. Frye, like Schiller before him, sees "free play" as a necessary precondition of moral growth, growth predicated on man's inherent powers rather than on those surrendered to, or arrogated by, the church or the state.

This concept of "free play" underlies the stress in Frye, as in the Romantic tradition generally, on the fact that mental growth is possible only when the mind "Seeks for no trophies, struggles for no spoils/ That may attest her prowess."[17] In Wordsworth, as throughout Romanticism, beauty is a force that is discovered by being surrendered to. Nor does this surrender amount to passivity: it is the very seeking after ends and purposes which blocks our most powerful potential for growth, as both Coleridge's Ancient Mariner and the speaker in "Frost at Midnight" find out when they surrender to the beauty of their surroundings and suddenly, as a consequence, find their power to grow has been triggered.

This notion of the liberating power of "free play," seen as issuing from "disinterestedness" and the disengagement of "purpose" from "purposiveness," so prominent in Kant and in European Romanticism, is very representative of Frye's thinking. His 1985 essay "The Dialectic of Belief and Vision," for example, makes a direct reference to Kant's formula: "The element in experience that we call aesthetic, the ability to see the world around us as beautiful, is not ... purely in the eye of the beholder, but is an objective fact as well. The world makes human sense, but there is nothing of the fallacy of trying to reduce the beautiful to the functional: there is rather that sense of purposiveness without purpose that Kant recognized as central to beauty" (*MM*, 105). Elsewhere, Frye speaks of the aesthetic imagination as "the constructive power of the mind set free to work on pure construction, construction for its own sake" (*EI*, 50), while in *Words With Power* he argues in the same vein that "the poetic is playful, and therefore should be taken in a different spirit from discursive verbal structures"; and so "however ironic or anxiety-ridden the fiction may be, the positive impulse behind it, the impulse to express a concern for more abundant life, is still a *gaya scienza*, a form of play or self-contained energy" (36, 43). "The world of imagination," as he says in *The Critical Path*, "is partly a holiday or Sabbath world where we rest from belief and commitment, the greater mystery beyond whatever can be formulated and presented for acceptance" (169). In the *Anatomy*, Frye talks of the need to "transmute ... routine into play" in order to discover "the sense of buoyancy or release that accompanies perfect discipline, when we can no longer know the dancer from the dance" (93–4). Finally, in his 1984 essay "The Expanding World of Metaphor," Frye describes poetry as "a form of play" that is "detached from the kind of commitment that we call 'belief'" (*MM*, 112). In other words, "poems are as silent as statues" because their verbal structures are "autonomous"—that is, structured ("purposive") but independent of centrifugal reference ("without purpose") (*AC*, 4, 74).

Thus, Frye's and Kant's aesthetics join on an important point: excluding the ephemeral from the aesthetic allows aesthetic judgments to emerge as qualitatively different from transient judgments of taste, which are predicated on mere personal preference. In aesthetic judgments, as Frye says, "what I like or don't like disappears, because there's nothing left of me as a separate person: as a reader of literature I exist only as a representative of humanity as a whole" (*EI*, 42). And it is precisely because there is no private preference involved in aesthetic judgments that they are regarded in this tradition as transpersonal and transhistorical.

The notion of "free play" which descends through the Kantian notions of "disinterestedness" and "purposiveness without purpose" feeds directly into Frye's most characteristic thoughts about the power of and need for a liberal education. Detachment is, he says, the only authentic goal of education, which accounts for the persistent emphasis in Frye on the liberating function of education, which for Frye was simply guidance towards "the disinterested use of words." The teacher, consequently, is not "someone giving out information to someone else who doesn't have it" but one who must "help create the structure of the subject in the student's mind" (WE, 63, 543). Thus, the teacher's "ultimate goal" is "the abolition of himself, or the turning of himself into a transparent medium for his subject, so that the authority of his subject may be supreme over both teacher and students" (550). For in the final analysis, all that the teacher has to teach is "the verbal expression of truth, beauty and wisdom: in short, the disinterested use of words" (63).

Thus, in the humanist tradition adumbrated by Kant and Frye, the love for literature leads, if not to the love for man, certainly to the discovery of "renewed ways of extending the expression of our energies and vision" (WP, 228). For literature, in teaching us to "distinguish ideology from myth" (MM, 103), helps us perform "the work of civilization." By placing the individual work of art into "the total form of the art," the educated imagination promotes the work from "an object of aesthetic contemplation" into "an ethical instrument" (AC, 349). Or, in the words of Kant, "The beautiful arts ... make man more civilized, if not morally better, win us in large measure from the tyranny of sense propension, and thus ... make us feel an aptitude for higher purposes which lies hidden in us" (CJ, 284).

I began this paper by referring to Frye's first-known piece of academic writing, the student composition in which he cites Kant's work as providing "the matrix of Romanticism." Sixty years later, in his final published work, The Double Vision, Frye refers to Kant as "the greatest of all philosophers" (32). By drawing out the most productive and fruitful implications of the transcendental philosophy, by mapping out for us the crucial milestones on the critical path, and by emphasizing and clarifying the social and moral implications of Kant's centralization of the aesthetic function, Frye revealed the full richness and value of the long and distinguished tradition of German idealist aesthetics which Kant initiated.

NOTES

1 Hayden White, "Ideology and Counterideology in the *Anatomy*," in *Visionary Poetics: Essays on Northrop Frye's Criticism*, ed. Robert D. Denham and Thomas Willard (New York: Lang, 1991), 106.

2 *CP*, 157. Cf. Immanuel Kant, *The Critique of Pure Reason*, trans. Norman Kemp Smith (New York: St Martin's Press, 1965), 668. Hereafter referred to as *CPR*.

3 Frye owned copies of *CPR* and of the *Critique of Judgment*, trans. J.H. Bernard (New York: Hafner, 1966), hereafter referred to as *CJ*. Neither is heavily annotated. However, his copy of Herbert Marcuse's *Eros and Civilization*—especially chapter 9 which deals with *CJ*—and his copy of Susanne Langer's very Kantian *Feeling and Form* are comparatively well-annotated.

4 Imre Salusinzsky, "Frye and Romanticism," in *Visionary Poetics*, 58.

5 Oskar Walzel, *Deutsche Romantik*, 2 vols. (Leipzig: Teubner, 1918), 1:11. My translation.

6 William Blake, *Jerusalem*, plate 12, l.13, in *Complete Writings of William Blake*, ed. Geoffrey Keynes (London: Nonesuch, 1958), 631.

7 Ernst Cassirer, *Kant's Life and Thought*, trans. James Haden (New Haven: Yale University Press, 1981), 273. Goethe, for example, saw in *CJ* "[his] most diverse thoughts brought together" (quoted Cassirer, 273); Crabb Robinson quotes Coleridge as finding it "the most astonishing of Kant's works" (qtd. in Gian N.G. Orsini, *Coleridge and German Idealism* [Carbondale IL: Southern Illinois University Press, 1969], 159); as did Fichte, Schelling, Hegel, and Schopenhauer. And Friedrich Schiller acknowledges at the very beginning of his *On the Aesthetic Education of Man* (ed. and trans. Elizabeth M. Wilkinson and L.A. Willoughby [Oxford: Clarendon Press, 1967]) that his aesthetic theories are largely "based" on Kantian principles (3).

8 John Crowe Ransom, "The Concrete Universal: Observations on the Understanding of Poetry," in *Poems and Essays* (New York: Vintage, 1955), 161.

9 H. Marcuse, *Eros and Civilization* (New York: Vintage, 1962), 159. Frye's copy is annotated # 1059 in NFF.

10 S. Langer, *Feeling and Form* (New York: Scribner, 1953), 49. Frye's copy is annotated # 1717 in NFF.

11 Bernard's translation is not clear, but the meaning here is evident: the realms of nature and freedom cannot, theoretically, impact on each other.

12 Marcuse's statement of this problem is underlined in Frye's copy of *Eros*: see 158.

13 Blake, *A Vision of the Last Judgement*, in *Complete Writings*, 609.

14 As Kant put it (in a passage underlined in Frye's copy of *CJ*), "the beautiful

is the symbol of the morally good, and ... it is ... in this respect ... that it gives pleasure with a claim for the agreement of everyone else" (*CJ*, 198–9).

15 S. Körner, *Kant* (Harmondsworth: Penguin, 1955), 188. Frye's copy is annotated #736 in NFF.

16 As it is to Romanticism generally: one thinks immediately for example of Keats's insistence in his oft-quoted letter to John Reynolds of 3 Feb. 1818 that "We hate poetry that has a palpable design upon us—and if we do not agree, seems to put its hand in its breeches pocket. Poetry should be great & unobtrusive" (*Letters*, ed. Hyder Edward Rollins, 2 vols. [Cambridge: Harvard University Press, 1958], 1:224). Schiller says similarly that "only inasmuch as it is honest [*aufrichtig*] (expressly renounces all claims to reality), and only inasmuch as it is autonomous (dispenses with all support from reality), is semblance aesthetic. From the moment it ... has the need of reality to make its effect, it is nothing but a base instrument for material ends, and affords no evidence whatsoever of any freedom of the spirit" (*Aesthetic Education of Man*, 197).

17 William Wordsworth, *The Prelude*, bk. 6, ll. 610–12, in *Poetical Works*, ed. Thomas Hutchinson, rev. Ernest de Selincourt (London: Oxford University Press, 1960), 535.

JEAN O'GRADY

Northrop Frye on Liberal Education

Northrop Frye, many have claimed, was a liberal humanist. Whether this label is affixed as the validation of a noble lineage, or on the contrary as a sign that his time has passed,[1] it is nowhere more germane than in regard to his thoughts on education and on the role of the university. Drawing largely on a tradition of British liberal thought that runs through Milton, John Stuart Mill, and Matthew Arnold, Frye defines an ideal education as "liberal" in the sense, among others, of being "a disinterested pursuit of truth as its own end, in contrast to the attempt to manipulate it or press it into the service of an immediate social aim" (RW, 311). He was also an eloquent spokesman for the humanities in an age of science: though he bends over backwards to admit the claims of scientific truth in all disciplines, Frye points at the same time to another kind of knowledge equally vital to humankind.

In this paper I propose to discuss some of the key concepts in Frye's liberal humanist vision of the university, and his view of the social role of knowledge. The main issue I take to be the socially disengaged university. Frye was driven to elaborate his theories partly in response to the student-radical demand for a university committed to worthy causes, and he consistently defined his ideals against the Marxist model of a university engaged in a revolutionary struggle to build a better society. In what way, then, did he see the university contributing to society? That many specific benefits and technological advances are made possible by the spread of education goes almost without saying, but in the broadest sense, does society improve as the number of university graduates increases? Whether Frye believed human progress was possible at all is discussed in the last part of the paper. I should like to suggest finally that, while Frye offers no apocalyptic hopes, his humanist vision remains relevant both to Western-style democracies and to other societies.

Frye often pointed to the importance of examining the metaphors used in discursive thought as well as those in literature. His own metaphors for the university are revealing; the universisty is "the engine-room of the world," "the powerhouse of freedom" (WE, 280, 99). For Frye as much as for any Buddhist, ordinary life consisted largely of illusions: the superficial changes of politics, the passing show of fashion and celebrity, the inane din of advertising and entertainment. The arts and sciences studied in a university, on the other hand, present a body of knowledge that is rationally organized and that examines the reality behind the illusions. Like most Romantic or post-Kantian thinkers, Frye rejected naive notions of the mind as a blank tablet receiving sense-impressions and stressed the fact that the mind shapes the reality that is perceived. The arts and sciences look at the constructs, theories, and myths by which mankind has ordered experience and are themselves the source of new constructs. "The university informs the world, and is not informed by it," Frye said in 1957, with a majesty worthy of Queen Victoria (WE, 64).

To return to Frye's metaphor for the university, our contemporary image of an engine-room, with its banks of humming computers, bears little resemblance to the engine-room of Frye's day, which produced power by shovelling coal into red-hot furnaces. The metaphorical equivalent for coal, the source of fuel, is a motivating vision.[2] Without exhorting its students in any way, the university provides the means for the individual to form such a vision. In his most celebrated work, Frye suggested the possibility of seeing literature as a total order of words. A student who has approached literature in this way acquires a synoptic view of the images by which we live, ranging from what is most desired to what forms the stuff of nightmare. It is less widely recognized that for Frye, the other humane disciplines also yield myths and models, mental constructs that outline projects of civilization and ideal goals. In this sense of offering hypothetical models, Frye maintained that at university "what we are trying to teach is a vision of society" (WE, 190).

Frye's writings sometimes seem to suggest that the attainment of vision—a far-reaching Blakean transformation of perception—is the goal and supreme attainment in life. I will return to this issue later, but provisionally I want to point out that Frye did not hold up knowledge or even wisdom as an end in itself. For one so cerebral, he was surprisingly earthy, or at least Aristotelian. Ideas must issue in action, and visions struggle to be embodied. Thus he suggested that our real self may be found, not in some inner psychic realm, but in our reputation and influence: in what others think of us, and in what we contribute to society (*WE*, 295). He insisted that what we believe is shown not by what we say or by the creed we subscribe to, but by what we do (*NFR*, 349).

In a similar way, Frye posits that the possibility of a redeemed society glimpsed at university should inform a student's whole life. It will not necessarily do so if the will to act properly is lacking, for education does not automatically improve the character: "education makes a bad man more dangerous; it does not make him a better man" (*NFR*, 308). It is possible to maintain the "aesthetic" attitude described in Kierkegaard's *Either/Or* and to remain otherwise uncommitted to what one studies, like the legendary Nazi prison guard who admires Goethe. But in his addresses to graduating classes and elsewhere, Frye suggested that a two-stage process generally takes place. University education itself is addressed to what he calls the "speculative reason," the power of understanding that grasps a subject intellectually and contemplates patterns in themselves. But after the details of particular studies have been forgotten, there remains ideally a desire and an ability to contribute to society that Frye called the "practical reason." Professional people work in the light of a mental model, derived from their studies, of what they hope to achieve (*WE*, 174, 502). In its after-effects, the university is profoundly social.

Frye's views of the university were generally welcomed during the 1950s, but they were severely challenged when the climate of opinion changed during the student protest movement of the late 1960s and early 1970s. This movement, a worldwide one stretching from North America and France to China, where it fused with the Cultural Revolution, involved an attack on the disinterested stance of the university, which was interpreted as a cloak for complicity with the established powers. In pursuit of their own moral imperatives, student radicals demanded choice in the curriculum, student parity on decision-making bodies, instruction by seminar and discussion, and above all, politically correct actions and the forwarding of social justice on the part of the university. Frye was at the epicentre of the resulting disturbances, as he was teaching at Berkeley in the spring of 1969, when the first major confrontation erupted. Here helmeted police used tear-gas and bayonets on embattled students while helicopters droned overhead, a spectacle that Frye said a few months later (reflecting on both sides) reminded him of a sentence in an old cook-book: "Brains are very perishable, and unless frozen or precooked, should be used as soon as possible."[3]

Frye's reaction to these activist demands was to dig in his heels and defend traditional liberal education. He was often called upon to address the issue, and he responded to the call not only because he was horrified at the anti-intellectual violence, but also because he believed that there was a truth beyond ideology—whether the ideology was that of the established society or that of the counterculture—which could best be approached by the sort of free discussion offered by the uncommitted university. As he discussed this deeply held belief in addresses to students and at conferences on the role of the humanities, he introduced the terms "concern" and "freedom" to characterize the competing demands of social commitment and intellectual independence. These concepts were thus born at a time of crisis. But they continued to dominate his thinking long after the student movement had evaporated, and they are equally relevant today, when the perceived threat to the university is not so much the premature moralizing of its role as its harnessing to programs of job creation or its capture by the agenda of multinational corporations.

To summarize briefly an argument that is most fully worked out in *The Critical Path* (1971), Frye posited two basic myths that govern individuals' relation to their society. The myth of concern includes all that holds society together: religion, political ideals such as democracy or Communism, folk heroes, social practice, patriotism. The myth of freedom constitutes a kind of liberal opposition, criticizing the shared myths and preventing them from hardening into dogma. It is individualistic, rational, and, since the Renaissance, usually scientific. Both myths are necessary for a healthy society, Frye argued, and intelligent individuals are likely to be in a constant state of tension between them, balancing their loyalty to their community against their instinct to criticize its accepted wisdom. But the university, to carry out its function, must remain in the realm of the myth of freedom. That is, scholars must not be required to conform to any ideology, and as scholars their primary loyalty must be not to society but to their discipline. Frye urged scholars to resist their "nervous itch . . . to help turn the wheel of history" (*WE*, 575). Julien Benda's *La trahison des clercs* [*The Treason of the Intellectuals*] (1928), with its strong criticism of the "politicizing" of the once independent thinking class, was a favourite exhibit in this argument. To act we must commit ourselves, however blamelessly, to one facet of the truth, whereas the university's sphere is the realm of the mind, where all possibilities are kept alive.

In late 1968, Frye introduced the term "educational contract" to help define the myth of freedom. This term is a counterpart to the traditional "social contract," which posited a fictitious agreement in the past among the different elements of society. Whereas the social contract rationalizes the existing balance of power—or, as Frye puts it, hallows the transient *appearance* of society—the educational contract is a fictitious agreement to build the "real form" of society (*CP*, 156), an unrealized ideal found in its culture or its arts and sciences. According to the educational contract, all scholars agree to respect "the authority of logic and reason, of demonstrable and repeatable experiment, of established fact, of compelling imagination" (*WE*, 372). In the world of scholarship, truth must always prevail over social goals.

This concept, though simple enough in bald outline, obviously harbours complex issues when scrutinized. For instance, three of the four criteria of truth—fact, logic, and experiment—pertain more to the sciences or social sciences than to the humanities. It is generally agreed that the sciences need to function on the level of the myth of freedom, but Frye's inclusion of the humanities in the educational contract is more tendentious. Far from abandoning the controversial contention of the *Anatomy* that literary criticism should become more scientific, Frye argued, for instance at a conference on the role of the humanities in 1965, for a general advance of scientific method into all liberal arts subjects, which "have to be as scientific as the nature of their subjects will allow them to be, or abandon all claim to be taken seriously" (*WE*, 246). The distinction between sciences and humanities, he held, lay not in methodology, but in the fact that science studies nature, or the world that is given, while the humanities study the world of culture, which is a human creation. The *subject-matter* of the humanities lies in the realm of concern: poetry, painting, music, law, the acts that history studies, all entail committed attitudes to society and controversial ethical choices.

Frye struggled with difficult distinctions as he tried to promote the dispassionate attitude of scholars working within the humanities. The authority of "the compelling imagination" is more problematical than that of logic, fact, and experiment. The term seems to refer to the personal authority exercised by the great visionary authors in their works of art; presumably Milton has an authority that Harlequin Romances lack.[4] But this brings up the *bête noir* of Frye studies, the role of value judgments, since without a value judgment there is no criterion for deciding which works of imagination are, or should be, compelling. In a similar way, Frye pictured the literary critic as surveying all of literature and mapping its genera and species without championing one movement or denigrating another. Yet there is a taxonomic problem in that the field has first to be defined, at least tentatively, by means of judgments between what is literature and what is not. And the critic's whole enterprise depends on the ability to read these creative works in the first place, on a passionate, imaginative response which Frye can only label as pre-critical.

Frye recognized in fact that humanists will always be torn between the scientific demands of their discipline and the personal imperatives of their subject-matter. Even scientists, he conceded, will face some of these dilemmas: they may study the atom scientifically, but they cannot be blind to the possible use of their research in warfare. Frye did not elaborate as much as might be wished on this point, but he did suggest a consciousness of a broad social context that should in some way govern all scholars.[5] And he made a distinction between the teacher or student as a scholar and as an individual. Just as value judgments should remain personal and tentative, rather than being enshrined in the discipline where they may prematurely define a canon, so convictions should motivate individual actions but not guide research or suggest conclusions. That this distinction is difficult to make in practice is a consequence of the fact that the scholarly task is enmeshed in all the perplexities of the human situation.

Thus Frye tried to build a bridge between contemplation and action, knowledge and commitment, *theoria* and *praxis*, keeping the university in the realm of pure knowledge while showing how that knowledge informs society. The discussion so far might lead one to conclude that Frye believed university graduates, armed with their vision and aware of their social conditioning, could go out and transform the world. Some of his own statements—for instance, the remark that "We cannot discuss educational theory simply in relation to an existing society, for no educational theory is worth anything unless it can be conceived as transforming that society" (*WE*, 265)—support this view. Does this mean, then, that with the spread of education we can expect to advance towards a just society, and usher in an era of universal peace and good will? Unfortunately not, as Frye denied categorically that the world can or should be transformed. He was thinking, of course, of mental and moral progress. He did not deny the improvements evident in medicine, life expectancy, and general comfort, at least among developed nations, but he argued that every such advance created another problem. Thus in place of the plague we have heart attacks, nuclear power unleashed the Hiroshima bomb, and war and oppression remain the human lot. Frye used two specific arguments against what he describes as "the moral horrors of a theory of progress" (*RW*, 312). First, the notion of social progress often implies an automatic or inevitable advance, onwards and upwards, on the analogy of biological evolution. In the opening chapter of *The Modern Century*, Frye showed at length that this mechanical idea robs humans of dignity and freedom. Second, the idea of progress may be used to justify atrocities, on the grounds that we must take some unpalatable actions now for the sake of a brighter future. In his resolute rejection of this ideology, Frye seems to deny overall progress in human affairs and to imply that the Neanderthal era was on much the same mental and moral level as the present one, though its evils were different.

Frye also rejected the idea that a just society can be created on earth on the grounds that it would involve unbearable tyranny. If such a society were not repressive, the wrong choices and anti-social acts that are an inevitable consequence of freedom would soon destroy it. His position is clear in his remarks on Utopias, a literary genre that interested him greatly. One of the first English classes Frye taught as a young lecturer was on Sir Thomas More's *Utopia*; his first substantial paper on critical theory concerned this work and related forms of prose fiction; and in his last years he was contemplating a book on the subject.[6] He begins by positing two poles in the myth of human history, as presented in the Bible—the expulsion of Adam and Eve from paradise, and the re-establishment of the City of God. The fall of mankind inspired the social contract, a conservative notion appealing to concerned individuals whose loyalty is to their existing society; the City of God inspired the various Utopias, which attract those more detached individuals, operating in the myth of freedom, who envisage a different society. Frye argues that Utopians would simply assimilate themselves to the first group if they realized their Utopian dream: one social contract or ideological straitjacket would be replaced with another. A Utopia should properly be seen as a mental model, a projection into the future of the educational contract of the present, in which the arts and sciences form a spiritual and non-coercive authority in society (*CP*, 160–3; *WE*, 371–3). That first class on More's *Utopia* turned out to be a paradigm of Frye's theory of education, for in it students were, quite literally, discussing a hypothetical model of society. Far from being idle dreaming, such modelling is an attempt to focus on ultimate values: "without Utopian hopes there can be no clear vision of social reality" (*WE*, 272). But when the model is used as a basis for coercing others, it becomes pernicious.

This anti-Utopian temper is often taken to be anti-Marxist, and certainly it exhibits a *prima facie* hostility to planned and totalitarian societies. But Frye's words are equally directed against the prevailing ideology of Western societies. His strictures against the idea of progress were initially made in reaction to sub-literary theories popular in nineteenth-century Britain, as promulgated by neo-Darwinians and imperialists heralding the spread of the British empire among benighted "savages." The idealism of the sixties' counterculture in North America only intensified his sense of the futility of premature, wholesale movements of social transformation. It is the fate of all political revolutions, in Frye's thought, to subside into a new orthodoxy, just as it is inevitable that any actualized Utopia will become an anti-Utopia.

Does this mean, then, that Frye holds out no hope at all for an improvement in actual human society, and that the vision of improvement must remain for ever just that—a vision in the minds of enlightened individuals? If so, this position would be consonant with his general tendency to interpret supposedly physical events as metaphors—heaven and hell, for instance, being not places we go to after death, but realities we can experience now. Just as he read the Bible's history and prophecy not as descriptions of what has actually happened or will happen, but as images of an inner transformation that may occur now, so he pointed out that when we think we are working for the society of the future, we are really fulfilling ourselves in the present (*WE*, 516). The thrust of Frye's argument, especially in his later books, with their emphasis on kerygma and the actualization of myth and metaphor, is on the attainment of a Job-like consciousness that allows one to live fully and without despair in the flawed present. Truly educated individuals act as if the just state existed and thus live out their imaginative ideals, while being fully aware that Astraea will not return to the earth and the general course of human life will remain as it has always been.

This seems a reasonable, Frygian conclusion, but I should like to suggest two qualifications that mitigate what social progressives may take to be its bleakness. The first qualification simply stresses the degree to which, for Frye, individual vision is in fact social. Fredric Jameson is far from the mark, for instance, when he criticizes Frye for negating and "re-privatizing" the social vision of his archetypal level by culminating, on the anagogic level, with the figure of a giant man.[7] This figure is no mere private individual or "isolated body," as Jameson argues, but the body of humanity itself—-the collectivity of mankind, apprehended as both one and many. Frye's image owes much to

St Paul's conception of the body of Christ in the New Testament, but it is not doctrinal; it draws on a tradition of literary, religious, and kabbalistic symbolism that tries to envisage the individual as part of the larger whole.

This aspect of Frye's thought may be illuminated by an analysis of his use of the concept of freedom. "Freedom" is obviously one of his key words, having great positive emotional resonance, whereas its opposite, bondage or tyranny, was for him the very essence of hell on earth. Frye espouses both of the contrasting types of freedom described by Isaiah Berlin in "Two Concepts of Liberty." Negative freedom, or "freedom from," the absence of compulsion championed by John Stuart Mill in *On Liberty*, is central to Frye's concept of the scholar unconstrained by social pressures and constantly informs his defence of free speech. Yet this kind of freedom, which Frye considers vital on the social level, is less relevant for him on the level of the individual psyche. He points out that an individual who thinks he is doing what he likes may really be enslaved by his own compulsions. Moreover, the idea that freedom is essentially "what [the individual] wants to do minus what society stops him doing" (*RW*, 358) implies that society is the antithesis of the individual rather than the soil from which the individual grows. On the intellectual level Frye prized another kind of freedom, positive "freedom to," or what Berlin calls "power through self-mastery,"[8] which is more austere and less idiosyncratic, involving a certain sacrifice of arbitrary, wilful choice. In the explanation Frye often used, an individual is not free to play the piano until he or she has undergone a long apprenticeship in playing the right notes. Even when the former apprentice has become a virtuoso, it makes no sense to say that she is now free to play the wrong notes. Similarly, free creative artists are not so much following their own bent as doing what their material or their theme demands; thus the poet is the voice through which language itself speaks.[9] In all areas, Frye would argue, empowerment comes when we escape from our own ego and enter a wider, non-personal sphere which exercises a spiritual authority over us. The acceptance of this authority collapses the antagonism between freedom and necessity: what you want to do is also what you must do.

On the academic level, the concept of an austere "freedom to" explains why Frye disapproved of radical demands for freedom to make up an individual curriculum. In the citadel of freedom there is a good deal of necessity, though, let us hope, not tyranny. The student must master a body of material with a given structure; only through this laborious apprenticeship does he become free to engage in creative action. And on the personal level, it means that the mature individual is not one who has attained a kind of isolated selfhood, but rather one who has found his identity in a larger whole. The scholar is a contributor to his or her discipline, the worker is a genuine member of his society, the mystic attains some sense of the oneness of mankind, and in this way the social ideal is kept alive.

The second factor mitigating the potential bleakness of Frye's vision is the fact that, although Frye did not believe that progress is an inevitable phenomenon or characteristic of human history so far, he left the door ajar to allow a glimpse of its possibility. In a world of competing ideologies, the preliminary question is perhaps whether mankind can agree on what is wanted. Frye's whole endeavour is posited on the notion that myth and literature embody transnational and in some sense universal desires. But—leaving aside the much-canvassed question of whether literature can transcend ideology—Frye is not forthcoming in translating these desires into social terms. Initially, he suggested that literature addressed four primary concerns basic to all humanity: food, shelter, sex, and property. He admitted that these are almost too banal to be stated, but he did not immediately address the problem that, if these concerns are so universal, they hardly demand the whole panoply of imaginative and artistic endeavour that poets have lavished on them and that critics have laboured a lifetime to elucidate. In *Words with Power*, however, he introduced a new category of spiritual primary concerns, including art, love, and freedom; it is these extended primary concerns that literature and myth address and that imaginative perception can uncover. According to Frye, they have social aspects that can be found in all cultures. Events like the protest in Tienanmen Square demonstrate that a more generalized democracy, not as a political system opposed to Communism but in the sense of respect for the individual and the prevalence of the rule of law, is a basic human goal (*WE*, 615).

In *The Critical Path*, Frye remarks that "the concept of evolution is of little use to a literary critic, for much the same reason that the measurement of a light year is of no use to a carpenter" (85), and that art has not improved since cave times. But sometimes the perspective of a light year may be refreshing, and in terms of defining human rights and aspirations, we may have gained a little ground since the cave men, even if only as dwarfs standing on the shoulders of giants. Frye admits that the growth of literacy is an advance, written texts being one of the essential safeguards of democracy (*SM*, 64–5), and the development of universal education is thus "one of the few really convincing arguments for progress" (*WE*, 318). The abolition of slavery and the granting of the vote to women were, he concedes, steps towards the abolition of oppressed minorities (*WE*, 288). His desideratum of what, following Karl Popper, he calls an "open," or a "mature," society (*CP*, 136; *WE*, 292, 305), in which different myths of concern are tolerated, is at least partially realized in the societies taking shape today. And the very existence of a conference such as the one at which some of the papers published in this volume were presented points to a cross-cultural dialogue all too rare in the past.

Without holding out delusive hopes of an end to history, Frye occasionally implies that these steps towards a less constricted social life go beyond the value-neutral changes that characterize progress as usually understood and indicate that, with the spread of liberal education, human life has the capacity to improve. In an unusually expansive moment in 1976, he remarked to the Modern Language Association that "whatever man has been capable of in imagination he can realize in life. In the future there is the possibility of an ideal society in which man's vision of his culture has liberated and equalized his social existence" (*WE*, 485). More characteristic is his modest assertion that society "can come to a certain point of increased coherence and common sense" (*WE*, 301), can offer freedom, the tools for learning, space for the imagination to grow. If such a society could be sustained, Frye suggested in *The Modern Century*, we could turn out to be "the cave men of a new mental era" (*MC*, 96).

The meaning Frye attached to this figure of cave men, as opposed to what its originator Wyndham Lewis meant, is made clear in two earlier statements. In a 1949 review in the *Canadian Forum*, he remarked of Spengler's theory of a series of growing and declining cultures, "It is also possible that behind this organic rhythm, which is seems to me certainly does exist in history, there may be an evolutionary one, and, without vulgarizing this into a theory of progress, we may perhaps see in the Industrial Revolution the beginning of something that makes us, in the words of Wyndham Lewis, the cavemen of a new mental era."[10] In his CBC lecture on Spengler in 1955 Frye elaborated on this idea: "Perhaps our science and technology will bring in a new phase of human life, which will supersede the history of cultures just as the history of cultures superseded the Stone Age. And perhaps that's the whole point about science: that it's a universal structure of knowledge that will help mankind to break out of culture-group barriers, and get rid of war by moving into a higher area of conflict" (*RW*, 324).

The future tense in this suggestion is, however, important. Surveying the panorama of wars, pogroms, torture, and mass exterminations that characterize the twentieth century, Frye was not about to stress the historical likelihood of such a new stage of human life. What was important for him was the timeless vision of an ideal society, which has the power to illuminate each individual life. The non-progressive arts, or culture in general, are the source of this vision, and the university is the centre of culture—the university being a metaphor for an academy without walls, "a society of students, scholars, and artists" (*MC*, 102–3) encompassing all who have accepted the educational contract. It was loyalty to such a society that led Frye to dedicate his life to the university, and to write so often and so compellingly on the vital importance of its liberal education.

NOTES

1 For a criticism of Frye's liberalism, see, e.g., David Cook, *Northrop Frye: A Vision of the New World* (Montreal: New World Perspectives, 1985), chap. 4; Terry Eagleton, *Literary Theory: An Introduction* (Oxford: Blackwell, 1983), 199–200, 207–8; and Shaobo Xie, "History and Desire: Fredric Jameson's Dialectical Tribute to Northrop Frye," *Cultural Critique* 34 (Fall 1996): 138. Recent vindications include Graham Good, *Humanism Betrayed: Theory, Ideology, and Culture in the Contemporary University* (Montreal: McGill-Queen's University Press, 2001), chap. 7; and Douglas Long, "Northrop Frye: Liberal Humanism and the Critique of Ideology," *Journal of Canadian Studies* 34, no. 4 (1999–2000 Winter): 27–51.

2 In a variation of the figure that Frye used in 1952, "the draft that draws the fire of freedom is liberal education," but to complete its work it needs "a chimney reaching into the sky" (*RW*, 312).

3 Address to Acadia University (6 May 1969), NFF, box 3, file ca.

4 See "Education and the Humanities" (1947), *WE*, 50–2, for an early statement of this personal authority.

5 "The Knowledge of Good and Evil" (1966), *WE*, 281–96, is his most extended discussion of the moral responsibility of the scholar.

6 The paper was "The Anatomy in Prose Fiction," *Manitoba Arts Review* 3 (Spring 1942): 35–47; see 41–2. For his early class on More, see *MM*, 289. For the planned book on Utopias and educational theory, see *LN*, 229, 404.

7 F. Jameson, *The Political Unconscious* (Ithaca, N.Y.: Cornell University Press, 1981), 72–4, discussing *AC*, 119, 125–6.

8 Isaiah Berlin, "Two Concepts of Liberty," in *Four Essays on Liberty* (London: Oxford University Press, 1969), 134. Obviously the attempt to impose this

intellectual model on all mature members of society, deplored in Berlin's essay, would lead to the kind of supposed Utopia or authoritarian society that Frye too deplores.

9 Frye adopted the notion of language itself speaking from Heidegger. For the poets' own testimony to this phenomenon, see, e.g., *RW*, 267.

10 "Two Books on Christianity and History," *Canadian Forum* 29 (Sept. 1949): 139. For Lewis, the new era ushered in by Newtonian science and industry is a disaster, characterized by vacuous subjectivity and loss of community: we have been "driven down into our primitive private mental caves, or the unconscious and the primitive. We are the cave-men of the new mental wilderness" *Paleface* (London: Chatto & Windus, 1926), 103. For Frye, the reconnection with the primitive and the mythic that he discerns in modern art means that we could be at the start of a better, unknown culture.

GLEN ROBERT GILL

Beyond Anagogy:
Northrop Frye's Existential (Re)visions

One of the most contentious issues in contemporary literary theory has been the question of whether the positivist continuum of history and ideology is the sole context of human experience, or whether transhistorical states of being (to which the terms "mythic," "mystical," "metaphysical," or "imaginative" variously adhere) are attainable through language. The debate is far from settled, but proponents of the former perspective clearly hold the field at the moment, and the result has been the exile of what has traditionally been called "myth criticism" to the theoretical wasteland. A major step in this expulsion has been the dismissal of myth criticism's most influential theoretical text, Northrop Frye's *Anatomy of Criticism* (1957). Once deemed to be "an unassailable presence in the universities" and to have "an absolute hold on a generation of developing literary critics,"[1] *Anatomy* is now routinely critiqued in surveys of contemporary theory as typical of myth criticism's reliance upon "critical principles which stand free of ideology."[2] Terry Eagleton's popular *Literary Theory* is representative of this critique. Frye's *Anatomy*, according to Eagleton, theorizes that

> Literature is not a way of knowing reality but a kind of collective utopian dreaming which has gone on throughout history, an expression of those fundamental human desires which have given rise to civilization itself, but which are never fully satisfied there. It is not to be seen as the self-expression of individual authors, who are no more than functions of this universal system: it springs from the collective subject of the human race itself, which is how it comes to embody "archetypes" or figures of universal significance.
> Frye's work emphasizes as it does the utopian root of literature because it

is marked by a deep fear of the actual social world, a distaste for history itself.[3]

Readers of the *Anatomy* will recognize that what is being critiqued most aggressively here, with the mockingly reductive phrase "collective utopian dreaming," is Frye's theory of anagogy, the concept that the metaphors of literature, functioning at the universal level, compose a self-contained imaginative verbal universe. Such a concept is clearly anathema to the tenets of poststructural and cultural materialist theory; these critical perspectives typically emphasize both the instability and inefficacy of metaphor, and the position that, even if there is experience to be had outside the material conditions of history (which, they typically argue, there is not), to pursue or cultivate such experience is to evade the responsibilities of living a genuine material and political existence. Thus the forced exodus of myth criticism in general, and Frye's theories in particular, from the centres of critical debate.

As every student of mythology knows, however, exodus is merely the first stage of a purgatorial journey that concludes with an entry into a promised land. If Northrop Frye's last major work, the elder-statesman-like *Words with Power* (1990), has a primary intention, it is to conduct this passage for myth criticism, which it stands ready to lead into a fuller awareness of the relationship between mythology, ideology, and reality. Despite its subtitle, "Being a Second Study of 'The Bible and Literature,'" Frye informs us in his preface that *Words with Power* is not merely a sequel to *The Great Code: The Bible and Literature* (1982), but also "a successor" to the *Anatomy of Criticism* (*WP*, xii). A detailed consideration of the thesis and implications of *Words with Power* suggests, in fact, that Frye read and absorbed critiques of the *Anatomy* by critics like Eagleton, and revised and broadened his theories to account for them, or more accurately, to swallow them whole on the way to a more inclusive vision. *Words with Power*, as the discussion that follows will demonstrate, chronicles Frye's stepping behind literature to configure the relationship between mythology and ideology, idealism and materialism. This in turn leads him to a new theory of metaphor and hence a new concept of what the sum of metaphors creates. The result is the revision of the concept of anagogy into the theory of kerygma, a radical mode of language out of which springs the *axis mundi*, a verbal cosmology of intensified metaphoric and spiritual consciousness.

Frye begins *Words with Power* with a survey of the various modes of language that expands a similar sequence presented in *The Great Code* and, more importantly, broadens considerably the purview of the *Anatomy*'s second essay, the "Theory of Symbols." While the second essay is intended to be a "systematizing of literary symbolism" (*AC*, 71), the sequence with which Frye begins *Words with Power* sets for itself the broader task of laying out "the different idioms of linguistic expression" (*WP*, xxi). The sequence of the *Anatomy*, we may recall, consists of four phases (the literal and descriptive, the formal, the mythic or archetypal, and the anagogic), and takes its form primarily from the medieval theory of polysemous meaning used in the exegesis of Biblical texts; it operates along an axis of aesthetic and formal referentiality. The broader sequence of *Words with Power*, however, fuses that medieval polysemous schema with a Viconian theory of the role of language in society that sees its descent from and *ricorso* to a mythological mode. The result is a series of linguistic modes that not only identifies the contexts in which the literary symbol operates, but also outlines an evolution and structure of language based not on its historical development but on its capacity to present different realities to the mind and generate different kinds of discourse in society.

The sequence consists of five successive linguistic modes, each of which has a primary focus or explicit purpose as well as an "excluded initiative"—an unacknowledged motive that emerges in, and becomes the focus of, the subsequent mode. The sequence thus proceeds dialectically, with each new mode becoming a fuller realization of language's creative potential. The process begins with the descriptive mode, which aims to provide an accurate verbal replica of the external reality outside language, to which it ultimately refers; its excluded initiative is the reconstitutive word-ordering process itself, the fact that our perception of reality is determined by how we structure it in language. The conceptual mode makes this word-ordering process its focus, and thus withdraws from the task of referring to the external world in order to posit abstract concepts; its excluded initiative is the human subjectivity concealed beneath its presumably objective conceptual authority. In the rhetorical or ideological mode, this subjectivity becomes the focus, as its purpose is to articulate and rationalize structures of social authority to the subject; its excluded initiative is myth, which ideology concretely and selectively applies to accomplish this. The imaginative or metaphoric mode makes the hypothetical postulates of myth and literature its focus; its excluded initiative is the radical notion that such postulates need not remain merely hypothetical, but are posed with the prospect of being realized. When the reality of myth and metaphor becomes the focus of a final mode, the apotheosis of language is reached in kerygma, the language of "the myths we live by." A process that began with a simple recapitulation of reality in the descriptive mode concludes with a total recreation of reality in the kergymatic mode.

Frye devotes the entire first half of *Words with Power* to articulating the increasing potency of each phase in this linguistic process. So concerned was he with addressing the critique that his theories ignore the ideological dimensions of language and "the actual social world" that, while he devotes only the first ten pages to outlining the clear distinction between the descriptive and conceptual modes, he spends the next seventy configuring the interplay of purpose and excluded initiative in the rhetorical and metaphorical modes. At issue in these early pages, therefore, is the distinction between ideology and myth.

Myth, Frye discerns, is prior and anterior to ideology, because ideology descends from it. Myth, through the metaphorical mode, "outline[s], as broadly as words can do, humanity's vision of its nature and destiny, its place in the universe, its sense both of inclusion in and exclusion from an infinitely bigger order ... [T]he imaginative mode [is] the basis of any sense of the reality of non-human personality, whether angels, demons, gods, or God" (*WP*, 23). Ideology, however, is a derivative of myth, because "An ideology starts by providing its own version of whatever in its traditional mythology it considers relevant, and uses this version to form and enforce a social contract. An ideology is thus an applied mythology, and its adaptations of myths are the ones that, when we are inside an ideological structure, we must believe, or say that we believe" (*WP*, 23). The derivative condition of ideology leads Frye to call it, in a memorable pun, "myth-begotten" (*WP*, 32). Mythology is "a structure of practical human concern" expressing human needs and desires, and hence speaks, simply put, to the way we think things ought to be (*WP*, 32) . Ideology, on the other hand, is a rationalizing and compelling verbal mode, articulating in essence the message: "Your social order is not always the way you would have it, but it is the best you can hope for at present, as well as the one the gods have decreed for you. Obey and work" (*WP*, 24). Insofar as the general goal of ideology is to solicit and maintain acceptance of the status quo, it must privilege itself and the historical continuum of its evolution as having priority over the interests of the individual and collective human subject. It is the role of myth, by contrast, to exert "a counterbalancing force to such history" in its expression of universal human needs, desires, and perspectives (*WP*, 26).

Frye's distinction rings true for anyone who has studied mythology, but there are many questions to be answered for it to become a tenable principle. For example, what specifically are these universal human needs and desires that myth expresses? How exactly does it express them? And is not the social order, a product of ideology, a human need and desire? In Frye's theorizing of these and other specifics of the mythology/ideology relationship, we observe the application of his characteristic lucidity to a critical issue that is often obscured by political agendas and by abstract over-intellectualizing. It is not only one of many examples in *Words with Power* of his articulating something so obvious that we are shocked that everyone, including ourselves, missed it, but also the point at which the potential of his revised myth criticism begins to emerge.

Frye starts by outlining the elements of a satisfactory human existence, which he calls "concerns." Based on the derivative relationship between mythology and ideology, concerns are also configured in terms of priority: primary and secondary. "Secondary concerns," Frye explains, "arise from the social contract, and include patriotic and other attachments of loyalty, religious beliefs, and class-conditioned attitudes and behavior. They develop from the ideological aspect of myth, and consequently tend to be expressed in [the] ideological [mode]" (*WP*, 42). Prior to and more urgent than these, however, are "primary concerns," which, Frye explains,

> may be considered in four main areas: food and drink, along with related bodily needs; sex; property (i.e. money, possessions, shelter, clothing, and everything that constitutes property in the sense of what is "proper" to one's life); [and] liberty of movement. The general object of primary concern is expressed in the Biblical phrase "life more abundantly." In origin, primary concerns are not individual or social in reference so much as generic, anterior to the conflicting claims of the singular and the plural. But as society develops they become the claims of the individual body as distinct from those of the body politic. A famine is a social problem, but only the individual starves ... The axioms of primary concern are the simplest and baldest platitudes it is possible to formulate: that life is better than death, happiness better than misery, health better than sickness, freedom better than bondage, for all people without significant exception. (*WP*, 42)

While ideologies express secondary concerns, often to rationalize them over primary concerns, "the longer we look at myths," Frye insists, "the more clearly their links with primary concern stand out" (*WP*, 43). Works of literature, being composed in the metaphorical mode of myth, reflect the secondary ideological concerns of their time, but "relate those concerns to the primary ones of making a living, making love, and struggling to stay free and alive" (*WP*, 43). The primary concern for food and drink, for example, is the motivation for the vast number of "dying god" myths assembled by mythologists such as James Frazer, which then develop into archetypes and rituals like the Eucharist symbolism of the New Testament. "The metaphorical or 'spiritual' direction" of this development, Frye explains, fulfils "the physical need in another dimension of existence: it may require sublimation, but it does not cut off or abandon its physical roots" (*WP*, 45). Nor can it, it seems, for etymologies typically reveal those physical roots; "the metaphorical kernel of [the word] spirit, in all languages, is air or breath," Frye reminds us, and "breathing is the most primary of all primary concerns" (*WP*, 126). The role of myth and myth criticism, Frye concludes, is not to eradicate the conditions of ideology or to abolish secondary concern, but to increase the awareness and satisfaction of the primary concerns through the experience of metaphor.

It is reasonable to pause at this last point and inquire as to whether we have understood Frye correctly here: is Frye actually proposing that the metaphoric mode of language not merely expresses but might go some way towards fulfilling primary concern, if only "in another dimension of existence"? In fact he is, and this notion demands a significant if not radical reconceptualization of his original theory of metaphor. The metaphoric theory of *Anatomy of Criticism* is based primarily upon the Aristotelian notion that metaphor is mimetic, that is, a word identified with or as a thing in an imitative verbal relationship. In the descriptive phase, this usually makes it a verbal imitation of specific human actions and forms outside the text. In the formal phase, the imitation is not of specific actions and forms, but typical and idealized ones, dislodging metaphor's referentiality to specific things in the external world. In the archetypal phase, the imitation is of those actions and forms as found in other poems (now called archetypes) which over time begin to give us "a vision of the [larger] goals of human work" (*AC*, 113). In the phase beyond this, the anagogic, Aristotelian mimesis is pushed to its hypothetical extreme, to its point of inversion in fact, and thus literature fully swallows the actions and forms of the world outside the text. A self-contained verbal universe is the result. "This is not reality," Frye writes; it is "a literary universe [but] not a separate existential universe," even as it establishes "the conceivable or imaginative limit of desire, which is infinite and eternal" (*AC*, 125, 119).

In *Words with Power*, however, Frye counsels that "we have to ... consider an extension of the use of metaphor that not merely identifies one thing with another in words, but something of ourselves with both." A metaphor functioning in this way opens up the possibility of a "merging of the [literary] work with ourselves" (*WP*, 75). Frye calls this "existential metaphor," implying its passage from literature into human experience (*WP*, 76). Later, as he begins to explore its potential, he renames it "ecstatic" metaphor, a term borrowed from Heidegger and Longinus which is used more often in discussions of religious and mystical experience (*WP*, 82). For Frye the term retains the sense of its Greek original *ekstasis*: to be taken or lifted out of one's place. The "central axiom [of ecstatic metaphor] is ... something like 'One becomes what one beholds,'" Frye writes, re-wording the Hindu Upanishadic principle *Tat Tvam Asi* (Sanskrit, "Thou Art That") into something that sounds as if it might (or should) be found in the Gospels. The point is that "consistent and disciplined vision ends in ... identification," which involves an upward journey of consciousness into a world where subject and object are at one (*WP*, 86). "This takes place," Frye explains, "through an interchange of illusion and reality. Illusion, something created by human imagination ... becomes real; reality, most of which in our experience is a fossilized former human creation from the past, becomes illusory" (*WP*, 85).

Having exchanged the representational principle of mimesis for the experiential principle of *ekstasis*, Frye then considers what happens when we combine this experience of metaphor's reality with the knowledge that myth is the metaphoric language of primary concern. The answer takes us into the verbal mode Frye calls kerygma (Greek "proclamation"). Here the creation of metaphors of primary concern, and the recognition of those metaphors as "extending bodily experience into another dimension," begins to look like "the revelation of a paradisal state ... where all primary concerns are fulfilled" (*WP*, 128, 88). Kerygma is thus both the medium and the message of a collective humanistic epiphany, the creative Word that brings the world we desire into being in the middle of the world we have to settle for. "The principle that opens the way into the kerygmatic," Frye explains, "is the principle of the reality of what is created in the production and response to literature. Such a reality would be neither objective nor subjective, but essentially both at once, and would of course leave the old opposition of idealism and materialism a long way behind" (*WP*, 128). It also leaves the theory of anagogy a long way behind; or more accurately, radically revises it through a new metaphoric theory to meet the challenge of manifesting its imaginative world as reality. In kerygma, the myths and metaphors we read and write become, Frye says, the "myths we live by" and "metaphors we live in."

It should be clear by now that the theory of *Words with Power* represents myth criticism's engagement of its antithesis, materialist criticism, and its carrying forward of the indispensable aspects of both positions into a theoretical synthesis. By theorizing archetypal metaphor's connection to the materiality of primary concern, and confronting the dangerous tendency of those metaphors and concerns to be ideologically utilized, Frye finally introduces into myth criticism the capacity to account for the material and ideological conditions of living in an "actual social world." This breakthrough does not come, as we have shown, at the risk of turning myth into yet another discourse of the positivist continuum or of forsaking myth criticism's articulation of the transhistorical and the ideal. Through the theory of ecstatic metaphor, Frye demonstrates the potential of myth criticism not only to prioritize the primary concerns but to access higher realities where those concerns are fulfilled. Naturally, this process is not limited to the material aspect of primary concern; as the Gospel of Matthew says, Man does not live by bread alone. Thus in the second half of *Words with Power*, Frye details how the metaphors that fulfil the primary concerns of the physical body expand to convey the spiritual, intellectual, aesthetic, and communal experiences that are the primary concerns of human consciousness.

To satisfy the full range of primary concern for body and consciousness, nothing less than a complete metaphorical superstructure is required, which is, of course, the whole verbal cosmos of myth. Frye adopts the traditional mythographic term *axis mundi* for this structure, which he sees as consisting of four vertically arranged archetypal spaces: the Mountain, the Garden, the Cave, and the Furnace. Each level or station corresponds to one of the primary concerns, which is either fulfilled, denied, or ideologically compromised, depending on the quality of metaphorical identification achieved by consciousness. In other words, the *axis mundi* has three possible aspects relative to the question of metaphor and concern. There is, first, the potential for "authentic myth," the peak, kerygmatic experience that fulfils primary concern, the models of which are drawn from the comic resolutions of Biblical and Classical mythology. Secondly, there is the absence or failure of this fulfilment, the "demonic parody," a vision of the denial of primary concern resulting from the separation of subject and object, as is depicted in the tragedies of mythology. Lastly, there is the possibility of an "ideological adaption," the social structure that typically results when an ideology appropriates the metaphors of myth to rationalize secondary concern. Even a brief survey of these three experiential dimensions of the *axis mundi* (the kerygmatic, the demonic, and the ideological) will demonstrate the theoretical coherence of this vast metaphorical universe.

The metaphors that express the concern for freedom of movement are images of heavenly ascent, such as mountains, towers, ladders, staircases, upward spirals, and "world trees." The archetype here is the cosmic ladder of Jacob's dream in Genesis 28. Fulfilment of the concern for freedom of movement ideally modulates into the experience of being in perfect accord with the primary categories of consciousness, time and space. This includes aesthetic epiphanies in dance and music, an uninhibited participation in a world of play, and other experiences of total presence in a total present that is the nature of heaven and eternity, or at least a vision of the original unfallen order of creation. The demonic parody of this myth is the experience of falling into complete discord with time and space, the perception of them as oppressive and alienating categories of being that occurs when we sever the material and physical from the imaginative and the spiritual. The archetype in this instance is the collapsing Tower of Babel and its concomitant world of babble, miscommunication, and conflict. The ideological adaptation of these metaphors results in what in the Renaissance was called "the chain of being," a concretizing of the metaphorical/spiritual ladder to heaven into a static social hierarchy. Such structures, it goes without saying, are typically more concerned with rationalizing the authority of tyrants and political leaders, and with fixing the subject to a certain station in society, than with providing freedom of movement.

The concern for sexual fulfilment is expressed through imagery of gardens and other natural, earthly paradises; its spiritual intensification is erotic love, the *hierogamy* or sacred marriage of lovers, and the equally sacred sense of concern for the ecology of "Mother Earth." These are relationships of ecstatic union that liberate rather than subordinate, and which are therefore more aptly imaged as the unity of centre and circumference than as vertical or hierarchical structures. The archetypes of this authentic myth are the harmonious relationships of Adam and the feminized garden of Eden, of Adam and Eve before the fall, and major antitypes of these, the relationship of Solomon and his bride in the Song of Songs and of Christ as bridegroom to humanity itself (what organized religion calls "the Church") as bride. The demonic parody is "the sado-masochistic cycle, in which the female may tyrannize over the male or vice versa" (*WP*, 218). This includes the sword of the Oedipal Complex, with the son's possessive lust for the mother cutting one way, and the mother's domination of the son the other. Frye describes this circumstance as the "inferno of damned lovers in the setting of a bleak landscape of exhausted fertility" (*WP*, 219–20). The archetypes of this demonic experience, in addition to the Oedipal struggle, include the fiery, doomed relationships of Samson and Delila in the Bible and of Hercules and Deianeira in Classical mythology. Ideological adaptations of this myth result in the many social institutions dominated by incest-taboo imagery and metaphors of strict maternal and paternal authority. Among these, of course, are all the socialized forms of censorship and prudery that attempt to separate sex from spirit and promote the systemic exploitation of the natural world.

The concern for food and drink is metaphorized by descents into, and returns from, caves, waters, and other "lower kingdoms." These are narratives derived from the disappearance of vegetable life into the ground in winter and its rebirth in spring, which in turn expand into recuperative psychological and spiritual journeys into dream states and the unconscious. Its authentic myth is the narrative of *katabasis*, the movement into a lower world for the purpose of recovering something which has been suppressed, repressed, or otherwise lost, but which is essential to the fertility of the upper world. Its archetypes include the *nekyia* or summoning of the prophet Tiresias by Odysseus, the Old Testament's descent into and exodus from Egypt, the experience of Jonah, and, most significantly, the Resurrection. The demonic parody can take several forms: one results when the spiritual elements of hope and learning are missing from the descent structure and thus, as with vegetable life, the descent must be made over and over again in an endless cycle that resolves nothing. The devouring and regurgitating vortex of Charybdis in the *Odyssey* is an apt metaphor. Another is the direct inversion of the fertility god whom we eucharistically eat and drink (or who is otherwise associated with the miraculous provision of food): the figure of death that eats us, the representative of the consuming hell that lurks behind all the demons, cannibal giants, gobbling sea-monsters, and hungry tyrants of myth, from Egypt's Pharaoh to Jonah's "great fish" to the Hell that Christ harrows. The authentic myth of descent and return is ideologically adapted when the anxiety connected with the disappearance of food gives rise to an obsessive, compensatory need to create and preserve continuity in social institutions and ideological causes (which often results in a devaluation or consumption of the individual in the process).

The concern for property is represented in images of furnaces, fire, and other spaces and voids at the very bottom of creation. These involve narratives of descent into and return from worlds located below even the lower kingdoms of the previous variation. The fulfilment of the physical component of this concern unfolds into and enables the higher achievements of technology, education, and the arts—the properties of civilization itself. The Classical archetype of this authentic myth is the work of the titan Prometheus, the bringer of fire to mankind (technology), the god of forethought (education), and the creator of man (the arts). The Biblical archetypes are the miracle of God's creation of the universe *ex nihilo* and the experience of Job, stripped of every scrap of property and human dignity and then miraculously restored to an abundant material and spiritual life. The demonic parody is therefore not merely the demons and tyrants of the lower world, but Satan or Lucifer, the Antichrist himself, a figure-complex whose origin lies at the very outset of creation and who enters it through the void, not to construct but to corrupt. The ideological adaptation of this variation is the anxious aligning of our Promethean powers and civil achievements with specific ideological and political positions. This culminates in a final dystopic concession, the radical social *skepsis* that all the properties of civilization are inevitably corrupted by the nature of power itself, and that absolute power corrupts absolutely.

The all-too-familiar world depicted by this and the other ideological adaptations, with its uncanny similarity to the demonic reality, is the result of the long history of our mismanagement of language and subject-object relations. If there is a fear of the social world and a distaste for history in Frye's mystic vision it is because Frye recognizes that our social world is fearful and our history is distasteful. "Hell is in front of us because we have put it there," Frye writes succinctly in the conclusion to *Words with Power*, "paradise is missing because we have failed to put it there" (*WP*, 312). This failure occurs because we have continually focused not on the higher reality we might create, but on the lower reality we have been taught to accept—a reality that insists on regarding myths as rationalizations of authority, a body of unattainable dreams, or even outright lies, and metaphor as the merely rhetorical use of language. It is a world-view that materialist criticism has done much to reinforce, even as it goes about the important task of keeping us mindful of these dangers as aspects of life in the field of time. But with the revelation that authentic myth speaks for our health and freedom, that metaphor is not just a turn of phrase but a higher state of awareness, we find that we are not consigned to this world-view. We discover that it is within our power to kerygmatically create a paradisal world from the archetypal blueprint of the *axis mundi*, the spiritual inheritance bequeathed to us by our mythological and sacred traditions, our artists and visionaries, and our better selves.

Words with Power is, ultimately, Northrop Frye's *summa*, both in the sense of the summit of his theorizing and the summation of his contribution to the study of mythology, literature, and culture. It provides as much emphasis on material concern as cultural materialism could ask, and yet uses myth's defence of those concerns and its consciousness-raising verbal authority (and myth criticism's awareness of those qualities) as a springboard to higher states of being, gathering the incomplete perspectives of both modes of reading into a single fulfilling vision in the process. Although he died only a few months after its publication and would not have known how his book was received, Frye knew well that he had led criticism to the brink of a promised land. His legacy to us as critics and readers, like that of Moses to the Israelites, is the invitation to step inside it and get on with the business of living there.

NOTES

1 John Ayre, *Northrop Frye: A Biography* (Toronto: Random, 1989), 296; Murray Krieger, *Northrop Frye in Modern Criticism: Selected Papers from the English Institute* (New York: Columbia University Press, 1966), 2.

2 Frank Lentricchia, *After the New Criticism* (Chicago: University of Chicago Press, 1980), 17.

3 Terry Eagleton, *Literary Theory: An Introduction* (Oxford: Blackwell, 1983), 93.

MICHAEL DOLZANI

On Earth as It Is in Heaven: The Problem of Wish-Fulfilment in Frye's Visionary Criticism

Midway along the journey of our life, Dante tells us in what is perhaps the most famous opening sentence in Western literature, he woke and found that he had lost the way. "So here I am, in the middle way," T.S. Eliot, echoing Dante, tells us in "East Coker," "having had twenty years—/ Twenty years largely wasted .../ Trying to learn to use words." Midway in his life's journey, Northrop Frye had taken twenty years to write two of the greatest of all works of literary criticism, *Fearful Symmetry* and *Anatomy of Criticism*. He was in his late forties: what next? As we now know from his unpublished notebooks, what he conceived was a project bigger than either of them. Both Dante and the Eliot *Quartets* were to serve as models; at one point it was even to be called *The Critical Comedy* and to be written in a hundred parts. I am especially interested in this project because I am currently editing the notebooks of the late 1960s and early 1970s, during which period he referred to it most often as simply the Third Book. Frye spent the last thirty years of his life tinkering at this work, if "tinkering" is the right word to describe the filling of notebook after notebook with attempts to realize this opus. Close to half of all the notebook material we have, some two thousand of four thousand pages, is devoted to the Third Book. The material in these accumulating pages remains largely the same: Frye just keeps rearranging it, trying to find a containing pattern that satisfied him. He never did. Even though a good deal of the material became, in a significantly altered form, the second half of *Words with Power*, the Third Book remained an unpublished quarry for the books of the second half of Frye's career. Moreover, during this same mid-life period, Frye was beginning to face the fact that the "ogdoad" of eight definitive and interlocking books he had contemplated writing since his teenage years was never going to be written. He also wanted to leave behind at least one novel, but he never got beyond a few sketchy story ideas. We think of Frye's public career as one of the most successful on record; after all, he was still writing great books up to his death in his late seventies. But he failed to do what he set out to do, and his life did not have the shape that he hoped and planned for it. It is unlikely to be an accident that the plot outline, so to speak, of both the Third Book and of his life became unmasterable at the same time. It seems reasonable to say that in mid-life Frye awoke to find that some-how he had lost the way.

This crisis interests me not only as editor of the Third Book note-books, but on other levels as well. In fact, I am not going to focus on the Third Book in this essay; rather, I am going to use the Third Book as a springboard from which to dive into the deeper waters of a question that has intrigued and sometimes troubled me since I first began to read *Fearful Symmetry*. The original "plot" of the Third Book was summed up in a diagram that Frye whimsically referred to as the Great Doodle. In the simplest terms, it can be described as a circular diagram of the hero's quest, closely related to the Monomyth diagram Joseph Campbell uses in his *Hero with a Thousand Faces*. The heroic quest traverses a diagram which is really a mandala, for the circle is divided into quadrants by horizontal and vertical axes. These four quadrants are four *topoi*, or regions of poetic and mythological imagery: Eros (E–N), Adonis (N–W), Hermes (W–S), and Prometheus (S–E), consti-tuting a total birth-death-rebirth pattern. Though the descending movements of Adonis and Hermes are tragic or ironic in themselves, they are part of a total pattern which is that of comedy and romance, the pattern of the happy or desirable ending. As Frye says in the open-ing of *A Natural Perspective*, his study of Shakespearean comedy and romance written during the years of the Third Book notebooks, he has always been temperamentally attracted to comedy and romance. But the Third Book was not to be another version of the *Anatomy*, a study of literary patterns in themselves; it was to go beyond that by studying how the patterns of myth and literature inform life as we experience it outside of books, how they become "myths to live by." As he says in Notebook 19, "AC dealt with the internal structure of literature & this deals with its external relations" (*TBN*, 20). Later, he breaks down these relations into a tentative sequence of chapters: "Chapter Two is anthro-pological, dealing with myth in society & history; Three is psychologi-cal, & deals with the conflict of the quest myth in the mind with ordinary life. Four returns to society & history; Five to the mind again; Six, dealing with education, is again socially oriented, & Seven returns to religion" (*TBN*, 84). Is this, however, exactly where Frye's ambitions ran into an obstacle?

In real life, the happy ending never occurs. To say this is not to deny, out of cynicism or melancholic despair, that good things sometimes happen. But they are random and cannot be relied on; they are not part of a providential plot. In book 24 of the *Iliad*, Achilles tells the parable of the two jars of Zeus. One holds good fortune; the other holds bad. Zeus throws them out arbitrarily, and some days we get the good luck, some days the bad. That is the view of human existence in the *Iliad*, a book Frye expressly admits in the notebooks that he hates for this very reason. The *Iliad* influenced the later development of Athenian tragedy, and all three Greek tragedians were fond of such aphorisms as "Count no man happy until he is dead." The attitude is ancient, yet also strikingly modern, for it matches both existentialism and the scientific world-view, which see no pattern or purpose in human existence, let alone a redeeming one. As Heinz Pagels puts it in *Perfect Symmetry*, "Steven Weinberg, a theoretical physicist and a Nobel laureate, spoke for many scientists when he wrote, 'the more we know about the universe the more it is evident that it is pointless and meaningless.'"[1] Considering himself a scientist, Freud in *Civilization and Its Discontents* accuses the arts of escapism insofar as they indulge in such illusions as happy endings. At one point he calls art a narcosis—in other words, the escapism of a drug trip. For the theme of *Civilization and Its Discontents* is that the limitations of reality make human wishes unfulfillable: adult maturity demands constant repression of all our deeper desires if civilization is going to remain possible, a prospect about which Freud was not overly optimistic.

Freud can perhaps be dismissed as a neurotic pessimist. But what if we turn to Jung, who, like Frye, was so much more open to visionary possibilities that many dismiss him as a mystical irrationalist? In his great essay "The Stages of Life," Jung says that happy endings, at least as we normally conceive them, are for the young. Marriage, family, money, fame, success in a career: typically, these things have already been accomplished by mid-life, and the mid-life crisis deepens as one realizes that the objects of desire do not constitute a happy ending even when possessed. First of all, life is a series of compromises. Pick into any happy ending, a marriage for example, deconstruct it, as they say, and one will discover various ironies and limitations beneath the surface about which the parties involved are either resigned or in denial.

Shakespeare's *Much Ado About Nothing* is supposed to be one of the so-called festive comedies, yet it can achieve its happy ending only by marrying one of its heroines to a man who has behaved selfishly and callously towards her for the whole play, and who seems more chastened than redeemed at its end. She wants him, but we ask ourselves privately what this marriage is going to be like, because we have all been to weddings like *that* in real life.

Second, Jung says, even those whose wishes have been fulfilled are now faced with the question of why people live to seventy or eighty if their goals have already been achieved at half that age? "We have to grant these people," he says, "that it is hard to see what other goal the second half of life can offer than the well-known aims of the first. Expansion of life, usefulness, efficiency, the cutting of a figure in society, the shrewd steering of offspring into suitable marriages and good positions—are not these purposes enough? Unfortunately not enough meaning and purpose for those who see in the approach of old age a mere diminution of life and can feel their earlier ideals only as something faded and worn out."[2] The journey of middle to old age is one of progressive loss: the body ages and declines; the family undergoes a diaspora; in work one learns the Citizen Kane lesson that worldly success does not satisfy human needs; and one gets more and more accustomed to going to funerals as every friend, and, finally, even one's best loved are lost to the ultimate unhappy ending of death. It is silly to dismiss this thinking as neurotic and morbid when decay and death are the normal and inevitable course of every human life. All life is sorrowful, the Buddha said. *All* life. Indeed, to dismiss this fact, Jung says, leads, especially in America, to the real neurosis, a panicky refusal to grow old, what Ernest Becker called the denial of death.[3] American film scholars have often criticized a trend in the 1980s and 1990s towards "feelgood" movies, films that achieve their happy ending either by simplifying the ironies and limitations of the human condition or by manufacturing magical means by which they can be transcended. Such attacks are not necessarily motivated by intellectual snobbery; what the scholars fear is the falsification of history. Once we say it is acceptable to believe what we want or need to believe, there is no delusion that human beings are not capable of, not even something of such magnitude as the denial of the Holocaust. One popular film of the period, *Back to the Future*, goes even further: not only can the failures of the past be repaired and its wounds healed, history can be changed so that the failures never really happened. There is actually a profound insight latent in this piece of light entertainment, for it is arguable that the deeper wounds suffered in life are not capable of being healed. In the vision of tragedy, Lear's daughter Cordelia can "Never, never, never, never, never" be alive for him again. Contrast the happy ending of the Book of Job, in which Job learns that, to the contrary, dead daughters are as replaceable as automatic coffeemakers. Frye notes (*GC*, 197) that in real life, three replacement daughters, even if they are new and improved models, are not going to compensate for the wrenching loss of the old ones. Even if Job had got the old ones back, the trauma of the loss might have hurt him beyond repair, as the loss of Cordelia shattered Lear.

Providential views of history, whether religious or Marxist, Hegelian or Wordsworthian, imply that the ideal future goal justifies all the sufferings and losses that led to it. But that is history from the point of view of the winners. There is, as usual, a parallel in private life: in comedies, we are led to sympathize with the winners, that is, with the lovers who are going to achieve the happy ending. But what about the rival who loses out, the one who is not loved? In the spirit of the moment, the audience usually does not care, because the author has been careful to portray him unsympathetically. Comedy focuses on the triumph of desire over the blocking character—but what if someone discovers that, to the love of his life, *he* is the blocking character? The point is that in many cases, happy endings could only be conceivable not by virtue of consolation in the future, but by ensuring that certain suffering will never have happened. Thus, the ultimate enemy of the happy ending is time, because time is the irrevocable fabric of the human condition. In the tragic vision we are exactly what the title of Frye's book on tragedy calls us, fools of time.

In the structure of comedy, the happy ending typically begins when the action has reached its lowest, darkest point, and by now my argument has perhaps become so melancholic that it is time to seek what Aristotle called the *peripeteia*, the turning point, which comes suddenly, and from the least likely quarter. The least likely quarter here is a novel by, of all people, Edith Wharton, an author in whom Frye had no apparent interest and probably would not have liked, for the same reason that he disliked the *Iliad* and Thomas Hardy. To say that Edith Wharton is not known for her happy endings is like saying that *Titus Andronicus* is just a little bit violent. Wharton's short novel *Summer* is the story of Charity Royall and the man in whose house she has grown up, Lawyer Royall. Royall, to Charity's disgust, is in love with her, although he is old enough to be her father. Charity is eighteen, and her coming-of-age story consists of a passionate relationship with the young and desirable Lucius Harney. As everybody but Charity can see, Lucius can never marry her because she is not of his elite social class. Predictably enough, she gets pregnant and he abandons her. Charity now has few options. If she stays in her rural village community of North Dormer, she will be slandered and ostracized like Hawthorne's Hester Prynne. If she flees to the next town, she has no means of providing for herself and her child except prostitution. To many readers' horror, Charity's fate is precisely that which she had tried her whole life to escape: trapped in the ignorant, insular world of North Dormer, married to a man old enough to be her parent, Lawyer Royall. So much for happy endings. Of all the writers I know, Hardy and Wharton insist most unremittingly on the inescapable fatedness of life's limitations.

That is the entire story, yet not the entire picture. At the point in the book at which it is becoming clear that Charity's hopes will be dashed, Lawyer Royall gives a speech at an Old Home Week celebration. The speech goes on for so long, and at that point seems so unrelated to the main action, that the reader is puzzled. Only after the novel is finished can one go back and see its full significance. This is the final part of that address:

> Gentlemen, let us look at things as they are. Some of us have come back to our native town because we'd failed to get on elsewhere. One way or other, things had gone wrong with us ... what we'd dreamed of hadn't come true. But the fact that we had failed elsewhere is no reason why we should fail here. Our very experiments in larger places, even if they were unsuccessful, ought to have helped us to make North Dormer a larger place ... and you young men who are preparing even now to follow the call of ambition, and turn your back on the old homes—well, let me say this to you, that if ever you do come back to them it's worth while to come back to them for their good ... After a while, I believe you'll be able to say, as I can say today: "I'm glad I'm here." Believe me, all of you, the best way to help the places we live in is to be glad we live there.[4]

This seems a kind of Stoic resignation, and on one level it is. But that is not the final level of the novel's vision, for both Charity and Lawyer Royall have been transformed from what they were at the story's beginning. Charity's name of course means "love," and a Northrop Frye would observe that she is associated throughout with the Eros colours of red and white. Yet while Charity has an erotic and romantic awakening, she is anything but charitable in the compassionate sense. On the very last page of the book, both characters' experiences have granted them not a reprieve from their fate, but an expanded vision within it. We know this because they are now able to say to each other, using the very word that Royall's speech made double meanings of, what they could never have said while locked into their previous self-interested desire: "You're a good girl, Charity," he says. "I guess you're good, too," she says. No tragedy has been averted, no fate consoled; Wallace Stevens's "things as they are" remain all around them. But as Blake said, "As the Eye, Such the Object," and their vision has been enlarged. Romantic love is not necessarily bad, but it at least begins as self-centred: the loved one is an object that will fulfil my needs, my desires, and this leads to a dangerous possessiveness. Charity loses forever her object of romantic desire, and the rest of her life closes down as a result. But her name now stands for another kind of love.

The final insight is actually very simple. In ordinary experience, there is no happy ending, because ordinary experience means the ego or subject alienated from its object, which it consequently either fears or desires, or both at once. The ego cannot close that gap between itself and the object without ceasing to be an ego; its very nature is by definition alienated self-consciousness: that is what the Freudian poststructuralist Jacques Lacan meant when he said that the subject is *constituted by* a split. We can never become whole because being split off, being what Heidegger calls "thrown," is our very nature. Even if we attain the object of desire, we are still alienated from it.

But what if the happy ending of comedy and romance does not refer to the ego's wishes at all? Another way of asking the question is, to whom does the happy ending happen if not to the ego, to the "I"? And what good does it do *me* if it happens to some *other*? The ego is not bad, but it is by nature self-centred. After all, what else could the "I" be? It defines itself as the reality principle; whatever the ego is conscious of is real, and whatever is outside conscious experience is unreal and false. Historically, egocentric consciousness has been notoriously reluctant to admit the reality of anything beyond the direct evidence of the senses; science has had to go to the length of inventing and exploding nuclear bombs to convince the ego of the reality of invisible forces like electrons and quarks. Confronted by something transcendent, whether the unconscious or God, the ego stubbornly says, "Show me. I demand evidence, not just assertion. I stand for what is provably real, and all else is superstition." Clearly, the ego evolved because this attitude is practical. At the same time, it is not always realized that such a seemingly noble attitude is limited by a built-in arrogance: to measure everything by our own standards of reality is to declare those stan-

dards absolute and infallible. I may change my mind about the interpretation of this piece of evidence or that one, but the one thing I never
doubt is that my ego consciousness is the only competent, indeed the
only possible judge or what is real or unreal. What other standards can
I go by?

Yet even the ego finds it hard to deny that the ego is not only far
from being the only reality but is in the end something of a conjuror's
illusion. As Frye says on the final pages of *The Double Vision*, "We are
born on a certain date; ... then we move into an 'after'-life or 'next'
world where something like an ego survives indefinitely in something
like a time and place. But we are not continuous identities; we have
had many identities, as babies, as boys and girls, and so on through
life, and when we pass through or 'outgrow' these identities they
return to their source" (84–5). Not a day goes by when the ego does not
have to deal with some mood-swing or wayward impulse that beto-
kens psychic realities outside the ego's control and to a large extent
outside its line of vision.

Christianity, Jungian psychology, and Frye all agree that in addition
to the ego or natural self there is a second and spiritual self. Jung refers
to the two identities simply as ego and Self; as readers of *The Great Code*
and *Words with Power* are well aware, St Paul speaks (I Cor. 2:14 and
15:44) of the *soma psychikon*, or natural man, and the *soma pneumatikon*,
or spiritual man (*GC*, 20; *WP*, 124). Our life task, what Jung would call
the process of individuation, is to undergo a death-and-rebirth process
from the former into the latter. In an early notebook from the late
1940s, largely concerned with religion, Eastern and Western, but composed during a period when Frye was considerably preoccupied with
Jung, Frye observes, "But, as Jung says, the subconscious has its root in
the unconscious, & once the cruder forms of repression are abolished
the impulses from 'below' surge up & we become conscious of something, first 'compensating' for our conscious deficiencies, then expanding & bursting the ego so that the ego becomes revealed as the really
inert principle, the subjective seed in an objective reality which is to the
work of art what the censor is to the dream" (3.100).[5] "Bursting" is a
rather violent metaphor, but it may be that sometimes the ego's para-
noid clinging to its defences can only be broken through the hard way,
by the force of suffering. This is what happens to King Lear. The ego
cannot have the happy ending, which, we have seen, means that it cannot possess its objects of desire. We cannot possess anything in this
world, and sacrificing the happy ending means, for the ego, undergoing a dispossession. We are back in the world of the Eliot *Quartets*

again, where, in the well-known lines from "East Coker," "In order to possess what you do not possess / You must go by the way of dispossession." We have to relax the egocentric will and stop trying to hold on, not just to material possessions or worldly success but to those whom we most deeply love, and, finally, to the last possession, which is the ego itself. As Eliot says, "In order to arrive at what you are not / You must go through the way in which you are not." King Lear learns that to be dispossessed of all is to become "nothing," a leitmotif repeated endlessly in the text of the play. Nor is Eliot the only poet of Frye's period to affirm this negation, so to speak. In "Vacillation," Yeats's Great Lord of Chu says, "Let all things pass away," and "Lapis Lazuli" says that "All things fall and are built again, / And those who build them again are gay." Both poems link this vision to the wisdom of Chinese sages, and in Notebook 3 Frye was more preoccupied than in any other work with Eastern sources that could provide a parallel to his vision. His central interest lay in Zen Buddhism—in paragraph 110 he goes so far as to wonder if Protestantism and Zen "aren't the same thing, possessed by the same Saviour." This is the notebook which first mentions the Lankavatara Sutra, a principal Zen source for the doctrine known as Cittamatra, or Mind-only; but the Mind which is the only thing that exists is, again, not the ego but an infinitely larger self.

To use the appropriate figure, let us return full circle to the problem of the mid-life crisis of the unwritten Third Book and its attendant diagram, the Great Doodle. I would like to venture a tentative speculation about the reason that project could never be completed as originally conceived. Frye had never been fully comfortable with the heroic quest of the Great Doodle: its cyclical form indicated that it was still caught in the categories of the ego or natural self. The ego always thinks of itself as the hero, and thus falls into what Jung calls inflation. The Great Doodle as the quest of the natural self for the ego's wish-fulfilment is not the true way or journey but a parody of it that Frye sometimes called the Druid analogy, a term out of Blake referring to the Druids' worship of the natural man. For example, in Notebook 12, Frye qualifies his "cycle of topoi, what I used to call the Druid analogy" with the following description: "It's Druidical & mother-centered because it's a cycle, a spatial & temporal cycle of then & there. So it's really a kind of Inferno, for all its ending in heaven, an Inferno close to FW [*Finnegans Wake*] & the Yeats vision" (*TBN*, 240). It took thirty years, but Frye finally rearranged the four quadrants of the Doodle into a vertical *axis mundi*. This is the form in which they appear in the second half of *Words with Power*. When the walls of the ego begin to dissolve, what begin to appear are levels of consciousness that lie both above and below the horizontal level of ordinary experience. Frye now uses the metaphor of a vertical Jacob's ladder to refer to ascent and descent among these various levels. These appear as alien and other to the ego, but they are far from non-human; on the contrary, we use only a fraction of our mental capacity, and these vertical levels, if recovered, would represent a recovery of full mental functioning. In a metaphor that occurs everywhere from Shakespeare to Blake to the contemporary fantasist John Crowley, in his novel *Love and Sleep*, it is as if we have always been asleep and suddenly wake up; as if we have been lying down, horizontally, and suddenly take up our pallet and walk.

Nor is such an image of an awakened human body incidental. When we ask what it is that the ego is unconscious *of*, and therefore what is recovered or remembered when the walls of the ego become permeable, we begin to realize that we cannot stop with the repressed or forgotten thoughts that make up the Freudian unconscious. Jung calls this the personal unconscious because it is just that: parts of the ego, and partaking of its nature, that have become detached from the ego but that remain "personal" and are not truly "other." But a mind which is truly beyond the ego is beyond the ego's categories of time and space, mind and body, self and other, and so on through all the classic dualities posited by the Western cultural tradition. If "things as they are" are only appearances, products of the ego's organizing categories, then the reality that lies beyond them is paradoxical, and can be expressed only as a union of opposites. One form of this occurs in Zen, and in Notebook 3 Frye explains Aldous Huxley's failure in *The Perennial Philosophy* to make much of a particular Zen passage by saying that "The road to this kind of spiritual energy lies through paradox, & Huxley has no feeling for paradox" (3.52). The paradoxes occur when we begin to realize that we are not different either from our physical environment or from other people; we are only unconscious of the fact that they are part of us and we are part of them. This amazing passage occurs in Notebook 3:

I notice that Jung also speaks of the shift from ego to self as a geocentric-heliocentric metaphor. Surely there are many layers of unconsciousness. On top, below the personal unconscious, is the family & racial unconscious; our heritage from parents & the mental & physical makeup that says I, for instance, will resemble the English and not the Zulus or Siamese. Below that is the human unconscious, then the animal unconscious, then the organic unconscious & finally the material unconscious. (3.93)

The passage goes on to speak of the progressive awakening of these deep levels. Other people, animals, plants, even matter itself: these are other, yes, but not *merely* other. When the mental walls go down, there is a recognition that is in fact a remembrance of kinship, even communion.

Let us focus for the moment on our recovered relation to other human beings. To the ego, other people are objects to be desired, possessed, and mastered; objects which resist possession are to be feared and perhaps destroyed. Egocentric consciousness therefore perpetually vacillates between narcissism and paranoia. The reversal of this begins when we speak, in a meaningful phrase, of finding kindred spirits in the world. When it becomes intense enough, kinship turns into actual communion, and two people feel that, though remaining two, they are also somehow one, not only one mind but also one body, the "one flesh" of the marriage ceremony. The usual way of experiencing a sense of this is of course through sexual intercourse, as described in poems like Donne's "The Extasie" and Shakespeare's "The Phoenix and the Turtle."[6] But sexual experience is a transient epiphany of something that must be far more permanent.

The title for this essay comes from the following passage of *The Double Vision*:

> The growth of nature from a manifestation of order and intellectual coherence into an object of love would bring about the harmony of spirit and nature that has been a central theme of this work. Some recent writers have been deeply impressed by the conception in Chinese culture of a harmony between two similar worlds, usually translated as "heaven" and "earth," which is the goal of all genuinely human aspiration. We should perhaps not overlook the fact that what seems like the same kind of harmony is prominently featured in the Lord's Prayer. (*NFR*, 234)

The natural self or ego lives on earth; the spiritual Self lives in a higher order of reality we call heaven. But the kingdom of heaven is not otherworldly; it is within and among us, here and now, even if the ordinary self remains unconscious of it.

It seems likely that most conceptions of heaven are pitifully inadequate, given the complexity of human needs. Take the need for love: the most common notion of its eternal fulfilment is being with a spouse in an eternity of middle-class monogamous marriage. For some people, this could be a genuine image of fulfilment. But it did not take the divorce generation of the 1990s to begin to see some of the oversimplifications here. The Pharisees confronted Jesus with the problem of the woman who had seven successive husbands: what is to be her final fate in heaven, especially if, as is perfectly possible, she loved all of them? Jesus' answer, that in heaven there is to be neither marriage nor giving in marriage, is usually interpreted as meaning that we will all be disembodied souls and beyond such things, but that is not very satisfying either. If the higher Self is to be seen as a unity of selves that to ordinary consciousness seem isolated islands of consciousness, perhaps we have part of the answer. In Blake's poem *Milton*, the spiritual form of John Milton returns, through Blake, to reclaim his emanation Ololon, who is both his lost love and the feminine aspect of his own greater identity. But Ololon is sixfold, because there were six women in Milton's rather complicated personal life, three wives and three daughters. What he is reunited with is a total form of which all the women he had loved somehow form a part. Some may find this merely bizarre; for others it may be deeply suggestive and moving, not least because his relationship with one of those three wives had been so problematic that Milton had been inspired by it to compose his four tracts arguing for freedom of divorce. What gets in the way of love is always the will-to-power of the egocentric self. In *Words with Power*, Frye writes that "The Song of Songs tells us that love is as strong as death, but immediately adds that jealousy is as cruel as the grave, and sexual relations in themselves appear to be inseparable, according to the testimony of the poets, from the tension of egos, the sense of ownership and possession, the panics of status" (222–3). When a relationship comes to its final grief out of this tension of egos, the greatest heartbreak is often that the couple really did love each other. Blake seems to suggest that even such "divorces" have a redeemed aspect: when Jesus denied marriage in heaven, perhaps he meant that the power-brokering of egos will be dissolved. This would not eliminate what was genuinely loving between two people, but transfigure their love by removing it from the squabbling and arguments of damaged selves. As St Paul says, "We shall be changed," and our communion with other human beings shall not stop with the twofold, or even the sixfold. We are all members of one mystical body, one total self. In his two Bible books, Frye calls this the royal metaphor because of the old doctrine that the king was the embodiment of both his land and his people. In *Summer*, Charity's last name is Royall, at first signifying that she and Lawyer Royall are kindred spirits because they think they are better than anyone else in the town. But the climax of the novel is the burial service of Charity's mother, in which Paul's words about the transformation of the natural into the spiritual body are quoted for something close to two pages straight. Nothing is spelled out, but it is after this terrible epiphany on the mountaintop that Charity and Lawyer Royall are able to transcend their egos and call each other good.

In the Third Book notebooks, Frye repeatedly links Blake's *Milton* with two other works: *Paradise Regained* and *The Tempest*. *Paradise Regained* is the ultimate poem of dispossession; in it, Milton's Christ, again in a vision on a mountaintop, rejects every form of egocentric happy ending that Satan can tempt him with, saying instead to his higher Self, which he calls his Father, "Thy will be done, on earth as it is in heaven." And the Father's will was not marriage, success, and security, but crucifixion. In *The Tempest*, Shakespeare's Prospero renounces his magic and dispossesses us all by saying that we are such things as dreams are made on. But dispossession, when the ego says to something greater than itself, Thy will be done, is only the first half of a double movement. The second half is a reversal, in which our consciousness gets turned inside out in what Blake called a vortex, Eastern thought calls a *paravritti*, or turning about, and the Bible calls *metanoia*, or conversion. Decreation, then recreation: this is a continuous, dynamic, dialectical process. It slowly becomes apparent that the true form behind *Words with Power* is neither the cycle of the Great Doodle nor the simple vertical of the *axis mundi* with which it begins, but the spiral. As usual with Frye, there had been intimations of the spiral many years before: paragraph 45 of Notebook 3 says that "There is a third movement which is neither straight nor curved but vortical." The spiral is a mandala become open-ended and dynamic. In "The Symbol Without Meaning," Joseph Campbell claims that we have to go beyond the Jungian mandala and its closed, static perfection.[7] Symbols, he tells us, may function for engagement, like the mandala whose circle returns upon itself with safe enclosure, or for disengagement. But if the latter,

> That is the victory of yoga. And one cannot gaze on the world, after that,
> with any of the fears and pieties of the virtuous citizen of the mandala, who
> has not yet watched God himself, together with his universe, evaporate like
> dew at dawn. As we read in a celebrated Buddhist text [*Vajracchedika*]:
>
>> Stars, darkness, a lamp, a phantom, dew, a bubble,
>> A dream, a flash of lightning, or a cloud:
>>   Thus should one look upon the world.[8]

But actually the spiral is Jung's final symbol also, an image of the dynamic alchemical process of transformation that was for him identical to the psychological process of individuation. The spiral has closure and therefore form, because it returns upon itself; yet it is also open-ended.

In a key passage of Notebook 3, Frye says, "There doesn't seem to be a recognized yoga of art, not that it matters, for there is one anyway ... Suppose I call it Sutra-Yoga. Sutra, like strophe & verse, means the turn, the vortical twist of the mind in the imagined form. Sutra-Yoga, then, is identical with what I have been calling anagogy, & I have to discover its principles—in a sense have already done so" (3.47). Forty years later, in the final chapter of *Words with Power*, Frye is still speaking of this yoga of art as a spiral that he calls the purgatorial process, likening it to Dante's climb up a spiral mountain. But it is really more like Yeats's image of the double gyre, two interpenetrating spirals, descending and ascending movements of creation and recreation. Frye defines apocalypse in *The Great Code* as what the world looks like after the ego has disappeared. The spiral may seem a rather abstract image—though in fact it is one of the oldest of all human symbols, dating back into the Paleolithic—but it is the pattern of the happy ending insofar as it means anything profounder than the ego's wish-fulfilment. We may possess nothing, and in light of this knowledge ordinary consciousness is elegiac, a perpetual grieving for the transience of everything we love, which is at all moments saying goodbye. The usual consolation is the hope for possession in an afterlife, but that is a false solution to the problem. In the final paragraph of the final book he ever wrote, Frye says in *The Double Vision*:

> If death is the last enemy to be destroyed, as Paul tells us, the last metaphor to be transcended is that of the future tense, or God in the form of Beckett's Godot, who never comes but will maybe come tomorrow. The omnipresence of time gives some strange distortions to our double vision ... There is nothing so unique about death as such, where we may be too distracted by illness or sunk in senility to have much identity at all. In the double vision of a spiritual and a physical world simultaneously present, every moment we have lived through we have also died out of into another order. Our life in the resurrection, then, is already here, and waiting to be recognized. (*NFR*, 235)

The happy ending will never happen to the ego. But it is here and now, nevertheless, to some other part of ourselves, though we may spend our lives spiralling ever closer to an understanding, which is also an experience, of what that can possibly mean. If ever we could experience it fully, it would mean that we would finally have returned for good to our true home.

NOTES

1 Heinz R. Pagels, *Perfect Symmetry: The Search for the Beginning of Time* (1985) (New York: Bantam, 1986), 383.
2 C.G. Jung, "The Stages of Life," in *The Structure and Dynamics of the Psyche*, vol. 8 of *The Collected Works of C.G. Jung,* ed. Herbert Read et al. (London: Routledge & Kegan Paul, 1960), 400 (par. 789).
3 Ernest Becker, *The Denial of Death* (New York: Free Press, 1973).
4 Edith Wharton, *Summer: A Novel* (New York: Harper & Row, 1979), 194–5 (chap. 13).
5 As in Robert Denham's essay, unpublished notebooks are cited in the form "Notebook number.paragraph number." All notebooks are in NFF.
6 In "The Survival of Eros in Poetry," Frye says of "The Phoenix and the Turtle," "there the biblical metaphor of two people becoming 'one flesh' in marriage is applied, in an erotic context, to the union in 'death,' which can mean sexual union, of a red bird and a white bird on St. Valentine's Day ... Donne uses the same kind of imagery, especially in 'The Canonization'" (*MM*, 50). Elsewhere he says, "In Donne's poem 'The Extasie' two bodies joined in sexual union produce two souls that merge into a single entity. The barrier between subject and object disappears, and the single entity is thereby enabled to enter an experience that is not wholly in time ... But of course the clock still goes on ticking in the ordinary world, the united soul dissolves and returns to the two bodies, and ordinary experience is reestablished" (*MM*, 26).
7 Joseph Campbell, "The Symbol without Meaning," in *The Flight of the Wild Gander: Explorations in the Mythological Dimension* (New York: Viking, 1969), 189–90.
8 Campbell, "Symbol without Meaning," 176–7.

JAN GORAK

From Escape to Irony: Frye's "The Argument of Comedy"

At the start of September 1948, the English Institute met at Columbia University in New York. The purpose of the institute, founded in 1939, was to reorient the discipline of English in the United States from its positivist, philological bias towards a more speculative, theoretical method of inquiry. Columbia had provided early sponsorship, with distinguished faculty members past, present, and future—including James Clifford, Carl van Doren, Marjorie Hope Nicolson, and William York Tindall—supplying strong participation. Cleanth Brooks and Robert Penn Warren, at that time still at the State University of Louisiana, and René Wellek, then at Iowa, were also early leaders of the organization. W.H. Auden, at the time attached to the New School of Social Research in New York, read a paper on "Allegory and Mimesis" at the second meeting. Early contributions show an institution still in search of an identity: some papers were hangovers from the age of *belles lettres*, while others make rather imposing contributions to the history of ideas. After a wartime hiatus, however, many of the institute's early intellectual objectives were coming to fruition. Its membership continued to draw on a wide constituency. William Carlos Williams delivered "An Approach to the Poem" at the 1947 session, whose participants included distinguished foreign critics attached to American institutions, like the Scottish David Daiches and the Canadian E.K. Brown, then both teaching at the University of Chicago. A spine of central problems and directions for future study—the role of myth, the relationship between literary history and literary criticism, the theory of fiction—was clearly beginning to take shape.

At the 1948 meeting session leaders were David Daiches, René

Wellek, and Philip Wheelwright. Featured speakers included R.S. Crane, Leslie Fiedler, Robert Heilman, and William K. Wimsatt. Wallace Stevens delivered the keynote address, a difficult and challenging lecture on "Imagination as Value." One of the participants was Northrop Frye, whose pathbreaking book on Blake, *Fearful Symmetry*, had, after many delays, appeared to considerable acclaim the previous year. Frye's trenchant reclamation of myth and vision as the neglected foundations of English poetry made him a natural contributor to the proposed section on myth and literature in Shakespeare. His paper, "The Argument of Comedy," the first paper delivered to the institute by a teacher from a Canadian university, was duly assigned to this section.

From this point my story assumes the shape of scholarly dream: after its publication in 1949 "The Argument of Comedy" quickly became one of the classics of postwar criticism, reprinted in anthologies on Shakespearean drama, tragedy, and comedy alike, and, as George Hunter has observed, "drawn on in a thousand student papers" ever since.[1] Its status as a pedagogical tool and a theoretical breakthrough can hardly be disputed. Possibly one of the reasons for this unprecedented success lies in the simplicity that Frye himself would argue underlay even the most ambitious intellectual structures.[2] Cutting through a mountain of materials about comic sources, influences, the charm of the heroines, and the pallor of the heroes, Frye instead considered the structural properties of Shakespeare's comedy, noting that it "begins in a world represented as a normal world, moves into the green world, goes into a metamorphosis there in which the comic resolution is achieved, and returns to the normal world."[3] Frye's "green world" serves as the location for the myths of rebirth and renewal that he sees as the comic counterpart to the myths of dismemberment and annihilation enacted in tragedy. But he also suggests that this account of comic structure subserves "a profounder pattern" of considerable significance to a postwar world. Through the typical comic journey from oppressive normality, liberating escape, and ultimate return to a transformed normality, Frye perceives "the vision of a free society" snatched from the repressive machinery of ordinary social reality. Not only does Frye's structural analysis enable him to unify the bewildering course of Shakespearean comedy from *The Comedy of Errors* to *The Tempest*, but his account of the purpose of comedy raises the genre itself to a new level of social concern, integrating Shakespeare's *play* with the *serium ludere* and Utopian world-view of Renaissance humanists like Erasmus, More, and Rabelais. As C.L. Barber observes, Frye's is "a brilliant, compressed summary of the whole literary tradition of comedy and Shakespeare's relation to it."[4]

These facts are anything but new to students of Frye. Two issues remain less explored by his critics, however. First, what is the relationship of Frye's essay to the broader seam of twentieth-century concern with comedy and laughter that begins with Bergson's *Le Rire* (*On Laughter*) (1900) and extends to the publication of Edmund Wilson's *The Wound and the Bow* (1941)? Frye's methods of composition, his habit of absorbing his predecessors rather than citing them, his rapid transit from aphorism to aphorism, are scarcely calculated to signal visible lines of intellectual descent. Yet bringing Frye's latent affinities with his predecessors into the foreground can only assist in consolidating his status as a major twentieth-century critic, since awareness of his precursors serves to intensify the conviction that Frye's contribution to a substantial critical twentieth-century discussion about comedy is unique. My second question explores Frye's relationship to his contemporaries rather than his predecessors. What does Frye's essay tell us about the nature of post-war criticism in general? George McFadden, who sees Frye's as a "redemptive theory, and far and away the most studied theory of comedy in America during recent years," nonetheless links it to an American tradition "according to which if one wants a dream to come true ardently enough to imagine it and to act vigorously upon one's imagined projection of it, one's belief ... may indeed bring the dream into being as the new reality."[5] As McFadden hints, a closer look at this influential essay might yield some important understanding about the interpretive procedures and ideological allegiances of postwar criticism in North America.

The late nineteenth and twentieth centuries mark the extension of scientific investigation into the analysis of social phenomena. One of the unexpected consequences of this extension was to bring social science more into line with the consciousness of social constraints previously acknowledged chiefly by the Victorian sages—Mill, Carlyle, Arnold. In *The Rules of Sociological Method* (1895), Emile Durkheim emphasizes that the social scientist's field of investigation begins where "ways of acting, thinking and feeling ... present the noteworthy property of existing outside the individual consciousness." Durkheim notes that this zone is not purely one of obligation or legal constraint, but that it pervades many social transactions previously considered as voluntary. He notes, "I am not obliged to speak French with my fellow-countrymen nor to use the legal currency, but I cannot possibly do otherwise. If I tried to escape this necessity, my attempt would fail miserably. As an industrialist, I am free to apply the technical methods of former centuries; but by doing so, I should invite certain ruin. Even when I free myself from these rules and violate them successfully, I am always compelled to struggle with them."[6] Durkheim's account of social performance and social institutions begins the long and steady erosion of the autonomous subject of nineteenth-century social thought, free to spend his money as he likes and to speak as he likes.

With the application of the methods of social science to non-Western societies, as in Bronislaw Malinowski's *Crime and Custom in Savage Society* (1926) and *Sex and Repression in a Savage Society* (1927), even the cherished distinction between primitive and civilized societies begins to look less stable. As Malinowski describes them, the Trobrianders begin to sound much more like Victorians than otherwise: theirs is a culture of enterprise, although their market is in fish rather than iron or steel and their method of transport canoes not railways. Trobriander clan loyalties are no less fervent than the loyalty of upperclass Englishmen to Eton or Harrow, and no less strategically advantageous. Moreover, Malinowski's Trobrianders do not shy away from a little gunboat diplomacy when disputes with neighbours rise to uncomfortable levels. Nevertheless, whether in Western Europe or the South Seas, human societies consist largely of law-abiding citizens for whom public order has rarely to be maintained by bloody penalty, but functions more continuously as unconscious constraint. "The threat of coercion and the fear of punishment do not touch the average man, whether 'savage' or 'civilized,'" Malinowski comments. "On the other hand, they are indispensable with regard to certain turbulent or criminal elements in either society. Again, there is a number of laws, taboos and obligations in every human culture which weigh heavily on every citizen, demand great self-sacrifice, and are obeyed for moral, sentimental or matter-of-fact reasons."[7] The whole tendency of early twentieth-century social science was to describe society—any society—in terms of unconscious constraint and invisible regulation. The "secret sharer" in any transaction is the group whose expectations and manners confer identity, sustain privilege, and discipline infraction by means of internal persuasion that rarely reaches the point of direct prohibition or punishment. Unconscious conformity rather than expanding liberty is the principal characteristic of both primitive and civilized societies. The nineteenth-century vision of mobility for the individual and progress for the species recedes before the imposing mechanism of Durkheim's oppressive social machinery.

The substitution of an all-encompassing policing mechanism for an expanding zone of ascending individual freedom differentiates twentieth-century social science from its predecessor. Consequently, when Henri Bergson decides to investigate the phenomenon of laughter, his search begins with "a logic of the imagination" that "obeys laws, or rather habits, which hold the same relation to imagination as logic does to thought." Bergson's search leads him to posit comedy as embedded in "something like the logic of the dream, but not that of a dream which would have been abandoned to the caprice of an individual fantasy, but the dream of an entire society." When Bergson's society dreams, however, it is not of freedom, but of constraint, since "laughter is, above all, corrective,"[8] its corrections aimed at reining in the individual whose pursuit of private obsession or lapses into inelasticity must be somehow reclaimed for the social fold.

Five years later, Freud, in *Jokes and Their Relation to the Unconscious* (1905), turned his attention not to Bergson's laughter, but to the structure of the joke and the psychology of the joker. In the very structure of the joke as narrative—its brevity, transparency, audience inclusion, stylization, and careful plotting—Freud discerns a speech act constructed to please an audience and in so doing release the tension of the speaker. Comedy, in Freud's theory, becomes a desperate bid to court favour, to dissolve the self once more into the protective cocoon of the social group. He notes that "Everything in jokes that is aimed at gaining pleasure is calculated with an eye to the third person, as though there were internal and insurmountable obstacles to it in the first person. And this gives us a full impression of how indispensable the third person is for the completion of the joking process."[9] One of Freud's most significant insights is into the impasse or blockage so central to the comic imagination. Pleasure itself thus becomes something to be courted, to be harried into being as the most fleeting and precious of social benefits. Hence too the natural bond that ties comedy to drama, the genre that uniquely requires an audience for its performance and reception.

To this Freud adds the unique hold that joking and comedy possess over consciousness. Freud's comedian seeks to attain through artifice what once was acquired easily enough through nature. He posits that "the euphoria which we endeavour to reach by these means is nothing other than the mood of a period of life in which we were accustomed to deal with our psychical work with a small expenditure of energy— the mood of our childhood, when we were ignorant of the comic, when we were incapable of jokes and when we had no need of humour to make us feel happy in our life."[10] Bergson's understanding of the great policing mechanism that underprops comedy clears a path for Freud's analysis of the ambivalent emotions of loss and euphoria that nurture it, and his explanation of the neurotic aim to please that makes the comedian, according to all received wisdom, the saddest and most harassed of social performers. Freud's analysis also supplies one of the leading images of the comic imagination, the child-adult represented in the work of Shakespeare, Dickens, Chaplin, and Keaton. Finally, if Freud raises the stakes concerning the complexity of needs and desires released in comedy, he potentially stifles any impulse to take comedy seriously as an art. Rather, *Jokes and Their Relation to the Unconscious* alerts its readers to the deeply symptomatic signals emitted by the joke, and the accumulations of anxiety and the quest for release that gather inside the joker.

The influence of social philosophy and psychoanalysis is soon registered by literary historians. F.M. Cornford's *The Origin of Attic Comedy* (1914) emphasizes the recurrent types and situations of ancient comedy, where tricky slaves, rebellious children, and ineffectual parents and masters recur in comic action with timeless, even shameless frequency. Cornford's attentiveness to structure, however, leads him to detect a recurrent moment in comedy in which the chorus steps back from and out of the dramatic action and addresses the audience directly. For Cornford, this split in the action highlights the ritual origins of comedy, and its status as a literary form that derives from ritual. Comedy points to the community and the satire of public personalities known to residents of *polis* and *forum*. But it also concerns itself with deep structures of revival and renewal, with an order that precedes civil society.

In subsequent decades, the influence of Bergson, Freud, and Cornford was felt on the tradition of American humour. Works like Van Wyck Brooks's *The Ordeal of Mark Twain* (1920) or H.L. Mencken's many volumes of *Prejudices* (1919–) are evidence that comedy is no longer regarded as clowning or elegance by twentieth-century criticism. But they are evidence, too, that to the twentieth-century critic comedy offers primarily the image of art and society in chains. Mencken's essay on American humorist and short-story writer Ring Lardner (1926), with which Frye appears familiar, praises the author's museum of American atrocities, "his incomparable baseball players, pugs, song-writers, Elks, small-town Rotarians and golf caddies." But beneath Mencken's relish for the individual awfulness of Lardner's protagonists is his assessment of their existence as collective testimony to the malaise of American culture. Mencken describes Lardner's characters as "flitting figures of a transient civilization"; "all his people share the same amiable stupidity, the same transparent vanity, the same shallow swinishness; they are all human Fords in bad repair, and alike at bottom."[11] Brooks's Twain, for all his liberating victories of style for a subsequent generation, is condemned to perform as the ritual scapegoat for Gilded Age America and censored by the crushing cultural decorum of the genteel tradition. The emphasis on recurrent types and situations identified as the basis of humour by Freud and Bergson merges with Durkheim's paradigm of social order as unconscious conformity to reach its apotheosis in Mencken's vision of an acquisitive society chained to its own acquisitiveness, or in Van Wyck Brooks's juggernaut mechanical order that endlessly reproduces itself at the expense of its citizens. The regular orderly society that had sustained so much of nineteenth-century social thinking becomes a coercive machine for twentieth-century North American literary intellectuals, who find in comedy the precise image of their frustrations with such a society. In such an America comedy is art manqué, its formal imperfections the visible signs of a blocked society.

For a younger generation that included T.S. Eliot, Edmund Wilson, and, as we shall see, Northrop Frye, apparent structural imperfection represents the essence of the comic vision. For both Eliot and Wilson, comedy is a mixed genre. In comedy these critics see unparallelled exactness in the representation of manners and mimicry of locutions. Eliot sees Marie Lloyd mimic a char lady before a working-class music hall audience mesmerised by its own image grotesquely raised to the power of art; Wilson praises Samuel Butler's meticulous reproduction of the mean self-approval of bourgeois idiom in *The Way of All Flesh*. They concur in seeing the exact reproduction of styles of living as the basis of comic art. But this is not all comedy does. To the precise representation of manners the comic artist adds his intuition of an alternative sphere of judgment from which to view the action. Where Cornford saw the heterogeneous origins of comedy in terms of a formal imperfection, his successors identify the unnerving properties of an absolute verdict or a penetrating glimpse of absurdity suddenly brought to bear on human transactions. Like Cornford, Eliot detects a sudden swerve outside the action in plays such as *Volpone* and *The Jew of Malta*. For Eliot, however, these are not flaws in artistic unity but survivals of "the old English comic humor, the terribly serious, even savage comic humor, the humor which spent its last breath on the decadent genius of Dickens."[12] The authority for this humour rests not on its ability to represent a society accurately, but in the power to judge it absolutely, in the unforgettable image of a Volpone crouched over his gold, Barabas's energetic mimicry of Christian piety and Christian rapacity, or Boffin's wealth-creating dustheaps in *Our Mutual Friend*. Wilson praises Shakespeare's power to enforce our sympathies with "those of his characters" who, like Falstaff or Shylock, "have been bent out of line by deformities or social pressures."[13] Of Dickens, in whom he sees a "childhood ... crushed by the cruelty of organized society," Wilson notes the power to fuse two heterogeneous activities—the farce of social manners and the psychological obsessions of the social actor—in an edgy, unstable humour where laughter supplies a momentary release from a life of slow mutilation by a victimizing society. In Dickens's laughter, Wilson detects "an exhilaration which already shows a trace of the hysterical. It leaps free of the prison of life; but gloom and soreness must always drag it back. Before he has finished *Pickwick* and even while he is getting him out of jail and preparing to unite the lovers, the prison will close in again on Dickens."[14] Where Eliot sees comedy as exposing humanity's vulnerability to a final absolute verdict, Wilson emphasizes the slow steady erosion of personal identity by unconscious neurosis inflicted by an impersonal social machine.

There was no shortage of serious critical responses to comedy, therefore, when Frye took to the lectern on 7 September 1948. Over sixty years of critical attention had transformed the supremely adult civilized monument to sparkling wit celebrated in George Meredith's "An Essay on Comedy" (1877) into the frantic cry for help of the essay on "Dickens: The Two Scrooges" that Edmund Wilson dedicated to the students of English 354 at the University of Chicago's Summer School. So what was Frye's contribution to the theoretical redefinition of comedy?

Frye's essay has an implicit three-part structure. In the first part, he describes the recurring types of comedy. Although his discussion of comedy's tricky slaves and impossible masters ostensibly derives much from Cornford, Frye adds his own significant contribution. For Frye, the recurring types of comedy belong to one seam of its structure. These characters are symptomatic of a fallen world, condemned to perpetual fantasies of power and dominance. But where the comic world of Eliot, Mencken, or Wilson saw little hope of emancipation from this fallen world, for Frye the characters associated with it soon shrink into insignificance, as the comic action relocates in a green world where a younger generation embodies hope for a renewed future. This change of place initiates a second stage of the action that propels a group of young people away from the imprisoning society of their elders into a world that—like Portia's Belmont or the forest of *As You Like It*—embodies an antithetical system of values from those represented in the opening of the play. When this youthful group returns from their interlude in the green world, they extend, humanize, and transform the world of power through the "spirit of reconciliation" acquired from outside its walls. Even society's most self-inflicted wounds can still be cured for Frye. These two parts of the essay add up to about nine-tenths of the whole. In the final page and a half, however, Frye offers some potent asides about the unreality of the green world and the world of power alike to the shaping power of the imagination.

Frye does not take issue with the assumption that comedy is a formulaic vehicle. Instead, he emphasizes the longevity of the standard comic formulas and their function in comic plotting and characterization. "The miser, the hypochondriac, the hypocrite, the pedant, the snob" are for Frye recurrent comic types from Aristophanes to Ibsen, who puts comic types to tragic uses in *Ghosts* and *Little Eyolf* with devastating consequences. But for Frye such types all exhibit "some kind of mental bondage." The emphasis on mental affliction rather than social malaise might not seem to carry us very far from Edmund Wilson or H.L. Mencken. Yet Frye gives these obsessions his own twist. He isolates the characters, and emphasizes not their accumulation into a society, but their self-insulating properties: "These are people who do not fully know what they are doing, who are slaves to a predictable self-imposed pattern of behavior" (61). The existing social world for Frye is more of an anti-society stripped to its drives and desires than an oppressive social machine.

Frye now pits characterization against plot in his description of comic action. He points to the recurrent comic typology of young love thwarted and young love united that has been the mainstay of comic authors for centuries. He contrasts the bonds freely accepted by the young lovers with the self-imposed neurotic shackles that afflict the older generation. He notes how, as the young hero and heroine come ever closer to each other, "all the right-thinking people"—including the audience—come over to their side. Even the blocked and neurotic adults who ruled the play world at the start of the comedy begin to lose their anti-social impediments. Accordingly, "a new social unit is formed on the stage, and the moment that this social unit crystallizes is the moment of the comic resolution. In the last scene, when the dramatist usually tries to get all his characters on the stage at once, the audience witnesses the birth of a renewed sense of social integration"

(60–1). Frye does not sever the bond that has linked the comic imagination to society for twentieth-century students from Bergson to Wilson, but channels it into a completely opposite direction. The originality of Frye's contribution derives from his argument that comedy dramatizes a society's capacities to grow and to transform, capacities he is unusual, maybe even unique, in recognizing among twentieth-century writers on comedy. For the policing of society that loomed so large in twentieth-century comic theory Frye substitutes a festive emancipation. "The impersonal laws of comic form," perceived by Bergson and Freud as a kind of disciplinary mechanism, become for Frye what Malinowski might call the social charters of a tolerant, expanded society able "to include as many as possible in its final festival" (62).

When Frye moves from a general sketch of comedy to a specific analysis of Shakespeare, the emphasis on myth and ritual relegates any talk of blocking figures to a marginal position. For Frye, Shakespeare represents the triumph of comedy and a moral norm he characterizes as neither conformity nor survival but what he calls "deliverance" (71). Frye's discussion of Shakespearean comedy emphasizes the sense of a transfiguring ending. In "the wonderful cosmological harmonies" that bring *The Merchant of Venice* to a close, the "carnival society, not so much a green world as an evergreen one" (68) of *Twelfth Night*, and "the halcyon peace" (72) at the conclusion of *Cymbeline*, Frye ascends nearer and nearer to a Utopian vision in which official social reality as administered by kings and parents is seen as a mistake, a temporary phase that a restored social organism will overcome.

When Frye turns his attention to the history plays, his iconoclasm stiffens. Acknowledging the "gigantic shadow" that Falstaff casts over the Henry plays, Frye raises him from the comic type of *miles gloriosus* to the status of a radical rebel, an "outlaw who manages to suggest a better kind of society than those who make him an outlaw can produce" (71). By his "temporary reversal of normal standards" Falstaff projects history backwards into a society of abundance and equality, "an original golden age which the normal world had usurped and which makes us wonder if it is not the normal world that is the real Saturnalia" (71–2). It is as if Frye has rewritten Freud and replaced the momentary freedom and long-term bondage of Freud's humorist with the eternal freedom and temporary constraints of a Falstaff. Falstaff thus offers an unofficial alternative to the accepted course of adult life, political history, and social reality. His challenge to the *status quo ante* could scarcely be greater.

Yet this does not exhaust all Frye has to say about comedy. In the last phase of his discussion, as he shifts from analysis of *Henry IV* to consideration of *The Tempest*, the two strands of Frye's vision appear to separate. At an assembly whose keynote speaker was Wallace Stevens, it is perhaps not surprising that Frye's ultimate vision of comedy in its final phase should not be of Falstaff, lord of misrule, but of Prospero, the prince of metadrama. In Frye's words, "For Shakespeare, the subject matter of poetry is not life, or nature, or reality, or revelation ... but poetry itself, a verbal universe" (73). Frye steps back from the vision of freedom embodied in festive comedy, and *a fortiori* from the militant counterhistory represented by Falstaff. At the apex of Frye's version of "the argument of comedy" is Prospero's stage-managed vision of the shifting traffic between reality and illusion:

> The famous speech of Prospero about the dream nature of reality applies equally to Milan and the enchanted island. We spend our lives partly in a waking world we call normal and partly in a dream world which we create out of our own desires. Shakespeare endows both worlds with equal imaginative power, brings them opposite one another, and makes each seem unreal when seen by the light of the other. He uses freely both the heroic triumph of New Comedy and the ritual resurrection of its predecessor, but his distinctive comic resolution is different from either: it is a detachment of the spirit born of the reciprocal reflection of two illusory realities. (72–3)

Phase one of Frye's comic theory brought the "pattern of a free society" (61) into his sights. The climax of phase two rests in Falstaff's golden age and its seriously anarchic challenge to the Tudor myth of Order. Phase three sees order and anarchy alike contained in "the detachment of the spirit" achieved through the shaping power of self-conscious imagination. Frye has liberated comedy from the images of social coercion that haunted Wilson and Mencken. But by the end of the essay he has transcended the notion of a liberal society as well. "The Argument of Comedy" is a fine example of the sceptical irony that so frequently bridled the Utopian impulses of post-war literary criticism in North America. Frye was always a critic much more willing than most of his contemporaries to entertain the prospect of Utopia encapsulated in an artistic work, and his ideas about comedy show this willingness stretched to a maximum. Ultimately, however, post-war criticism in English—and Frye's "Argument of Comedy" is no exception—remains an ironic, sceptical vehicle, committed to the power of imagination to present alternative perspectives on reality rather than to enforce its visionary truths in any one authoritative epiphany. Frye pins his faith on the artist not the dissident, because the artist recognizes the provisional status of his visionary kingdom, where the dissident or the rebel, like Caliban or Bolingbroke, merely wants to instal himself in power. Thus the play of imagination inside the artwork and across the Shakespearean canon gradually usurps Frye's vision of the world of play embodied in the dramatic action of any one protagonist or group of protagonists. Prospero comes to supplant Falstaff; the ironic artificer who can see that life is a dream marginalizes the subversive rebel. In 1948, when the Western world was still recovering from the giant shadow cast by Hitler, it is not really surprising that Frye should exhibit scepticism about rebellions "from below" and recast "the argument of comedy" as a dream vision rather than a social critique.

NOTES

1 George Hunter, "Northrop Frye's 'Green World': Escapism and Transcendence," in *Shakespeare: Le Monde Vert* (Paris: Les Belles Lettres, 1995). Professor Hunter's piece was a great help in the preparation of this essay.

2 In "Oswald Spengler," broadcast on CBC radio 23 Nov. 1955, Frye stated that "if we look at the thinkers who have permanently changed the shape of human thought ... we find, naturally, that their books are complex and difficult and require years of study. Yet the central themes of their work are of massive simplicity" (*RW*, 323).

3 Northrop Frye, "The Argument of Comedy," in *English Institute Essays, 1948*, ed. D.A. Robertson, Jr (New York: Columbia University Press, 1949), 68, 67. All page references to this article subsequently cited within the text.

4 C.L. Barber, *Shakespeare's Festive Comedy* (Princeton: Princeton University Press, 1959), 11n.

5 George McFadden, *Discovering the Comic* (Princeton: Princeton University Press, 1982), 159, 171.

6 Emile Durkheim, *The Rules of Sociological Method*, 8th ed., trans. Sarah A. Solovay and John H. Mueller (New York: Free Press, 1965), 2, 3.

7 Bronislaw Malinowski, *Crime and Custom in Savage Society* (New Jersey: Littlefield, Adams, 1962), 13–14.

8 Henri Bergson, *Le Rire: Essai sur la Signification du Comique* (Paris: Presses Universitaires de France, 1970), 32, 150. My translation.

9 Sigmund Freud, *Jokes and Their Relation to the Unconscious*, vol. 8 of *Complete Psychological Works of Sigmund Freud*, trans. James Strachey (London: Hogarth Press, 1960), 155.

10 Freud, *Jokes*, 236.

11 H.L. Mencken, "Lardner," in *Prejudices: Fifth Series* (New York: Alfred A. Knopf, 1926), 50, 51–2.

12 T.S. Eliot, "Notes on the Blank Verse of Christopher Marlowe" (1919), in *The Sacred Wood* (New York: Barnes & Noble, 1960), 92.

13 Edmund Wilson, "J. Dover Wilson on Falstaff" (1944), in *Classics and Commercials: A Literary Chronicle of the Forties* (London: W.H. Allen, 1951), 166.

14 Edmund Wilson, "Dickens: The Two Scrooges" (1940), in *The Wound and the Bow: Seven Studies in Literature* (Cambridge: Houghton Mifflin, 1941), 15, 14.

WANG NING

Northrop Frye and Cultural Studies

As one of the most important North American literary critics of the 1950s and '60s, Northrop Frye is closely associated with the rise of myth-archetypal criticism, which marked the demise of the New Criticism and which has always been thought of as elitist and thus confined to (elite) literary criticism proper. In the current context of cultural criticism and cultural studies, myth-archetypal criticism has been superseded—although it is still occasionally practised—and those who were active with Frye or who enthusiastically applied Frye's theory have almost been forgotten. Frye himself is still frequently cited and even now and then discussed, but usually in a negative manner, in the current debate on postcolonial studies and cultural studies.[1] It is not surprising that Frye's contributions to contemporary cultural studies on the lines of F.R. Leavis have been partially ignored. But as an independent scholar and cultural critic, Frye indeed played a significant role in the process of cultural criticism and cultural studies, especially in North America, as both A.C. Hamilton and Hayden White have acknowledged.[2] My intent in the present essay is to further this study from the wider perspective of cultural studies, crossing the boundaries between elite culture and folk culture, mainstream literature and postcolonial literature, literary discourse and cultural discourse, literature and other disciplines or branches of learning, and finally, between Oriental and Occidental literature, in an attempt to "rediscover" Frye's pioneering role and the significance of his works to current cultural studies.

Recoding Frye: Between Modernism and Postmodernism

In today's context "cultural studies" refers not to the traditional study of "canonical" or "elite" culture of which literature is one of the elegant products, but to studies of ethnicity, gender, media, area, Diaspora, identity, and other marginalized or repressed discourses. During his lifetime, Frye actually touched upon most of these topics in his writings. From a North American point of view, even from an international point of view, Frye should thus be regarded as one of the pioneering figures of contemporary cultural criticism and cultural studies. His category of literature includes such "low" and "marginal" cultural products as mythologies and folklores, even though he views them from the elitist perspective of high literature. Since a good deal of Frye's literary criticism was written and published in the period of "postmodernism," in which the modernist principles of totality or senses of centre have been severely challenged, Frye could not but be affected by this trend, whether consciously or unconsciously. Thus I will begin by discussing his relations with postmodernism/poststructuralism.

In my previous studies, I pointed out that, although Frye started his critical career by challenging New Critical formalistic doctrine and rose to the fore as an archetypal critic, his critical thinking is closely related to New Critical doctrine. Frye is often regarded in North American critical circles as one of the last important critics of New Criticism, and one of the first critics of structuralism.[3] However, as a transitional figure straddling literary modernism and postmodernism, he never totally involved himself in the tradition of the elitist New Criticism. Frye dealt simultaneously with issues in three relevant fields—English literature, Canadian literature, and literary theory and criticism—but he is famous chiefly for the archetypal criticism which, according to René Wellek, was in the 1960s as influential as Marxism and psychoanalysis. In contrast to the linguistic-centred New Critical doctrine, Frye's archetypal theory is more closely related to the anthropological approach, which has not only occupied an important place in contemporary cultural studies but even helped replace the "linguistic turn" with an "anthropological turn." His cultural criticism as well as his traditional literary criticism thus merits close attention.

Since contemporary cultural studies is heavily influenced by Marxist critical theory, especially the critical theory of the Frankfort School in Germany and cultural materialism in the English-speaking world, we might well overlook Frye's significant contributions. Frye always operated outside Marxist currents. But we should not forget that one of the aims of cultural studies is to break through the artificial "centre" of academia. Cultural studies thus take different directions and assume a variety of forms. To place Marxist critical theory under the umbrella of cultural studies is not at all surprising, given the works of such Western Marxists as Raymond Williams, Stuart Hall, Fredric Jameson, and Terry Eagleton. The same is true of Lacanian psychoanalysis in the poststructuralist sense. One might be tempted to place Northrop Frye's critical theory under the umbrella of the New Criticism and modernist critical theory, partly because of Frye's formalist criticism but primarily because of his persistent focus on literary criticism in its elite sense. We would probably conclude, however, that Frye cannot be positioned in the line of the elite New Critical discourse. One might then ask whether Frye could be regarded as a critical theorist with postmodern affinities, as he has enlarged the scope of elite literature.[4]

Generally speaking, the answer is no, as Frye never agreed with the critical doctrines formulated by such postmodern/poststructural critics as Jacques Derrida and Michel Foucault—although he was once highly praised by the Marxist postmodern critic Fredric Jameson for his innovation in traditional myth criticism. Why then should we continue to discuss Frye's relevance to current critical and theoretical debate, now that he is regarded as being out of fashion? In my view, the reason is that many of the issues Frye dealt with years ago are still significant to contemporary cultural studies. Apart from his other possible roles in the evolution of Western critical theory, Frye was one of the very few cultural critics who conscientiously positioned their critical practice within a broad context of cultural criticism of literary phenomena and their relations with social contexts.

Scholars of cultural studies usually agree that F.R. Leavis was a pioneering figure in contemporary cultural studies, despite his elitism. But what is Frye's place in the movement? To Leavis, culture is the product of a few people, and ordinary people can be better educated only by reading works of high literature. But to Frye, literature has a close relationship with myth and people's folklore; thus literary studies should be very much concerned with society and community life. In practice, Frye not only examined the work of Shakespeare, Blake, T.S. Eliot, and Yeats, but also paid particular attention to postcolonial Canadian literature. So we should certainly add Frye's name to the list of the pioneers of cultural studies if it is defined in its broader sense.

In positioning with Frye within contemporary cultural studies Hayden White tries to defend him against the accusations of contemporary practitioners of cultural studies that he "had trouble with history" and was thus "ahistorical" or even an "idealist." But White further argues, "Contemporary practitioners of what has come to be called 'cultural studies' have not on the whole found much of use in Frye's work. In part this is because cultural studies is a neo-Marxist activity, inspired by the example of such figures as Gramsci, Raymond Williams, Stuart Hall, Jürgen Habermas, and Louis Althusser, adamantly historicist therefore and paranoically hostile to anything smacking of formalism, structuralism, idealism, or organicism."[5] After a serious analysis of cultural elements in Frye's works that differ from Marxist doctrines, White points out, "Finally, and this strikes me as the most importantly realistic aspect of Frye's idea of cultural history (as against its alleged 'idealism'), the prefiguration-fulfillment model of cultural change, with its notion of retrospective expropriation of the products of past creative efforts, reminds us of the 'fallen' nature of any exercise of merely human creativity, namely, that it is always an exercise of power, that it is violent, and that it redeems itself only in the extent to which it 'makes new' the cultural artifacts it used as the material cause of its own operation."[6] Obviously, as I have mentioned, contemporary cultural studies take a variety of forms, ranging from cultural theory proper in regard to its aesthetic product, literature, to studies of mass media in the age of globalization; the recasting of literary cultures from the perspective of anthropology; and research on issues of gender, identity, and postcoloniality. Frye's own focus is undoubtedly on literary phenomena, which he interprets from the perspective of a literary or cultural theory.

Not all Marxists have neglected Frye's cultural criticism. Fredric Jameson, for instance, pertinently points out

The greatness of Frye, and the radical difference between his work and that of the great bulk of garden-variety myth criticism, lies in his willingness to raise the issue of community and to draw basic, essentially social, interpretive consequences from the nature of religion as collective representation. In so doing, Frye rejoins, although he would probably not enjoy the association, that more positive approach to religious symbolism which in the nineteenth century succeeded the essentially negative and destructive stance toward it of the Enlightenment, whose sapping of the ideological foundations of the *ancien regime* involved a systematic demystification and debunking of religious phenomena and a clear perception of the legitimizing relationship between what the philosophers conceived as 'error' and 'superstition' and the arbitrary power of hierarchical political institutions.[7]

It is true that Frye seldom involved himself in the critical debate on postmodernism which started in the late 1950s and early 1960s in North American cultural and literary circles. But his critical discourse is closely related to the postmodern critical strategy, which is characterized by crossing the boundaries between literary and non-literary discourse, between elite and canonical works of art and marginalized text, and between (imperial) English literary studies and (postcolonial) Canadian literary studies.[8] Frye's open attitude towards the various critical schools and his theoretical engagement with them is more pluralistically postmodern than simply modern. Like Bakhtin, he was never profoundly involved in any critical school, but Frye has been discussed and even studied by many contemporary critical schools, both in the modern and the postmodern periods. Frye, as I argued at the beginning of this essay, actually stood between modernism and postmodernism. His transitional status finds particular embodiment in the rhetorical tension of his writing and his pluralistic attitude towards the theoretic debate on contemporary critical orientation.

Frye's Study of Commonwealth and Postcolonial Literature

Scholars of cultural studies usually pay particular attention to non-canonical literature or marginalized writing/discourse, aiming at a new interpretation of these "non-stream" or "subaltern" phenomena. This focus has undoubtedly helped contemporary postcolonial studies to flourish in such "postcolonial" countries as Canada and Australia, where "English" sometimes appears as "english."[9] English literature in its traditional sense is classified into (British and American) "English" literature and (Commonwealth) "english" literature. Frye, as a leading Canadian cultural and literary critic, could not but speak on behalf of Canadian scholarship in the international forum and discuss Canadian literature as part of so-called Commonwealth literature or postcolonial literature in the English-speaking world. His effort coincides with the postcolonial attempt to demarginalize and deterritorialize Canadian culture and literature in the West. Unlike such postcolonial critics as Edward Said, who started his academic career in the United States, and Gayatri Spivak, who came to the imperial "centre" from a postcolonial country and has practised her postcolonial critique in the "other" (imperial) country rather than her (postcolonial) motherland, Frye never left his motherland, but always identified himself as a Canadian or North American critic speaking on behalf of Canadian scholarship. This stance finds particular embodiment in his various writings about

Canadian literature, especially his conclusions to the two editions of the *Literary History of Canada*, which Frye virtually co-edited with Carl F. Klink. These two conclusions highlight Frye's study of Canadian literature as part of "Commonwealth literature," which is of great significance to cultural studies today.

In speaking of the potential significance of Frye's two conclusions to contemporary postcolonial studies, Branko Gorjup points out that "According to post-colonial critics, the development of a national literature begins with the individual's desire for self-recognition within a post-colonial context, which, in turn, sets in motion the process for group identification. Members of such a group can then begin challenging forms of cultural imperialism still submerged in their society. ... In reference to Frye's brand of nationalism, however, the real threat to Canada's continuing existence as a nation no longer came from the British imperial connection—though frequently Frye would point out its frostbiting effect on the Canadian imagination—but rather from the 'new,' more aggressive type of American imperialism."[10] In Frye's view, to highlight the national and cultural identity of Canada and the distinctiveness of Canadian literature in an attempt to evade the shadow of American literature is to decentralize the imperial empire and decolonize Canadian literature, making it function both at the periphery and the centre. Although he did not involve himself in the debate on postcolonialism from a theoretic perspective, his practice is relevant to contemporary postcolonial criticism, which criticizes the imperial cultural hegemony and its dominance over the postcolonial discourse. Judging from Frye's reputation in today's academic circles, we could say that he has nearly realized his dream.[11]

In his first conclusion to the *Literary History of Canada*, Frye addresses the issue of postcolonial literature. Canadian literature, he argues, was inevitably influenced by others: "The simultaneous influence of two larger nations speaking the same language has been practically beneficial to English Canada, but theoretically confusing. It is often suggested that Canada's identity is to be found in some *via media*, or *via mediocris*, between the other two. This has the disadvantage that the British and American cultures have to be defined as extremes" (*BG*, 218). It is true that under the shadow of the United States, Canada's national identity, let alone its cultural and literary identity, is obscure. For many years, Canadian literature was not even taught as a graduate course in Canadian universities. And Frye himself was for a time regarded in China as an American rather than a Canadian critic. (Perhaps part of the reason is that Frye was once elected president of the

Modern Language Association of America.) Although Frye clearly realized the fact that Canadian literature was not as important as the English literature he studied for decades, he still thought it necessary to be one of the editors of a voluminous literary history of Canada in English, for this part of Commonwealth literature actually serves as a challenge to the imperial English literature.

Since Canada is a former British colony and has remained in the Commonwealth, and given its geographical proximity to and close economic ties with the United States, Canadian culture and literature cannot avoid British and American influence. Frye was always aware of Canada's postcolonial status. He writes, "After the Northwest passage failed to materialize, Canada became a colony in the mercantilist sense, treated by others less like a society than as a place to look for things. French, English, Americans plunged into it to carry off its supplies of furs, minerals, and pulpwood, aware only of their immediate objectives. From time to time recruiting officers searched the farms and villages to carry young men off to death in a European dynastic quarrel" (BG, 221).

Canada's postcolonial identity not only finds embodiment in its economy and politics, it is also represented in Canadian culture and literature. Canadian literature has been developing so quickly that it has to follow almost all the literary currents in the West in a way that obscures its own identity and national spirit. As Frye points out in his conclusion to the second edition of the *Literary History of Canada*, "Canada had no enlightenment, and very little eighteenth century. The British and French spent the eighteenth century in Canada battering down each other's forts, and Canada went directly from the Baroque expansion of the seventeenth century to the Romantic expansion of the nineteenth ... Identity in Canada has always had something about it of a centrifugal movement into far distance, of clothes on a growing giant coming apart at the seams, of an elastic about to snap" (DG, 77). Searching for a Canadian national and cultural identity has long been a task for historians of Canada as well as those of Canadian literature, and Frye's efforts naturally coincide with other postcolonial critics' attempts to highlight their national cultural identity. Speaking of her Indian "alien" status in the United States and her Hindu heritage, Spivak suggests in her recent book, "Since the 'national origins' of the new immigrants, as fantasized by themselves, have not, so far, contributed to the unacknowledged and remoter historical culture of the United States, what we are demanding is that the United States recognize *our* rainbow as part of its history of the present."[12] One cannot but recognize Frye's anticipation of many of the issues in today's postcolonial studies. As the study of postcolonial culture and literature is one of the most important issues in contemporary cultural studies, Frye's critical ideas in his later years appear a more and more significant heritage.

What I would like to emphasize before concluding this section of my paper is Frye's confidence in the rise of Canadian literature and its potential function in the future: "Canadian literature has always been thought of as having its centre of gravity in the future. Now that it has come into the present also, it may, by being where it is as well as what it is, help to make its own contribution to the future that we all hope for—not apocalyptic futures of fantasy and nightmare, but a future in which Western man has come home from his exile in the land of unlikeness and has become something better than the ghost of an ego haunting himself."[13] This remark reminds me of the pioneering figure of modern Chinese culture and literature, Lu Xun, who on the one hand sharply criticized the weak points of the Chinese nation, but on the other hand sincerely hoped that Chinese culture and literature would some day present itself to the whole world. I am sure that the wish of both these masters will materialize in the future.

Putting Literary Studies in the Broader Context of Cultural Studies

Frye's approach to literary studies, especially after the publication of *Anatomy of Criticism*, is opposed to the elite doctrine of the New Criticism and more attractive to cultural critics of later generations. While Frye seldom emphasizes the function of history in his analysis of literary phenomena, as Marxist scholars of cultural studies do, his view of history, as White has correctly pointed out, is a sort of "cultural history" of which literature is one aspect. Frye is among those far-sighted scholars who took the initiative in placing literary studies in the broader context of cultural studies. In today's atmosphere of globalization, cultural studies has been travelling farther and farther away from literary studies. Some traditional literary scholars in fact fear for the future of literary studies, which is being almost engulfed by cultural studies. In my view, by broadening literary studies, Frye paved the way for the possible fruitful confluence of literary studies with cultural studies. Thus, have we not received a revelation from Frye's theory and practice of cultural criticism?

Where F.R. Leavis speaks for (canonical) "English" literature, Frye speaks for (Canadian) "english" literature. Upon Leavis's death, his friend and colleague Raymond Williams wrote a short note praising

his contributions to contemporary cultural criticism and cultural studies and pointing out Leavis's stubborn devotion to an elite sense of literary and cultural studies. According to Williams, "The connecting
mode of the [Leavis] faction, serious, widely read and intelligent as
they all were, was a basic preoccupation with who was in and who
was out, and in this, of course, even in negation, they retained and
even emphasized the manners of their class."[14] Frye's attempt to
include non-canonical Canadian literature in the scope of literary studies anticipates his contribution to contemporary canon formation and
reformation, which is heatedly discussed among scholars of cultural
studies. Like Leavis, Frye adhered to his own view of cultural criticism
and cultural studies, which might well have been neglected by contemporary practitioners.

Last but not least, I should emphasize Frye's methodology in comparative literature, which breaks through the limited domain of literature proper and observes literature in a broader context of cultural
studies, in the process anticipating contemporary cultural studies in
the English-speaking world. In the final analysis, I would argue that
Frye's significance to cultural studies is as great as that of F.R. Leavis
and Mikhail Bakhtin, although it will only be "rediscovered" by future
scholars of both Northrop Frye and cultural studies.

NOTES

1 For this aspect, see Hayden White, "Frye's Place in Contemporary Cultural
Studies," in *The Legacy of Northrop Frye*, ed. Alvin A. Lee and Robert D. Denham (Toronto: University of Toronto Press, 1994), 28–39.

2 Cf. A.C. Hamilton's paper delivered at the International Conference on
Northrop Frye: China and the West (Beijing, July 1994). The Chinese translation appears in *Fulai yanjiu: Zhongguo yu xifang* (*Frye Studies: China and the
West*), ed. Wang Ning and Xu Yanhong (Beijing: China Social Sciences Publishing House, 1996).

3 Cf. Wang Ning, "Fulai de houxiandai chanshi" ("Frye Reinterpreted from
the Postmodern Perspective"), in *Frye Studies: China and the West.*

4 Cf. Linda Hutcheon, "Frye Recoded: Postmodernity and the Conclusions,"
in *The Legacy of Northrop Frye*, 105–21.

5 White, "Frye's Place," 29.

6 Ibid., 37.

7 Fredric Jameson, *The Political Unconscious: Narrative as a Socially Symbolic
Act* (Ithaca, N.Y.: Cornell University Press, 1981), 69.

8 Cf. Northrop Frye, "Conclusion to a *Literary History of Canada*" (*BG*, 213–51) and "'Conclusion' to *Literary History of Canada*, Second Edition" (*DG*, 71–88). Both may be found in *Mythologizing Canada: Essays on the Canadian Literary Imagination*, ed. Branko Gorjup (New York: Legas, 1997), 63–115.

9 It is very interesting to note that one of the most popular volumes on cultural studies is *The Cultural Studies Reader* (London: Routledge, 1993), edited by an Australian scholar, Simon During; and one of the most influential journals on postcolonial/Commonwealth literature studies is *Ariel*, edited and published in Canada.

10 Branko Gorjup, introduction to *Mythologizing Canada*, 12.

11 Regarding the worldwide quotation and discussion of Frye, see Robert D. Denham, preface to *Northrop Frye: An Annotated Bibliography of Primary and Secondary Sources* (Toronto: University of Toronto Press, 1987). According to Denham, "a recent study of 950 journals revealed that among the most frequently cited authors in the arts and humanities Frye ranked only behind Marx, Aristotle, Shakespeare, Lenin, Plato, Freud, and Barthes" (ix).

12 Gayatri Chakravorty Spivak, *A Critique of Postcolonial Reason: Toward a History of the Vanishing Present* (Cambridge, Mass.: Harvard University Press, 1999), 395.

13 Frye, "Haunted by Lack of Ghosts," in *Mythologizing Canada*, 135.

14 Williams's short note appeared in *Times Higher Education Supplement*, 5 May 1978. Quoted from Fred Inglis, *Raymond Williams* (London: Routledge, 1995), 266.

Frye and Canada

SANDRA DJWA

"Canadian Angles of Vision":
Northrop Frye, Carl Klinck, and the
Literary History of Canada

Although Northrop Frye is listed as one of the six editors of the *Literary History of Canada*,[1] it is not generally recognized that he was one of the two principal editors and, in the largest sense, the catalyst for the volume. Interviews conducted in the late seventies and Klinck's reminiscences, *Giving Canada a Literary History: A Memoir*, indicate that the literary history came into being as a result of a chance meeting between Frye and Klinck in September 1956. Klinck's letters on the development of the *Literary History* from its origins to publication in 1965 demonstrate that Frye's function was primarily that of a co-editor, albeit largely behind the scenes. He advised Klinck on the financing and organizing of the project, on the selecting of contributors, on the structuring of the book, and on the copy-editing of the completed text.[2] Moreover, remarks made by Klinck at the University of Leeds in 1965 suggest that he relied on the broad application of some of Frye's critical concepts to justify the editorial practices of the *Literary History*. Finally, Frye was assigned one of the most important tasks of a principal editor or co-editor, that of writing a summarizing conclusion for the first and second editions of the book.

The impetus for the *Literary History of Canada* was a wide-ranging paper, "Introduction: Lexis and Melos," given by Frye at a morning session of the English Institute at Columbia University in September 1956. Klinck was highly impressed by the paper and the two men had a brief conversation: "I asked him whether Canadian literature could be tested against international standards. Norrie replied, in effect, 'of course, why not?' He added, 'first of all there must be a great deal of research in basic facts.'"[3] In a later interview in 1979 Klinck added:

"I asked Northrop Frye whether Canadian literature could stand up respectably if it were subjected to a historical and critical survey? He agreed that the attempt should be made to obtain a good basis of fact and on that build a critical appreciation. We agreed on taking this step, we sold the idea to the University of Toronto Press and organized a board of editors shortly thereafter."[4] The pronoun "we," used by Klinck throughout this discussion, indicates that he saw the development of the *Literary History* as a joint endeavour by Frye and himself.

Klinck's conviction, reflected in his reminiscences, was that primary research in all historical periods was the first requirement for a literary history of Canada. He also believed that this research should be undertaken by a team of scholars along the lines of those assembled for the pioneering *Literary History of the United States* (1946) edited by Robert E. Spiller, Willard Thorp, et al. In his first handwritten notes on the subject (autumn 1956) Klinck listed a number of significant differences between the American and Canadian literary experience, including Canada's closer relationship with Great Britain, a lengthier colonial period, a significant relation to the United States, a division into English Canadian and French Canadian literature, and "a lesser intrinsic value as [an] imaginative production."[5] This last observation comes up in each of his accounts of the beginnings of the *Literary History*. It addresses what Klinck saw as the heart of the matter: was Canadian literature sufficiently developed to merit evaluation and how could, or should, scholars survey a field in which so little research had been done?

Following his initial discussion with Frye, Klinck made an appointment early in October to see the director of the University of Toronto Press, Marsh Jeanneret, to sound out the press regarding possible publication. This visit, and a following one, did not go well. Jeanneret expressed misgivings about team projects in Canadian literature; moreover, he was convinced that a literary history should deal with writings in both English and French. Klinck nonetheless wrote a detailed letter to Jeanneret proposing a small committee and suggesting that it might be joined by "opposite numbers" for French Canadian literature. He also explained his project in more detail: "There is a real difference between a 'history of literature' and a 'literary history' of Canada. The latter interprets Canadians in terms of the literary vision of those who have written here. We have never had such a study of ourselves, and I think it would be worthy of the best efforts of our scholars. It could be solidly based on a substantial body of Canadian writing, much of which would thus receive its first critical examination. Even if the works written in this country had no other value, they would still serve to reveal the Canadian mind."[6] There would be room for the "special talents" of a number of individuals: Klinck listed R.E. Watters, Northrop Frye, A.J.M. Smith, Claude Bissell, Roy Daniells, A.S.P. Woodhouse, Desmond Pacey, and a number of others, including Alfred Bailey. This group, headed by Watters and Frye, clearly represented Klinck's first choice for colleagues.

Watters had been Klinck's co-editor on the *Canadian Anthology* (1955), a collection of key texts in poetry and prose developed for the teaching of Canadian literature. The editorial work they had undertaken for this anthology had convinced both men that Canadian literary history lagged far behind American literary history. Midway through the project, Watters observed that "the whole of Canadian writing needs to be re-assessed and a decent History of the subject written. But that's a vast job, and one that must wait at least until the Can. Bibliog. is completed."[7] Just a few years earlier, the Humanities Research Council of Canada had supported the development of this comprehensive bibliography, *A Check List of Canadian Literature and Background Materials, 1628–1950* (1959). Although Watters strongly supported Klinck's proposal to start on a *Literary History*, in 1956 he was much too busy finishing his *Check List* to be of any help. As Klinck had been relying on Watters as a co-editor ("I almost dropped the project when I found that I could not rely on you"), this was a considerable blow.[8]

Klinck spent a few weeks mulling things over. Then, on 20 November, he took another tack. He wrote to Frye, attempting to pull him alongside, noting that "sound criticism alone could make the task worth doing." Klinck honestly (and shrewdly) flattered Frye: "I turn to you in the hope you can see in it a service to Canada which only you can perform ... I should like, therefore, to share the historical spadework with others so that maximum results may be obtained in our generation. The results, as I believe, would be not merely facts, but insights into what I am tempted to call Canadian angles of vision."[9] Klinck knew exactly what he wanted from Frye—validation of the project: "I should not ask you to take time from the work in criticism which has made you an international authority. Do you think that such Canadian concerns could be fitted into your programme if you participated chiefly in an editorial capacity by lending the project your authority, pointing up its possibilities, and protecting it from banality?"[10]

Klinck had sized up Frye's situation very well, and Frye was equally astute about Klinck. Some years later, in 1988, Frye recalled their first discussion on the *Literary History*: "I took to him so strongly":

> I thought here's a man who really cares about his subject. And after all that posturing and general nonsense that goes on at conferences and English Institutes and things, it was a very refreshing change to have him get so intense ... He was talking about the possibility of doing something about Canadian literature and I thought, "This guy has the guts to carry through what he starts." I've never lost that kind of affection and respect for him. Again, he cultivates a mask—he gave the impression of being much more innocuous than, in fact, he was. I knew that there was quite a strong will under there. That's why I was quite happy about joining his committee and then having him direct things.[11]

In fact, the two men had entered into a working partnership in which Frye became Klinck's adviser and confidante. Frye organized preliminary meetings at Victoria College and acted as a go-between for Klinck's next, predictably more successful, meeting with the University of Toronto Press. After initial discussions with Klinck, he made useful suggestions regarding the organizing and financing of the project. Most importantly, he acted as a sounding board, reinforcing Klinck's vision of what the *Literary History* ought to be: an indepth study of English Canadian literature only, covering successive historical periods and serving both as an introduction to the literature and as a reference text. A paper which Frye was then preparing for the Royal Society, "Preface to an Uncollected Anthology" (*BG*, 163–79), helped Klinck clarify his own position as a critic of Canadian literature and had important implications for the theory and scope of the book. Finally, Frye wrote two conclusions for successive editions of the *Literary History*, containing the most cited (and applied) passages in the volume.

Once Klinck established the *Literary History* in the mid-fifties, the study of Canadian writing shifted from impressionistic, often "Canadian" criticism to systematic national scholarship firmly anchored to bibliography, periodization, textual editing, and biography. Klinck assigned historical areas by chronology; provided proof sheets of Watters's *Check List* as the initial bibliography for each editor; insisted on original research; and structured his advisory board by geography. It can be argued, nonetheless, that the *Literary History* remained a transitional study, as a number of critics, including Frye in the conclusion, tended to favour the descriptive mode as opposed to the evaluative.

The *Literary History* also retained a vestigal nationalism, which appears both in Klinck's disclaiming introduction ("The editors and contributors have not joined in a chauvinistic hunt for ... 'Canadianism.' They wish to demonstrate, not to argue about, what and how much has grown up in Canada" [x]) and in Frye's conclusion—especially in his efforts to reveal the distinctive note of terror in Canadian landscape poetry. Frye's Canadianism ran second to his internationalism; paradoxically, however, this was not a matter of forsaking the Canadian, for "it may be that when the Canadian writer attaches himself to the world of literature, he discovers, or rediscovers, by doing so, something in his Canadian environment" (840).

As a product of the Canadian twenties, when the desire to affirm a national identity in literature was paramount, Klinck was a staunch literary nationalist: this was a large part of the impulse for undertaking the project in the first place. Nonetheless, as the son of immigrants and later a graduate of Columbia University (where he had trained as a Comparativist), he saw himself as "an outsider in Toronto."[12] Frye, however, by virtue of his position as principal of Victoria College, of his association with the *Canadian Forum* (where he set the direction for three decades of Canadian criticism with his review of A.J.M. Smith's *The Book of Canadian Poetry*, 1943), and finally, of his criticism of Canadian writing and the annual reviews of Canadian poetry contributed to "Letters in Canada" in the *University of Toronto Quarterly*, 1951–61, was a central figure in the Canadian literary establishment.

As such, Frye was a splendid adviser. In response to Klinck's first letter of appeal, Frye made three brief points. The first related to financing, and the second to contributors. Frye advised Klinck to structure the boards for the *Literary History* to reflect a distinction between a small but active nucleus of editors and a larger advisory committee to deal with policy. Frye suggested individuals appropriate for each board (e.g., Klinck, Watters, and Robert McDougall for the editorial board; others such as Roy Daniells and Malcolm Ross, whose scope he considered more deductive than inductive, for the advisory committee, possibly because the latter could be relied upon to draw the diverse chapters together). His third point related to the kind of writing to be included. When drafting a program comparable to the *Literary History of the United States*, Klinck should remember that Canadian literature has never been wholly detached from occasional writing. Indeed, Frye suggested that "the most important group, for quality of writing and value of subject-matter, were the scholars; then the political writers, then the journalists, from the diaries of explorers to modern columnists, and finally, after a long, thoughtful reluctant pause, the novelists."[13]

A week after Frye agreed to act as adviser, Klinck came to Victoria College to discuss the project. On 18 December, very likely with Frye's endorsement, he wrote to Roy Daniells at the University of British Columbia and Alfred Bailey at the University of New Brunswick asking them to join the project in an advisory capacity. Each of the three members of the advisory board—Bailey, Frye, and Daniells, representing the east, the centre, and the west of Canada respectively—were asked to nominate editors for specific sections of the text. By August 1957 Claude Bissell and Desmond Pacey had also been named editors and Klinck was nominated editor-in-chief. The editors, in turn, helped to recruit scholars, organized their area or period among contributors, and were responsible for indicating the degree of financial support required. The line between advisers, editors, and contributors was a very loose one, with Klinck, Frye, and Daniells performing all three functions. In addition, Daniells sought financial support for the project at the Humanities Research Council and eventually became the project's financial trustee. Advisers and editors agreed that no restriction was to be placed on contributors other than the approximate length of a chapter. As Klinck recalled, "we didn't want to impose a pattern, because people would write to it, that is, write up an old concept, instead of letting the content issue from the facts."[14]

Gradually the outline of the book began to take shape. By 5 September 1957 Klinck had unanimous approval from the editorial and advisory board committees of the *Literary History* for a book of about six hundred pages, divided into 50,000 words for the beginnings to 1880, 80,000 words for the period 1880–1920, and 100,000 words to cover 1920 to the present. For the early period he had contacted David Galloway, Victor Hopwood, Alfred Bailey, Fred Cogswell, and V.L.O. Chittick; for the middle period Claude Bissell, Gordon Roper, Roy Daniells, Desmond Pacey, Frank Watt, Malcolm Ross, Robert McDougall, and Alec Lucas, and for the last section Pacey, Hugo McPherson, Frye, Munro Beattie, Jay Macpherson, John Irving, and Millar MacLure. Not all were to accept, or to continue after acceptance, but a good beginning had been made.

As Klinck was later to recall, "Norrie's influence was ... strong in balancing the various topics and emphases in content." Of the advisers Frye had the most influence in naming contributors, in determining topics to be covered, and in offering suggestions regarding the shape of the completed text. Frye, as Klinck said at one point, was "our

Solomon, our last court of appeal."[15] By this Klinck seems to have meant that when issues were not resolved at the editorial level they were passed up to Frye for judgment. Frye, for example, working with Bailey, helped clarify the division of the early writings into Part I of the *Literary History*, "New Found Lands," and helped structure Part II as "The Transplanting of Traditions"; he agreed that Part III should be titled "The Emergence of a Tradition" and provided a title for Part IV— "The Realization of a Tradition."[16]

Frye's role in delineating possible topics and contributors is apparent in a December 1958 letter dealing with the treatment of Canadian history, in which he insists on original research and shows a willingness to allow contributors a free rein with their subjects. He also acknowledges that the *Literary History* was "for the younger generation."[17] Like Klinck, Frye believed the book would assume its own shape. That his views on structure agreed with those of Klinck is apparent from his response to a request by a contributor, Edith Fowke, for clarification of the boundaries of her subject: "Mrs. Fowke has outlined the very reason why we asked her to contribute to the book. She should use her own judgment about what borderline to draw, but the connection of folk-tale with such work as Sam Slick and Bob Edwards is one of the essential points about its literary relevance."[18]

The greatest problem faced by the editors was the small pool of contributors to choose from (there were sixty or more contributors for the *Literary History of the United States*). Fewer still of the available scholars were specialists in Canadian literature or cultural history. Consequently, the completed chapters varied dramatically in both style and critical approach. Early in the project Watters (who had been kept informed) had been irritated because he thought that the "Daniells-Frye-Pacey" group had been assigned responsibility for too large a proportion of the text.[19] Then, as the successive parts of the book began to take shape, Daniells became concerned: "Where is our boundary, the boundary between Canadian literature and Canadian writing? I don't think much of the production of our social scientists qualifies as literature."[20] When the completed chapters were submitted to the advisory board for commentary, he was alarmed. "I doubt if it is going to be possible substantially to harmonize styles (and approaches)."[21] However, as Daniells acknowledged, once the editors had decided "to let contributors go their own way within a simple limit of number of words" they had also decided "to run the risk of incompatible and incongruous contributions."[22]

The real issue, however, was the question of literary value. As

Daniells bluntly asked Klinck in early January 1963: "Is the book to be a *literary* history or a literary *history*?"[23] It was in this aspect of the whole undertaking that Frye provided the greatest critical support for Klinck, carving out a special place for the critic of Canadian literature "somewhere between" the descriptive function of the social sciences and the ordinary standards of literary judgment. Klinck was acutely aware of the "weak spots" of Canadian literature, but he believed in the surveying enterprise represented by *Literary History*. He pinned his hopes on the future, foreseeing that after the first version of the text had been published there would be other, revised editions where succeeding scholars could undertake evaluation in depth.[24]

Daniells, a Milton scholar, tended towards a "greats" theory of literature which distinguished between major and minor figures. He knew the Canadian field very well,[25] was an astute critic, and understood the probable role of the *Literary History*. "I doubt whether L.H.C. can be in any sense definitive. It will provoke discussion, reply, emulation and criticism; this is perhaps its main function, in the present dearth of real critical interest in Canada's literature outside the universities. I would be willing to accept some disproportions of emphasis and differences of approach for the sake of preserving the freshness of each contributor's contributions."[26] He followed up his question regarding "literary *history*" with a milder complaint: "What I am afraid of is that a reader in England might have difficulty in knowing who our major authors are and what they may be supposed to have accomplished." As a post-script to his query he cited the poetry of Roberts, Lampman, and Scott: "If ... you focus on the good poems, you see an absorption in landscape, little else; but this [is] of the utmost intensity and of the utmost importance in our cultural history."[27] However, Daniells went his own merry way in his contributions to the *History*, ignoring Klinck's editorial directives and writing his chapters on the major and minor poets of the Confederation precisely the way he felt they should be written—with appreciation, criticism, and judicious selections from the text. As Klinck ruefully concluded, Daniells's chapters, along with Frye's conclusion, were considered by critics to be the best pieces in the volume.[28]

Between 1956 and 1960, Klinck was so preoccupied with recruiting a team of scholars, raising funds, and setting out areas of research that he had little time to consider a theoretical justification of editorial practices. However, about 1961, he became aware of the need for some all-encompassing rubric for the project. It appears that Klinck then recognized that Frye's essay, "Preface to an Uncollected Anthology," provided a theoretical basis for the working principles on which the

Literary History had been structured. The *History's* editors had met in Montreal in June 1961 and Francess Halpenny, editor for the project at the University of Toronto Press, wrote Klinck commenting on the record of the discussion and reminding him that Frye had suggested Canada should be considered "'as an environment'—'the place where something happened'."[29] This summation was helpful to Klinck, as the *Literary History* was rapidly nearing publication and there were large areas in which the editors had been unable to reach general agreement.

In editorial practice, especially in the choice of contributors and subjects for chapters, Klinck had tacitly accepted Frye's conception of the Canadian critic as located between the social sciences and literature. Indeed, he held this view himself. In the autumn of 1956, in his first rough notes for the *Literary History*, Klinck noted that every writer of a chapter would be expected to deal with relevant aspects of Canadian art, politics, social conditions, economics, philosophy, religion, and criticism. But the extent to which he subsequently relied on Frye's theory and made it the official justification for his own practice is apparent in remarks he made at Leeds University in 1965.

In this talk, Klinck quotes from Frye's "Preface to an Uncollected Anthology," as indeed he does in his introduction to the *Literary History* itself: "The ... cultivated Canadian has the same kind of interest in Canadian poetry that he has in Canadian history or politics. Whatever its merits, it is the poetry of his own country, and it gives him an understanding of that country which nothing else can give him." Again citing Frye, Klinck remarked that "the environment that Canadian poets have to grapple with and many of the imaginative problems it presents have no counterpart in the United States, or anywhere else." As Klinck explained, "'Environment' provides the indispensable link with French-Canadians, who share with other Canadians much of this environment, as in Montreal, the chief centre of English and French literary production. It regards Canadian literature very properly as a North American literature, emphasizing its North American difference from Britain or Europe, but admitting whatever is United States American in Canadian life and literature." This concept also helped the editors resolve their ongoing debate about which authors were to be considered Canadian writers. In effect, they accepted "whoever or whatever is native or naturalized—whoever or whatever has its principal focus in Canada, although in some other context he could belong to some other country."[30]

Klinck's response to Frye's formulation about the position of the Canadian literary critic in relation to judgments of value is a little more cautious: "The historian of literature, like the Canadian at any time, may properly function 'somewhere between'; there will be times, of course, when he may step forth as a critic and deal with 'comparative value judgments'." In effect, Klinck accepts Frye's theory of "somewhere between" as the basis for his critical stance but reserves the right to invoke literary standards of judgment as required. Klinck summarized his application of Frye's thinking to the *Literary History* this way: "'Literary' has here been employed in a 'generic sense.' Authors and books of slight importance could not be set aside without investigation; this volume may give some names their first and last mention in a discussion of Canadian literature. Descriptive reference, however, without the addition of a specific claim for artistic value, must not be construed as anything more than an illustration of what was in the 'environment.' Whenever values were being critically assessed, 'literary' is used, of course, in its restricted meaning." It was the theoretical underpinning provided by Frye that led the editors, as Klinck says, "for better or for worse, [to call] our book, *not* a history of literature, but "a literary history of Canada"—our operation taking its place in an intellectual area "somewhere between" the historian or social scientist and the critic supremely devoted to value-judgments."[31]

In assembling topics for inclusion in the *Literary History*, Klinck admits the pragmatic nature of the approach: "an avoidance of head-on collisions with ideological differences; tolerance with regard to anomalies; acceptance of what is rather than straining for what might be." He believed that this editorial approach was "a Canadian way of working with our own literary output." Canadians, because of their geographic location, enjoy access to "the classical tradition through Europe; the British tradition back to *Beowulf*; the United States tradition back to John Smith, the French tradition back to the medieval epics and ... their own tradition developed over one hundred and fifty years."[32]

Although the origins of the *Literary History* and its practical procedures may seem "slavishly bound to the imperial pronouncements of Northrop Frye," Klinck emphasizes that these principles sprang also from "the unvoiced but private discussions of Canadian scholars."[33] This is largely correct: long before Frye's essay, Watters and Klinck had recognized the necessity of presenting Canadian literature within its cultural context. However, there is no doubt that without Frye to validate and conceptualize the positions taken the *Literary History* might well have been, as Frye says of Canadian literature in the slightly different context of his conclusion, "a poor naked Alouette" (822).

Frye's conclusion to the first edition of the *Literary History* recasts both Klinck's concerns and his own "Preface to an Uncollected Anthology." He states that the *Literary History* "is a tribute to the maturity of Canadian literary scholarship and criticism, whatever one thinks of the literature. Its authors have completely outgrown the view that evaluation is the end of criticism" (821). Daniells's arguments regarding the lack of a major figure are introduced, but ultimately reversed, in Frye's statement that "Canada has produced no author who is a classic in the sense of possessing a vision greater in kind than that of his best readers." Yet this is found to be an advantage; one can see all the more clearly, "in a literature that has not quite done it," what literature is trying to do (821). The usual distinctions to be made regarding a literary tradition are sidestepped by Frye's suggestion that Canada has undergone its cultural "revolutions" from wilderness to North American colony to internationalism "too quickly for a tradition of writing to be founded on any one of them" (826). As a result, Canadian writers are still attempting to assimilate the environment.

The argument, in fact, has been brought back to the thesis of "Preface to an Uncollected Anthology" and the greater part of Frye's conclusion deals with what he describes as "the imminence of the natural world" (846), that feature of Canadian poetry which Daniells had distinguished as "an absorption in landscape." The successive passages in which Frye elaborates upon what he finds to be the characteristic note of "terror" in Canadian nature poetry are not too different in sensibility from those of the avowedly nationalist critics of the 1880s and 1920s. Familiar also is Frye's reiteration of the perennial problem of the critic of Canadian literature—the obligation to work through the American example (in this case the American painting, "The Peaceable Kingdom") in order to distinguish Canadian differences and so elicit conclusions about a possible Canadian tradition. Despite these disclaimers, Frye concludes with tentative assertions of the continuity of a Canadian tradition: "A reader may feel ... unreality in efforts to attach Canadian writers to a tradition made up of earlier writers whom they may not have read or greatly admired ... Yet I keep coming back to the feeling that there does seem to be such a thing as an imaginative continuum, and that writers are conditioned in their attitudes by their predecessors, or by the cultural climate of their predecessors, whether there is conscious influence or not" (848–9). These summarizing remarks, Klinck stated, were "exactly what was needed to capture the spirit of the book ... written in Norrie's inimitable style."

In a letter to Daniells in the early seventies, however, Klinck was less circumspect, remarking that Frye's conclusion emphasized "not a factual-critical record, but more particularly ... a factual-descriptive record of what there is in English Canadian literature."[34] In a discussion with me in the late seventies he was equally frank about the conclusion, commenting: "Integration is something I think is necessary and we left that to Norrie [Frye] ... But mind you, it doesn't do justice to the material ... it's beautiful ... because ... of the insights from his point of view but it's far from being a literary history."[35] And Daniells continued unrepentant in his objections to the *Literary History*'s theory and practice, maintaining that Frye's chapter, although a splendid conclusion, really evaded the whole question of what Canadian literature was all about. When discussion of a revised edition came up in 1971, Daniells wrote to Klinck expressing the hope that a new literary history would "spotlight the best we can offer to the world" in a summary chapter quite different from Frye's:

> To present a record of the good, bad and indifferent in an undifferentiated continuum does, I think, drag down the whole operation ... I mention this, not with any thought of diverting the main-stream of opinion in the committee and without disrespect to those, like my dear friend Desmond [Pacey], who hold to the historico-informative concept. But I do think that problems remain and that some effort should be made to spotlight the best we can offer to the world, perhaps in an penultimate brief summing-up of a character and intent different from Norrie's.[36]

Daniells's objections are well founded and his Polonius-like allusion to Pacey's "historico-informative" bent is both witty and apt. The situation facing the editors had changed dramatically. The first edition of the *Literary History* had been published and reviewed during the time in which Canadian literature had come of age. It now seemed possible to make more specifically evaluative judgments in revised editions. As Daniells explained to Klinck, "I am regretfully in complete disagreement with Norrie's view that the revised version should be primarily descriptive and only secondarily critical ... I am now quite fervently of the opinion that evaluation and criticism and incitement to clearer views on the part of the reader are the desiderata for this decade."[37] As an example of a superior kind of literary history, Daniells cited what he elsewhere called the good "old golden baugh," Baugh's *Literary History of England*, "where a real and successful effort is made to keep author, critic and reader in one and the same intellectual context. If the new *Literary History* is to be the same there is much for Klinck and Frye to do in their joint conclusion."[38]

At this point in the planning for a second, augmented edition of the *Literary History* both Klinck and Frye were jointly responsible for the conclusion while Daniells remained one of the most active contributing editors. He objected to Frye's choice of Margaret Atwood as a poetry editor ("her theory of survival seems to me so monstrous that I find it hard to believe she can look at the poets with a clear eye"),[39] and pencilled some sixty editorial queries on the margins of one drafted chapter, nonetheless acknowledging, "I like [Malcolm] Ross' chapter ["Critical Theory—Some Trends"] very much. It is alive and kicking, mewling, puking, soiling its diapers, crowing with excitement and wanting to be picked up. Contrast [Thomas A.] Goudge's chapter ["Philosophical Literature"], a kind of still birth."[40]

However, when Klinck became overburdened with the practicalities of putting the volume together, Frye again came to the rescue of the editorial committee and wrote a new conclusion. He now recognized that "Canadian literature is here, perhaps still a minor but certainly no longer a gleam in a paternal critic's eye" (*DG*, 73), and, while making reference to separate chapters, emphasized the differences between Canadian and American cultural history. Klinck and Daniells again compared notes, and Daniells's letter indicates both reservations and tempered praise: "The conclusion strikes me as excellent of its kind and unexpected in its emphasis. Typically Northropian. The reader feels thrust into a number of fresh and unresolved questions rather than getting a firm grip on the knot at the end of the rope ... it will have to stand (in my opinion) and will certainly make the last pages an exciting and unexpected experience."[41]

In retrospect, it seems apparent that Klinck and Frye were satisfied with the primary mode established by the first edition of the *Literary History*—that of inventory and description rather than value judgment—partly because of Frye's own aesthetic and partly because both men viewed the project as a tentative exercise in canon making, an enterprise implied in Klinck's first question to Frye circa 1956. Was there a sufficiently substantial body of Canadian writing to justify sustained consideration in a history of Canadian literature? And if not, how best could one circumnavigate the problem in a literary history of Canada?

ACKNOWLEDGMENT

This article appeared in an earlier form in *English Studies in Canada* 19, no. 2 (June 1993). I should like to thank the editor, Mary Jane Edwards, for permission to edit, augment, and republish.

NOTES

1 *Literary History of Canada: Canadian Literature in English*, ed. Carl F. Klink et al. (Toronto: University of Toronto Press, 1965; 2nd. ed. 1976). Subsequent references to the first edition are given in the text. For reprints, see 91 n8.

2 "I dislike very much the style of the mass obituary, the use of the smarmy adverb. I dislike having a man four feet ten inches in height described as a 'towering figure.'" Frye quoted in Carl F. Klinck, *Giving Canada a Literary History: A Memoir*, ed. Sandra Djwa (Ottawa: Carleton University Press for the University of Western Ontario, 1991), 124.

3 Ibid., 103.

4 Carl F. Klinck to Sandra Djwa. Unpublished interview, May 1979.

5 Carl F. Klinck, "*A Literary History of Canada*. Handwritten notes, 1st draft. Autumn 1956." Carl F. Klinck Papers, J.J. Talman Regional Collection, The D.B. Weldon Library, University of Western Ontario (hereafter CFK Papers).

6 Carl F. Klinck to Marsh Jeanneret, 17 Oct. 1956. CFK Papers.

7 *Giving Canada a Literary History*, 92.

8 Carl F. Klinck to Reginald Watters, 21 Nov. 1957. CFK Papers.

9 Carl F. Klinck to Northrop Frye, 20 Nov. 1956. CFK Papers. This is Klinck's draft of this letter. In the sentence reading "I should like ... to share the historical" he has crossed out "share the" and "with others" and substituted a handwritten note, "lure others into."

10 Ibid.

11 Cited in *Giving Canada a Literary History*, xix. From unpublished interview, Northrop Frye to Sandra Djwa, 9 Sept. 1988.

12 Biographical Notes. CFK Papers.

13 Northrop Frye to Carl F. Klinck, 23 Nov. 1956. CFK Papers.

14 *Giving Canada a Literary History*, 111–12.

15 Ibid., 114, 134.

16 Northrop Frye to Carl F. Klinck, 16 Jan.1964. CFK Papers.

17 Northrop Frye to Carl F. Klinck, 17 Dec. 1958. CFK Papers.

18 Northrop Frye to Carl F. Klinck, 5 Jan. 1961. CFK Papers.

19 Reginald Watters to Carl F. Klinck, 30 Mar.1959. CFK Papers.

20 Roy Daniells to Carl F. Klinck, 30 June 1962. CFK Papers.

21 Roy Daniells to Carl F. Klinck, 24 Sept. 1962. CFK Papers.

22 Roy Daniells to Carl F. Klinck, 13 Nov. 1962. CFK Papers.

23 Roy Daniells to Carl F. Klinck, Jan. 1963. CFK Papers.

24 Carl F. Klinck, handwritten notes for a proposed essay on Roy Daniells. CFK Papers.

25 I was not aware , when first writing this paper, of the extent to which Roy

Daniells was a major commentator on Canadian literature in the 1940s and 1950s.

26 Roy Daniells to Carl F. Klinck, 3 Jan. 1963. CFK Papers.

27 Roy Daniells to Carl F. Klinck, 4 Jan. 1963. CFK Papers.

28 Carl F. Klinck. Handwritten notes for a proposed essay on Roy Daniells.

29 Francess G. Halpenny to Carl F. Klinck, 13 July 1961. CFK Papers.

30 Carl F. Klink, "To the English Graduate Seminar: The University of Leeds," 3 Mar. 1965, 11–12, 6, 7, CFK Papers. The two remarks quoted from the "Uncollected Anthology" essay are in *BG*, 163–4. Klinck uses his own concluding remark in slightly different words in his introduction to the *Literary History*.

31 "To the English Graduate Seminar," 8, 8, 9.

32 Ibid., 4, 5, 9.

33 Ibid., 10.

34 Carl F. Klinck to Roy Daniells, 3 July 1972. Roy Daniells papers, Special Collections, University of British Columbia.

35 Carl F. Klinck to Sandra Djwa. Unpublished interview, 18 June 1981.

36 Roy Daniells to Carl F. Klinck, 25 Oct. 1971. CFK Papers.

37 Roy Daniells to Carl F. Klinck, 22 Sept. 1972. CFK Papers.

38 Roy Daniells to Carl F. Klinck, 5 Sept. 1974. CFK Papers.

39 Roy Daniells to Carl F. Klinck, 8 Feb. 1973. CFK Papers.

40 Roy Daniells to Carl F. Klinck, 6 Feb. 1974. CFK Papers.

41 Roy Daniells to Carl F. Klinck, 5 Aug. 1975. CFK Papers.

THOMAS WILLARD

Gone Primitive: The Critic in Canada

When the United States celebrated its Bicentennial, in 1976, its neighbour to the north sent presents throughout the year. Many presents—for example, *Among Friends/Entre Amis*, a coffee table book of photographs shot along the border—emphasized their common experiences. But one of the last gifts stressed Canada–U.S. differences. A symposium on twentieth-century Canadian culture, held during the first week of February 1977 in the new Canadian embassy building on Pennsylvania Avenue in Washington, D.C., presented a series of distinctly Canadian "voices," English and French. The keynote speaker was Northrop Frye, of the University of Toronto, whose name was already well known in academic circles in the United States. The title of his talk was "Sharing the Continent" (*DG*, 57–70). But Frye quickly established that Canadians have a fundamentally different experience from Americans. Without a revolutionary heritage, Canadians do not feel the need to resist everything the Old World offers and to create everything anew. With their two national languages, they do not have the same drive towards assimilation and are more likely, in the current American phrase, to honour diversity. Moreover, given Canada's fragile landscape of frozen tundra and hardscrabble farms, they are less able to take the environment for granted.

Frye's comments cannot have seemed very surprising at the time, and the differences he identified may seem less pronounced after a quarter-century of Hispanic and environmental activism in the States. But Frye submitted that the arts are profoundly different in Canada, where the harsher environment imposes something more "primitive and archaic" on the imagination: "Everywhere we turn in Canadian literature and painting, we are haunted by the natural world, and even the most sophisticated Canadian artists can hardly keep something very primitive and archaic out of their imaginations" (*DG*, 68). When most guests at the Bicentennial celebrations wanted to appear as civilized as Uncle Sam, it must have seemed odd for a near neighbour to present itself as the *coureur de bois*. However, Frye's whole career had been devoted to the proposition that myths persist, especially in works of literature—and not only myths but other "primitive" forms like ritual and symbol. Frye's claims on behalf of myth entailed a reclamation of primitivism generally. Ironically, his primitivism was the flip side of modernism and internationalism. It was a distinctive product of the twentieth century, and showed the influence of his early absorption in the works of seminal thinkers. In the pages following, I shall first show how Frye's thinking was shaped by the books on myth and symbol he read as a student, and then turn to his emphasis on the role of myth in his criticism of Canadian poetry. The final part of the essay will consider the influence of Frye's comments on a generation of poets, critics, and readers in Canada.

Of course, Frye was well aware of the difference between primitive works of art, such as cave drawings, and primitive elements in modern art. He did not want poets to "go native" and would have grumbled at the title of my essay. But like many twentieth-century writers—D.H. Lawrence, for example, in the "Totem" chapter of *Women in Love*—he found useful analogies between the primitive and the modern. Frye often invoked the primitive elements in poetry to suggest that something very simple was at work in even the most sophisticated literary texts. He began his Massey Lectures, delivered over CBC Radio in 1963, by inviting listeners to imagine themselves on a desert island. As they explored it together, he explained that people develop the language they need to respond to their environment, participate in their society, and enter the world of the imagination. He conceded that a modern reader, with a set of modern-world associations, would not have the same experience of a desert island as "a genuine primitive" (*EI*, 12). But he insisted "that literature is still doing the same job that mythology did earlier" (22). He went on to suggest that literature is like magic because both depend on identification. "That's why literature, and more particularly poetry, shows the analogy to primitive minds that I mentioned in my first talk" (31). The dual concerns with primitive myth and modern analogies can be traced, in part, to Frye's early reading of Frazer and Spengler.

Two books appeared in the early 1920s that would affect the way people thought about culture for years to come: *The Golden Bough* and *The Decline of the West*. Immensely ambitious, they took shape during the period of the First World War. One was written in England, the other in Germany; one in a university office full of correspondence from researchers around the world, the other in nearly complete isolation. The authors, James George Frazer (1854–1941) and Oswald Spengler (1880–1936), went on to publish pronouncements about the state of modern society, but their words fell on deaf ears as the world again prepared itself for war. Ironically, both men predicted disaster. In the frenzy of mechanized society and the weariness of mass man they saw a dangerous break from the organic culture of Europe's past and the myths by which it lived for centuries.

Frazer and Spengler's messages to society at large were decidedly corrective. Europe was not set on an indefinite "onward and upward" trajectory. However, the implications for the arts and the arts critic were exhilarating. One did not have to go back to Homer to find the mythical stuff of heroism, be it the wrath of Achilles or the guile of Ulysses; mythic images could be found just below the surface of civilization, and not only in the dangerous atavism of political machinery and *Geopolitik* but in the dreams and customs of ordinary people. Although the two books were grounded in nineteenth-century thought, notably in that of Darwin and Goethe, they seemed absolutely contemporary to readers in the twenties, as contemporary as Joyce's *Ulysses* or Eliot's *Waste Land*, both published in 1922. It was inevitable that they would catch the conscience of the young Northrop Frye, a point noted by several contributors to the recent collection *Re-reading Frye*.

Frazer's great work, *The Golden Bough*, was a vast elaboration of his entries on "taboo" and "totemism" in the ninth edition of the *Encyclopaedia Britannica*. First published in two volumes in 1890, it was expanded into twelve volumes between 1906 and 1915 before being abridged into a single large volume in 1922. The subtitle of 1890, "A Study in Comparative Religion," recorded Frazer's debt to the developments of nineteenth-century comparativism, which had turned religious history into a semi-exact science. The final subtitle, "A Study in Magic and Religion," showed his true colours. An agnostic, Frazer regarded religion as the offspring of magic, and science as a distinct improvement on both: a more satisfactory way to understand nature and control it. His working formula, "from magic through religion to science," placed him among the progressives, an anthropologist reflecting on the "primitive modes" of thought in magic and their continuation in the Christian mystery of sacrifice and salvation.

Spengler published the second half of *Der Untergang des Abendlandes* in 1922, the year of Frazer's abridgement. *The Decline of the West*, an English translation by Charles Francis Atkinson, appeared in 1926 and 1928. Spengler dealt in places, dates, and events—the raw material of history—but always sought analogies and symbols. He approached "world-history" (*Weltgeschichte*) through "world-criticism" (*Weltkritik*); he paid careful attention to morphology, the study of forms, and to changes in art forms as nothing less than changes in modes of comprehending reality. His first volume devoted two chapters to the musical and plastic arts, showing how the "form-language" changed as culture changed. Some said this was his starting point: Spengler had pursued Goethe's interest in organic form and Nietzsche's passion for the genealogy of ideas into the writing of history generally. In any case, Spengler announced his departure from traditional history writing, which treated art as a parasite on culture. He insisted that art works held the key to understanding culture as an organism.

Frye encountered Spengler in his first year or two at university, when he found a copy of Atkinson's translation in the library of Hart House, the men's social and athletic centre at the University of Toronto. When he cited Spengler in the first of his surviving student essays, written during his fourth year at Victoria College, he wrote as a convinced Spenglerian: "we have seen the ultimate aim of romanticism to be, consciously or subconsciously, the philosophy of history, or the actualization of conscious life—the time-force aware of itself" (*SE*, 52). He started reading Frazer later, when he was a theology student at Victoria's sister college, Emmanuel. He followed Frazer's insights into the working of fertility cults, but did not hesitate to correct the "magic through religion to science" formula and suggested, "in opposition to Frazer, [that science] develops from magic and occultism" (*SE*, 137).

Frazer was far and away the more respected of the two scholars, the greatest living anthropologist in Britain, and the twelve-volume edition of *The Golden Bough* was being updated during Frye's years at Emmanuel. However, Frye owed more to Spengler inasmuch as Spengler taught him how to read Frazer—how to get beyond the imperialist mentality that thought the "scale of culture" culminated in the "Aryan race." Frazer identified "primitive modes of thought" only in the folk customs of Devonshire peasants and the like, though he hinted at survivals in High Church Anglicanism; Spengler, however, found primitive elements in various art forms, notably the ritual elements in drama that Cambridge classicists had also discussed in the wake of Frazer. In short, Spengler taught Frye to look for primitive elements in the midst of modern civilization. Where Spengler would speak of modes, Frye would talk of genres, and he soon assimilated both Frazer and Spengler into his own morphology. In a paper on the anatomy, written for his tutor at Oxford, he placed both *The Golden Bough* and *The Decline of the West* in that genre (*SE*, 400).

As Blake became the centre of Frye's attention, Frazer and Spengler faded into the background. Their names appear nowhere in *Fearful Symmetry*, except for a passing reference to the "Frazers" of eighteenth-century antiquarianism (174)—to Edward Davies, for example, whose *Celtic Researches* (1804) included "Introductory Sketches on Primitive Society." The modern mentors are everywhere present, however— Frazer in the human sacrifices associated with Blake's Druids, Spengler in the myth of decline that runs throughout Blake's prophecies. Frazer taught Frye that myth-making was above all verbal, not mystic in the sense of proceeding from a pre-verbal revelation, as earlier writers on Blake had suggested. He showed how certain myths, like that of Balder, are "dramatised in ritual," in ceremonies calculated to produce fertility or another desired end. He explained that magic worked by the principles of "similarity" and "contiguity," which a literary critic could easily recognize as the principles of metaphor and metonymy. Meanwhile, Spengler taught Frye that Blake lived in the late autumn and early winter of Western culture. In Spengler's scheme of things, the decline of the West was as inevitable as the fall of a leaf; indeed, the German title might be translated more literally, and poetically, as "Sunset in Evening Land" or "Winter in the West." Spengler identified four ages of modern or "Faustian" culture: the Gothic spring, the Renaissance summer, the Baroque autumn, and the Impressionistic winter. What follows is not a new spring but a new civilization, as distinct from a new culture. Civilized man is, strictly speaking, uncultured because not rooted in the land. Civilization is not organic, but belongs to the unreal city of modernity; it is inorganic, being built from stone, steel, and glass. In effect, Frazer and Spengler both contributed to "the case against Locke" that Frye elaborated in the first chapter of *Fearful Symmetry* (3–29).

Frazer followed Locke in regarding magic as a faulty association of ideas; Spengler identified Locke as the great upholder of European rationalism, whose main challenge came from Methodism and religious enthusiasm. Frye's famous defence of Blake's vision, which took the rising sun to be closer to a Hallelujah chorus than to a gold coin, was in effect a defence of personal associations that make one man's sun quite different from another's, but no less valid. The case against Locke became a case for metaphor, that is, a defence of poetry. Based solely on Frazer's insights, it might have become a case for Locke, running from magic through poetry to science. But with Spengler's morphology, poetry became a continuum, assuming new forms in new times. Spengler also suggested the possibility of cyclic return: when poetry was about as close to prose as it could come, someone might discover a very different sort of poetry. The "discovery" of Ossian during the Pre-Romantic period, which scholars now regard as the inspired recreation of the bardic voice by James Macpherson, is exactly the sort of cycling back that Spengler taught Frye to watch for.

Among Frye's lasting contributions to Blake studies is his description of the "Orc cycle" (*FS*, 206–35), a complex pattern of relationships within which the young Orc is repressed by the old Urizen and eventually disappears, only to return with the full force of Freud's "repressed." Behind the description of the cycle we may detect Frazer's seasonal myth, inasmuch as Orc is a dying and reviving god, and Spengler's historical myth, inasmuch as Urizen represents the soul-killing rationalism of modern civilization, from which Orc holds out the promise of liberation. Like Blake, Spengler regarded America as a site of transformation; Americans were not transported from Europe but were born in the revolution against European rule.

When Frye wrote about Canada and its poets, he was looking for signs of a new cultural cycle of this type. Could it be that Canadians, without ever having rebelled against their mother countries, England and France, were nonetheless quite distinct from the English and French? Or that Canada, so far removed from the great urban centres of civilization, possessed a new, springtime culture? And could a reader in Canada become a Spenglerian "microcosm," arriving at a new comprehension of the world? Such questions propelled Frye's first queries into the arts in Canada.

He conducted the search on the side, while writing about Blake and English literature, but he carried it on steadily until he gathered the occasional pieces in *The Bush Garden* (1971). Without a single reference to Frazer or Spengler, he drew attention to many "primitive" elements in Canadian poetry. In a series of five essays, written over a quarter-century (1943–68), he showed a marked preference for what Schiller called the "naïve" in poetry. Beginning with his review of a "critical and historical anthology" of Canadian poetry, and continuing with essays on narrative poems and ballads in Canada, he went on to imagine an anthology of his own, as yet "uncollected," and to celebrate the achievements of his Victoria College colleague E.J. Pratt.

European Romanticism gave poets the burden of being original— "absolutely original," said Rimbaud in the *Lettres du Voyant*. The New World gave poets the further compulsion to begin language anew, like

Adam in paradise, and to sound forth in something like Whitman's "barbaric yawp." Frye distrusted the latter development, remarking that American poets who seek to be "aboriginal" have been damaged in the process: "they have sought for the primitive and direct and have tried to avoid the consciously literary and speak the language of the common man," but have found to their sorrow that "the language of the common man is chiefly commonplace" (*BG*, 136–7). Canadian poets have been spared this error, for the most part, lacking the revolutionary legacy that would make them eschew the culture of England or France altogether. However, they have suffered the "frostbite" of prudery because the colonial mentality has created a nervous, often chilly reception for anything that originated inside the "garrison" (*BG*, 134).

Writing about narrative poetry, Frye suggested that Canadian poets might well seek models in older phases of English literature—that "the poetic forms employed in earlier centuries of English literature would have been more appropriate for the expression of Canadian themes and moods than the nineteenth-century romantic lyric or its twentieth-century metaphysical successor" (*BG*, 148–9). Frye often repeated this bold theme, but it was not his originally. He took it from John D. Robins, who came to Victoria College in 1925 and remained there until his death in 1962: "Robins' special fields were the ballad and oral literature, along with folktales and popular literature in that orbit, and Old English. This combination of interests was not an accident: through him I began to understand something of the curious affinity between the spirit of Canadian poetry, up to and including Pratt, and the spirit of Anglo-Saxon culture. In both the incongruity between a highly sophisticated imported culture and a bleakly primitive physical environment is expressed by familiar, even ready-made, moral and religious formulas which raise more questions than they answer" (*BG*, 183). Robins was a teacher of Old English and an authority on the ballad, interested in the famous poets as much as the anonymous. He was also a great raconteur, who could spin a tall tale as well as he could collect one; and he was an outdoorsman, who realized that the central challenge of Canada was in the north, where even mere survival could never be taken for granted.

In imagining his own anthology, Frye drew heavily on *The Book of Canadian Poetry*, edited by A.J.M. Smith. Like his Toronto colleagues Pelham Edgar and Ned Pratt, he had been an adviser to Smith when the book was in progress; like others, he reviewed it favourably when it appeared in 1943. Unlike *The Oxford Book of Canadian Verse, in English and French*, which Smith later edited (1960) and for which he is chiefly remembered, *The Book of Canadian Poetry* was not simply a chronological sequence of poems. It was also thematic. It began with translations of poems by Canada's first people, including the Inuit and Haida, and concluded with two parallel "traditions" in Canadian poetry: the "native" and the "cosmopolitan." In the native tradition in particular, where Smith placed Pratt, there was a "unity of tone" deriving from the experience of life in the new world (*BG*, 131).

As he imagined what his own ideal anthology would look like, Frye noted a central theme: "the winter, with its long shadows and its abstract black and white pattern, does reinforce themes of desolation and loneliness, and more particularly, of the indifference of nature to human values, which I should say was the central Canadian tragic theme" (*BG*, 171). This theme required an appropriate form, and thus placed considerable pressure on the poet: "The imaginative content of Canadian poetry, which is often primitive, frequently makes extraordinary demands on forms derived from romantic or later traditions" (173–4). Although Frye became known as a thematic critic, he recognized that "the poet's quest is for form, not content" (176), and he explained: "I mean by form the shaping principle of the individual poem, which is derived from the shaping principles of poetry itself. Of these latter the most important is metaphor, and metaphor, in its radical form, is a statement of identity: this is that, A is B. Metaphor is at its purest and most primitive in myth, where we have immediate and total identifications. Primitive poetry, being mythical, tends to be erudite and allusive, and to the extent that modern poetry takes on the same qualities it becomes primitive too" (177). Just as certain themes could be primitive, like that of survival in an alien landscape, so certain myths could have primitive content. The older poem did not necessarily include the more primitive content, however; for Canada's poets faced the challenge of handling themes treated in much earlier phases of European culture. With what seems a critical sleight of hand, Frye set Archibald Lampman's Byronic outpouring "Loneliness" (1894) against the first of Eli Mandel's "Minotaur Poems" (1964) and noted that the latter is clearly more "primitive" (177–8). He then moved quickly to a Haida poem in a recent translation. His classroom practice was similar. A handout for students in a modern poetry course began with Haida poems and moved directly to Pratt.[1]

When Frye celebrated Pratt's achievements, he stressed the poet's role as myth-maker in a "highly ritualized" culture (*BG*, 185), and the poet's relation to oral tradition:

> the oral poet does not deal in facts at all, as such: what he deals in are myths,
> that is, stories of gods, historical reminiscences, and concepts founded on

metaphors. Such myths are neither true nor false, because they are not veri-
fiable. Myths are expressions of concern, of man's care for his own destiny
and heritage, his sense of the supreme importance of preserving his community, his constant interest in questions about his ultimate coming and going.
The poet who shapes the myth is thus entrusted with the speaking of the
word of concern, which, even though in early times it may often have been a
word of hostility and a celebrating of war and conquest, is still the basis of
social action. Primitive myths are conservative because primitive societies
are conservative, and last a long time without much change. (*BG*, 194)

From this vantage, he could conclude of Pratt: "In this life he took his
place at the centre of society where the great myths are formed, the
new myths where the hero is man the worker rather than man the con-
queror, and where the poet who shapes those myths is shaping also a
human reality which is greater than the whole objective world, with all
its light-years of space, because it includes the infinity of human
desire" (197).

Frye never read a Canadian writer of the highest calibre, a "writer of
whom we can say what we say of the world's major writers, that the
reader can grow up inside their work without ever being aware of a
circumference" (*BG*, 214). But he knew a North American writer who
fit the bill. Wallace Stevens struck him early on as a poet with a comprehensive vision—one who could conceive a poem "of which all
imaginative work proves a part" (*FI*, 250). The last words are quoted
from Frye's gloss on Stevens's poem "A Primitive Like an Orb,"
in which the "primitive" is something like Kabbalists' primordial
man (Adam Kadmon) and the "sphere" indicates completeness. For
Stevens, as for Shakespeare, the poet is not far removed from the luna-
tic and the lover. For Stevens, as for Frye, all poems are interrelated:

> One poem proves another and the whole,
> For the clairvoyant men that need no proof:
> The lover, the believer, and the poet.
> Their words are chosen out of their desire,
> The joy of language when it is themselves.

This is primitivism of a sort that most critics can accept: a search for the
primal language of poetry and its joy. Frye offered glimpses of a poetic
vision which no Canadian writer had yet recorded at such length and
breadth.

Frye's dicta on the landscape of Canadian poetry influenced a great many poets and critics in the generation after him. In *Butterfly on Rock* (1970), the poet Douglas Jones documented the theme of terror that Frye had remarked (*BG*, 225). In *Survival: A Thematic Guide to Canadian Literature* (1972), Margaret Atwood took up Frye's riddling identity question, "Where is here?" (*BG*, 220). A few readers took Frye to task for his kid-gloves approach to Canadian poets—first in the field was Edmund Wilson in *O Canada: An American's Notes on Canadian Culture* (1965). Other readers, especially those whose texts were under review, claimed that Frye's criticism was better directed at classics of world literature. Frye was in fact writing simultaneously about Canadian and European (principally English) literature, and it should come as no surprise that he would treat issues of literary primitivism in *Anatomy of Criticism* (1957). He claimed to "find the primitive formulas reappearing in the greatest classics—in fact there seems to be a general tendency on the part of great classics to revert to them" (*AC*, 17). In proposing what he termed "archetypal criticism," he was pointing to "the possibility of extending the kind of comparative and morphological study now made of folk tales and ballads into the rest of literature" (104). Indeed, his approach to archetypal material in the literary classics made it seem that he was defining pre-literate material of epic and ballad, "admittedly in a rather circular way, as literature which affords an unobstructed view of archetypes" (116). The debts to Spengler's morphology and Frazer's comparativism are quite evident here.

Following Frye's keynote speech at the symposium on Canadian culture mentioned at the outset of this essay, a panel of poets addressed the question, "Is There a Distinctive Canadian Poetry?" All three of the English-speaking poets couched their remarks in the context of Frye's well-known pronouncements. Eli Mandel began with the "frostbite" of colonialism, Ralph Gustafson with a denial that all Canadian poets fear nature, Douglas LePan by insisting that the garrison is not important. All three echoed the indictment of Frye's and Atwood's "thematic" criticism that would reach a crescendo in Robin Mathews's stinging *Canadian Literature: Surrender or Revolution* (1978). Almost as if to assert that Canadian literature had come of age, LePan emphasized distinction rather than distinctiveness, the poet's stance rather than his geographical location.

The disagreement is not so much between critics and poets as between two separate traditions in Canadian poets—Smith had called them the cosmopolitan and native traditions. Gustafson had been positioned among the cosmopolitans, where the younger LePan and Mandel no doubt belonged, and Pratt among the natives. By 1977, Frye was no longer comfortable with the dichotomy. "We are no longer an army of occupation," he concluded the keynote address, "and the natives are ourselves" (*DG*, 69). He was a cosmopolitan figure, if anyone in Canadian literature could claim to be, translated into many world languages and studied in many countries outside the English-speaking world. Even when addressing fellow Canadians during the centennial of Confederation, in 1967, Frye had observed "that we are moving towards a post-national world, and that Canada has moved further in that direction than most of the smaller nations" (*MC*, 17). At the same time, he insisted on the perspective that came from local experience. As his criticism of European literature is reassessed in the twenty-first century, the reassessment is likely to focus on his Canadian perspective.

Of course, Frye was quite capable of integrating traditions, be they cosmopolitan and native, Aristotelian and Platonic, or Old Comedy and New. He certainly had no disagreement with LePan, with whom he shared much in common. (Both were English professors and college principals at the University of Toronto and senior fellows of Massey College.) He had written a sympathetic review of LePan's poetry, but very much on his own terms of symbol and vision (*BG*, 26–9). On LePan's seventy-fifth birthday, in 1989, Frye sent a note saying that, for someone who had once written a poem about "A Country without a Mythology," LePan had done a great deal to create myths for Canada.[2] LePan thanked him, but liked to remark that Frye missed the point of his poem, which referred to a wilderness landscape with no personal associations whatever. If Frye indeed missed the point, other Canadian writers did so as well: Robertson Davies had quoted the same poem to the same effect in the concluding remarks at the Washington symposium.

Frye had argued that a poet may be an indifferent critic of his own work (*AC*, 5). The obverse of this dictum, that a critic can be indifferent to the poetry in his work, not realizing that his words come from a deeply personal response to the world, may be applied to Frye himself. His vision of Canada and its poetry—a vision passed on to generations of fortunate students—is inseparable from his preoccupations with the mythical and the primitive.

NOTES

1 NFF, 1991, box 46, file 3.
2 NFF, 1991, box 7, file 1.

JAMES STEELE

Margaret Atwood's *Cat's Eye*: New Feminism or Old Comedy?

Northrop Frye's profound yet sometimes neglected insight that the many genres of literature are subsumed and shaped by only four narrative forms or *mythoi*—romance, tragedy, irony, and comedy (*AC*, 43–8)—can help to explain the problematic structure of Margaret Atwood's novel *Cat's Eye*. Although several critics, most of them feminist, have suggested that this fictional autobiography is the portrayal of a woman's developing self, the complex narrative structure as well as certain other literary features indicate that it is essentially a comedy: the story of how a hero forms a desirable new society by transforming, or escaping from, a defective old one. The protagonist, Elaine Risley, a painter by profession, descends to a mental underworld where she remembers encounters with persons in Toronto who made her feel weak, inadequate, and unhappy; then, mainly through an exhibition of her art, she struggles successfully for vindication and rises victoriously to form a new society. But this comic action is also ironic. The heroine treats her friends with good humour and her antagonists with varying degrees of ridicule and satire, while both her present-time story and her memories of past experiences are laced with parodies of characters and motifs from fairy tales and romance quests.[1] The society Risley finally forms excludes her Toronto circle and consists of her own fleeing self and fellow travellers content to mind their own business. *Cat's Eye* is therefore not a new feminine genre but a delightfully imaginative imitation of an old form of satirically comic story—one that also happens to do Atwoodian justice to both men and women.

Most analyses of *Cat's Eye* have been written from a feminist perspective. Critics have discussed what the novel reveals about social power in a patriarchal society,[2] commented on significant motifs and images that pertain to the development of the female protagonist,[3] and, above all, analysed Elaine Risley in relation to notions of the female self.[4] The assumption implicit—and sometimes explicit—in this topical criticism is that the novel's structure is essentially that of a *Bildungsroman* or *Kunstlerroman*: a fictional autobiography presented through numerous flashbacks. As one critic has remarked, Atwood, "instead of following a linear plot that emphasizes separation from the past as the mark of maturity, ... creates a circular structure emphasizing the protagonist's return to scenes of her childhood and her reunion, if only in her imagination, with key figures from her past."[5]

There are problems, however, with this reading and others like it. One is that there are few, if any, causal links between the remembered behaviour of the protagonist and changes in her mind or character. When away from home, the young Elaine is as much at odds with her society as is the older Elaine Risley, and for similar reasons. The theme of the novel must therefore be something other than the protagonist's growth or development as a person. A second problem is that the protagonist's main purpose in describing many events in her life seems to be to present a humorous contrast, usually ironic, between her own reasonable yet unconventional conduct and that of her conventional yet less reasonable acquaintances. Indeed, if the story is really about a developing self, then this protagonist, who manages in the end to portray herself as the double of the Mother of God, would be the most self-righteous woman ever described in a *Bildungsroman*. A third problem is that this reading does not explain the parodies of fairy-tale motifs and images used to describe the experiences of the protagonist at virtually every stage of her life, including her work as an adult artist. Nor can it account for the repeated metaphoric allusions to a psychological underworld explored by the protagonist, or explain her final escape from a society that she has deemed inferior. These structural features indicate that the novel has an underlying narrative pattern (in Frye's term, a *mythos*) that is more fundamental than autobiographical fiction or, for that matter, than elements of confession and lyrical dream vision, which are also present in this novel. It is possible, of course, for any of these genres to include comic and satiric elements, but to confuse these kinds of writing with the *mythos* that gives the work its coherent form is to miss the forest for the trees, and thus to lose much of the meaning of the text.

The dominant framing narrative in *Cat's Eye* is the four-day quest of Elaine Risley. Within this frame is the inner story consisting of hundreds of memories that come to her as she reviews her life. The action in the outer frame is a contest between Elaine, the protagonist—a self-deprecating *eiron* character in Frye's lexicon—and her antagonist, Cordelia, who is Elaine's flawed alter ego as well as her double. The young Elaine is threatened by Cordelia, who tries, in league with other, lesser antagonists, to dominate her in various ways and to make Elaine herself feel at fault. Elaine's counter-strategy is to find a coherent and vindicating shape to her life—a kind of understanding that will enable her to free herself from Cordelia's power and so achieve her liberation. She accordingly "descend[s]" for about three days to a lower world of memories to review her conduct. She says, in fact, that she is "dragged downward, into the layers of this place [Toronto] as into liquefied mud" and that before making this descent she feels as if she has been transformed into a light, semi-corporeal, shrunken entity that is filling "with cold air, or gently falling snow"[6]—a sort of gnomish, wintry spirit. After recalling her behaviour in many incidents, she achieves her goal through a Retrospective Exhibition held at the Sub-Versions Gallery. Elaine sees all art galleries as "frightening places, places of evaluation, of judgment" (20) and at the Sub-Versions her understanding takes the concrete form of pictorial judgments of herself and her several helpers and antagonists. She then settles the ghost of Cordelia and rises (as her surname Risley promises)—but only to escape to another society. The protagonist, after revealing the inadequacies of an inferior community, becomes part of a small enlightened society consisting of herself and, presumably, anyone who can share, or at least tolerate, her perspective. This comedy, however, is also ironic: the action of the frame is a realistic (or "low mimetic") and somewhat parodic version of the central stage of the quest myth—a hero's visit to a lower world to find the key to her liberation—and her struggle involves much satire.

The adventures of the recollected inner story, which comprise most of the novel, are distributed unevenly over some fifty years of the protagonist's life. They correspond to an earlier, preparatory stage of the quest and are likewise essentially contests between Elaine and her several antagonists. The latter include three neighbouring children—Carol, Grace, and Cordelia—as well as two adults—Mrs Smeath (the mother of Grace) and Miss Lumley (a teacher). They also include two of her three spouses (Josef and Jon), a group of feminist painters, and some journalists. What the adventures reveal are the relations between the protagonist and the various characters she encounters; what unifies them is her satiric attitude and the rationale behind it. Generally

speaking, the risible Elaine Risley uses humour in describing her helpers, especially members of her family, and irony and satire in describing her antagonists. Her satiric bite touches on moral, ethical, and
aesthetic matters as well as on schooling, religion, and relations
between the sexes.

A remarkable feature of both the inner and framing stories is that
they parody aspects of the fairy tale—a type of fiction that evidently
charmed Atwood as a child[7]—as well as features of the romance quest
(as noted above). The heroine is accordingly aided or hindered by
many conventional characters and/or motifs derived from this heroic
fictional world. On a spiritual level, these figures include virgins of
various kinds (who turn up as often in fairy tales as they appear in
romance quests),[8] apparitions (46–7, 417, 442–3), spirits of the dead,
emanations, vampires, and witches (202, 227, 249, 368). On a human
level, Elaine is helped or hindered by her kind parents and a variety of
doubles, the latter usually representing aspects of consciousness in
narratives about a psychological descent.[9] Her doubles include Cordelia, the Virgin in her various forms, and Elaine's helpful brother.[10]
Elaine is also affected by the magical number "9" (28, 420), the colour
blue (67, 51), an enchanted house (73), a magic plant,[11] "invisible
bloomers" (85), a "secretive watchful forest" (154), and several magic-
like transforming devices. In this last category are her mother's wash-
ing machine, Cordelia's sunglasses, and a perilous cemetery that can
transform the dead.[12] She likewise makes use of many mirrors (sur-
faces that can reflect truth and symbolize reciprocal self-awareness),[13]
special bridges (like ladders, bridges in fairy tales can facilitate tran-
sitions from one place or mental state to another),[14] transmissible
powers,[15] X-ray vision (408), buried treasures (216, 217, 354, 418),
voluptuous odalisques (372),[16] and a toy sword. She has numerous
prophetic dreams[17] and even finds a talisman, namely her cat's-eye
marble (151, 166), a recurring image in this novel. (The cat, an animal
of both good and evil omen, has symbolic properties that are also ironically ambivalent.)[18]

Like the framing outer narrative, these recollected episodes of the
inner story also parody elements of the romance but focus on the preliminary, pre-descent stages of the quest—the youth of the heroine and
her preparation for an underworld struggle. Elaine as a young child
lives happily with kind parents and a beloved brother at various places
in the woods, a condition that Frye, following Blake, would describe as
a world of "innocence" (WP, 244). The values of her family are based
on freedom, fraternity, and equality, and she grows up in a world that

makes human sense and seems to exist for her benefit. Nevertheless, she remembers her family with much humour, especially in her descriptions of their remarkable toilet habits, simple food, non-heroic clothing, and distinctive ears. Like Elaine, her family is admirable but less than heroic.

When Elaine then moves to a new city world, she enters a world of "experience"— a place where natural innocent desires come into conflict with oppressive and repressive forces as devious friends try to control and subjugate her. At school she encounters an unkind society in which she experiences a regimentation of her movements, an apartheid of the sexes, and an obligatory association with censorious girls (48–50). What make her feel especially uncomfortable are the perilous differences between her own attitudes and those of her "friends," especially about such matters as grooming, dress, wardrobes, church attendance, home furnishings, and boys. These differences are explored in numerous incidents, in each of which the satiric details suggest that Elaine's unconventional attitude is more reasonable or natural than the conventional perspective of her friends.

Eventually, a certain "energy" passes—mysteriously if not magically—from Cordelia to Elaine, giving Elaine the imaginative power she needs to begin to bring about her liberation through art (250, 274). After this parodied crisis, Elaine continues her satiric struggles against new antagonists, with even greater success. She effectively ridicules the two inadequate males in her life, the unprincipled, patronizing Joseph and the jejeune Jon. At her first art show, she likewise flays certain flawed feminists through artistic portrayals and verbal repartee. She also manages to laugh off her attempted suicide and to see humour in her marriage to the benevolent Ben. With the help of her dying, Demeter-like mother, she finds, or rather stumbles upon, a treasure in the depths of her mother's cellar: her cat's-eye marble. Although the marble symbolizes Elaine's valuable power of vision, it is an inherently worthless object and thus a parody of an underworld treasure. Elaine then returns in a non-satiric, elegiac mood to the place where her school once stood and climbs an old familiar hill. At its top, she has an epiphanic experience, an ironic vision of her life as a prison (422). With this brief and dark insight, Elaine has completed her preparation for her main struggle, and the inner narrative comes to an end.

The satire in this inner story is directed at many targets. Some relate primarily to a world of the young: unkind relationships among children or between children and adults, sexual stereotyping, snobbery, and pedagogical practices at both Sunday school and elementary school. Other targets concern adolescence: extraordinary fashions in dress as well as in speech and amusements; awkward relations between the sexes; and the presumptions of youth. Still others, which involve both young and old, ridicule class distinctions, colonialism, imperialism, feminism, "masculinism," and even "invalidism." Moral and religious hypocrisy as well as changing styles in art and art criticism are also targets. Even myth criticism comes in for good-humoured attack, when Elaine observes that some people have wrong-fully interpreted a series of her paintings of her mother as having to do with the "Earth Goddess," or the Demeter-Persephone myth (161).

A remarkable feature of this satire is the shifting norm or standard on which it is based. Sometimes the ironic Elaine depends on the reader's own common sense to make her point, and the satire is then essentially what Frye would describe as "low norm" (*AC*, 226). Her paraphrase, for example, of another painter's catalogue entry for her devastating pictures of Mrs Smeath ("It's good to see the aging female body treated with compassion, for a change" [368]) is effective because every reader knows that a picture of a fat, spam-like body wrapped in tissue paper could, in fact, only be ugly and therefore anything but an object of compassion. At other times, however, Elaine ridicules normal behaviour by applying a perspective that is as reasonable as it is unconventional, and the satire then becomes picaresque or "quixotic" (*AC*, 229–34). As Elaine recalls later in the novel, when she first arrived in Toronto she must have appeared to others as "a frazzle-headed rag-amuffin from heaven knows where, a gypsy practically, with a heathen father and a feckless mother who traipsed around in slacks and gath-ered weeds. [She was] unbaptized, a nest for demons" (427). The naive young Elaine, schooled only in the virtues of her own family, takes for granted the equality of male and female, the similarity of their dress when appropriate, and the interchangeability of their social roles; she therefore uses irony to describe the departures from these norms she observes in the city. As she grows older, her satiric attitude becomes less "quixotic"; even in the later chapters, however, her uncommon understanding of the spirit of equality that informs a good relationship between a man and a woman underlies her cheesecake attacks on Josef and Jon. It also underlies the satire in her "Falling Women" painting and her mockery elsewhere of domineering feminism.

When the humorous and satiric episodes of the inner story merge with the framing comic narrative at her Retrospective Exhibition, Elaine displays the full strength of her satirically comic vision. The Retrospective's early-period pictures—the paintings of banal domestic

appliances, the ridiculous renditions of Jon and Josef, and the carica-
tures of Mrs Smeath (now counterbalanced by Elaine's charitable comments [427])—remind the reader of the things and people in her past
whose inadequacies have already been revealed. The five "recent"
paintings, however, mark a new phase in the comedy. They are pictorial proof of the protagonist's power, but their remarkable parodic
qualities sustain the comic mood.

The first painting, "Picoseconds"—a picture of a northern landscape
with a window-like opening in the lower right-hand corner through
which can be seen Elaine's mother and father cooking lunch near their
Studebaker—is a reminder that the young Elaine was reared in a wilderness and that, at its heart, her loving and caring parents worked in
a spirit of equality. Although the images of the mother and father in
this idyll of innocence are certainly conventional,[19] their incongruous
windowed setting is a parody of post-modern juxtaposition. Even the
Studebaker contributes to the parodic mood. As a detail in an autobiography the car is, to be sure, a realistic touch. But, because it is also
the very automobile that carried Elaine between her wilderness homes
and her city dwelling, it must be a parody of such conventional, fairy-
tale transfer devices as the friendly bird, the convenient boat, the
accommodating horse, or the magic flying carpet.[20] When Elaine compares the marginal position of her parents in this picture to the disap-
pearing leg of Icarus in the painting by Breugel, she seems to be
implying, with good humour, that they are simply falling out of existence. (In an earlier dream, she had seen them "recede" by "sinking
down through the earth" [179].) Likewise, when she describes the row
of gas-pump logos placed beneath the inner picture of her parents as
being similar to a subterranean platform, the logos signify, on a literal
autobiographical level, merely that the young Elaine's nomadic family
once relied on service stations for food, fuel, and lodging. When she
observes, however, that they are "iconic-looking symbols painted in
the flat style of Egyptian tomb frescoes," the observant reader under-
stands that her representation of innocence is subject also to her satiric
humour.

The second painting, "The Three Muses," reminds the reader that
the protagonist was given an excellent education while gaining a deep
understanding of human equality. It depicts three persons influential
in Elaine's education: Miss Stuart (a Scottish teacher), Mrs Feinstein
(a kindly Jewish neighbour), and Mr Bannerji (an Indian graduate
student). She commemorates them because they gave her, respectively,
a knowledge of the arts (symbolized pictorially by a teacher's globe), a

sense of neighbourly kindness (symbolized by the orange donated by Mrs Feinstein), and some knowledge of science (symbolized by Mr Bannerji's microscope slide). Nevertheless, the picture is as much a parody as it is a celebration of kindly virtue. In her presentation, Elaine, playing God, raises her graceful tutors to a divine plane (428–9). The caricature lies partly in the outlandish costumes—including Miss Stuart's mask—in which she dresses her three saints, partly in the unconventional mixing of both the sexes and races of these divinities, and partly in the extraordinary features of two of the gifts they bear: Miss Stuart's orange is the size of a beach ball and the substance on Mr Banerji's slide resembles stained glass, although it turns out to be the guts of a spruce budworm. Elaine refers jokingly to this picture as a "translation." In Frye's terms, it is a parody of an apocalyptic epiphany and an integral part of the comedy.

In the third painting, "One Wing," the reader is reminded that the protagonist is also aware of the horrors of life. The central panel of the triptych depicts Elaine's innocent brother, having been thrown from a plane by terrorists, falling upside down through the air to his death. But there is parody here too. The aircraft in the right panel resembles one on a child's collector card, and the hand-held sword, a conventional romance weapon, looks like a child's toy (25). Even the luna moth in the right panel, a conventional symbol for regeneration, has extraordinary qualities: Elaine as a child describes this favourite moth as "huge and pale green, with crescents on its wings" (154). As an art form, the triptych has a strong ecclesiastical association; it is the kind of picture that might adorn a Chapel Perilous in a romance. Here it is used by Elaine for a non-religious purpose. Although it depicts the absurd killing of an innocent person, the triptych's parodic features lighten the burden and maintain the comic mood. In Frye's terms, "One Wing" is a "low mimetic" or realistic parody of a demonic epiphany—the protagonist's glimpse of Hell.

The fourth painting, "Cat's Eye," is a reminder that the middle-aged Elaine's power of ironic observation remains a vital force. In this picture, the only eyes are the aging ones in the half head of Elaine looking outward at the very bottom of the picture, the eye-like convex mirror that hangs in an empty sky at the centre, and, presumably, the eyes of her three reflected friends. Nevertheless, there is parody here too. The eyes and nose of the mature Elaine peering out over the bottom of the painting's border appear unconventionally as eyes observing a world outside the painting, and all portrayed eyes come from the unseen eye of the painter, the cat's eye that cannot be seen. The mirror in the painting, it is true, echoes Van Eyck's mirror in "The Arnolfini Marriage," but with a difference. Whereas Van Eyck's mirror reflects persons or things which are not in the painted scene but which could plausibly exist just outside it, the mature Elaine's mirror transforms her reflected image so that she appears much younger. Her mirror is thus magical, an instrument well suited to the hero of this satiric comedy.

In the fifth and final picture, "Unified Field Theory," Elaine again proves her strength through parody. This time she paints the Virgin of Lost Things, a form of Saint Mary. Even though Elaine herself is no virgin and certainly no Mother of God, her close link with this Virgin is clear: the good lady is Elaine's very own double. Since she hovers in the air, the Virgin of Lost Things must have supernatural powers, and the starlight shining through her cloak suggests an incorporeal quality reminiscent of Elaine at the time of her descent. Also, instead of cradling the infant Jesus in her arms, Elaine's most holy double holds only a large, worthless marble, the symbol of Elaine's satiric power. Even the wintry night setting, an appropriate time and season for this dark comedy, is paradoxical. In the upper part of the painting is an ordinary "night sky after sunset," with the lower half of a conventional moon at the very top. Across the middle runs a snow-covered footbridge, a variation of the conventional ladder or tower that links a higher spiritual sphere with a lower one (*WP*, 232). Below this bridge is the ravine where Elaine had a harrowing experience as a child. It is now presented, however, as a space organized by scientific intelligence: "the night sky as seen through a telescope. Star upon star, red, blue, yellow, and white, swirling nebulae: the universe in its incandescence and darkness." This starry space, which, we are told, is the artist's rendering of a magnified telescopic reflection of the sky above—and thus a product of one of the many mirrors in this novel—is totally displaced from its conventional upper position. Elaine, in fact, makes these magnified and coloured stars a part of "the underside of the ground" and mixes them with "stones, ... small roots" and even "beetles" (431), thereby suggesting that the traditional position of the starry heavens should be inverted.[21] Beneath this level, at the very bottom of the painting, in merging lighter hues, is a river of "clear blue water" that flows from "the land of the dead people," Elaine's good-humoured version, it would seem, of Hades. At the two sides of the picture, at the ends of the footbridge, are the leafless branch tops of snow-clad trees, a parodic version, perhaps, of a world-tree linking the four levels of a traditional cosmos in an *axis mundi* (*WP*, 232).

The picture's title, "Unified Field Theory," a phrase from the title of her brother Stephen's lecture on "The First Picoseconds and the Quest for a Unified Field Theory" (351), is also a part of the parody—a mock-heroic repetition of the name given by Albert Einstein to his great search for a way of synthesizing what was known about electromagnetism and gravitation. Einstein's quest involved ideas about quanta, relativity, mass, time, space, light, and energy; what Einstein's great problem and Elaine's little quest have in common are the last four of these subjects. Each of these has been an important motif in the novel prior to the presentation of this painting. At the very beginning of her story, Elaine explains that, for her, time has a spatial "shape" which she can see by looking "down through [time], like water" (3), and she refers to time repeatedly thereafter.[22] She also comments frequently on the dimensions of space,[23] on light,[24] and on energy.[25] She is aware that energy is physically related to mass and light, for at one point she tries to inform a totally uninterested Cordelia that Einstein's famous equation, $E=mc^2$ (in which E stands for energy, m mass, and c the velocity of light), can explain the explosive power of an atom bomb (260).

In this last picture, Elaine's entire life as well as the temporal coexistence of the living and the dead is given an expressive shape; in fact, Elaine insists here that her paintings are "the time she's made" (431). The coloured starlight of telescopic vision likewise falls within her powers of perception, and it is light of a special inner kind that enables Elaine, whose very name means "ray of light,"[26] to "see" with her satirical cat's eye. She also suggests that her whole painting is an aspect of energy, the "energy" which in this and other paintings "came out of [her]" and is now beyond her control. Energy produces all light in Elaine's time and space, and it is the ultimate source of her satiric power. Her attempt to find, through satire, a human meaning for "energy" in a scientific age is a continuing "quest," just like the scientific work of her brother, whom she likens to a "space twin" and thus another of her doubles (414). Yet, in keeping with her ironic attitude towards her less-than-perfect world, she has a titanic saturnine temptation to destroy her whole Retrospective by water or fire.[27] Even as parody, the title of her painting is apt.

Having vindicated her life's work through her art and thus proved her merit, Elaine's remaining task is to settle accounts with Cordelia. She wants her friend to present herself so that she can ask "why" Cordelia treated her with cruelty as a child, and she wants to give Cordelia a "reflection" of what she "look[s] like from the outside," that is, from Elaine's point of view. When she explains that "we are like twins in old fables, each of whom has been given half a key" (434), Elaine is not longing for a loving reconciliation or reunion (as some autobiographical readings of the novel have suggested), but simply observing that a good understanding of a relationship requires an appreciation of the perspectives of both parties. The implication here is that, just as Elaine has learned a lot about herself from considering Cordelia's point of view, she (Elaine) could now tell Cordelia a thing or two about Cordelia's own miserable self. Cordelia, however, does not appear. Elaine has a dream vision of her turning up dressed unrecognizably in the conventional attire of a proper, upper-middle-class matron—a damning image, indeed, from Elaine's perspective—but she does not experience a sense of closure after this vision, merely the frustration of "silence" and "absence" (435). Nevertheless, with a measure of admirable humility, she soon declares a victory over her non-appearing double ("got you back") and ambiguously pronounces her "dead." Then, to lay even the ghost of her defaulting friend to rest, Elaine returns to the ravine where she once nearly perished with Cordelia's assistance and imagines in a second dream vision that she sees Cordelia now embodying all her own former weaknesses and that she (Elaine) is strong enough to send her gently "home." (In this ironic comedy, the dismissed Cordelia is a pathetic basket case who comes close to being a scapegoat or, in Frye's term, a *pharmakos*.) With this vicarious settlement, Elaine snaps out of her trance, and imagined snow, which, it will be recalled, suffused her body just before her initial descent, "withdraws like smoke" (443). The protagonist's triumph is now complete.

Elaine is now entitled, according to one version of the comic *mythos*, to ascend to recognition by her community, to marry, and to live happily ever after. But this professional woman, who has long since married and mothered children, does not wait for approval from Toronto, a non-redeemable society she has referred to on an earlier occasion as "Gomorrah" (404). With characteristic irony, Elaine prefers a quick solitary escape: her final ascent is a night flight to Vancouver, with the assurance that the mere "echoes of [star]light shining out of the midst of nothing" are "enough [for her] to see by" (445). (Her victory is similar to that of the victorious Tukana woman in the ironically comic story of Eduardo Galeano quoted by Atwood as a preface to her novel. As this murdered old woman blew the blood from her beheaded body towards the sun, she made her own soul enter the bodies of her murderers, so that "since then anyone who kills receives in his body, without wanting or knowing it, the soul of his victim.") This dark resolution—the final spurning of an inferior community by a disdainful protagonist—is consistent with another version of the comic *mythos*, namely Old Comedy, a narrative pattern developed by the Greeks to accommodate an abundance of irony and satire (*AC*, 43–4; *SM*, 148–53).

Frye has suggested that, when the descending and ascending movements that underlie the *mythos* of comedy are essentially psychological, they are symbols of intensified consciousness. In his view, the Romantics and their modern heirs revolutionized the structure of human culture by transferring the ultimate source of the mind's power from a sky god to "a point of identity [in the human body] where human creation and imaginative power start." He further notes that this "point of identity" is sometimes "symbolized as [being] under the earth or sea, like Atlantis," or as a cave with primitive paintings, or as the subconscious mind with its dreams, fantasies, and memories (*WP*, 248). This insight is relevant to an understanding of *Cat's Eye*. It can explain why important elements of the traditional cosmos are inverted in "Unified Field Theory" and why there is no God in the painted skies of Elaine Risley. It accounts for the fact that her heavenly stars— another recurring image in this novel[28]—are generally related to night skies or astrophysics rather than to spiritual wisdom and that they can even be mixed up with the ground at the bottom of a ravine. It likewise explains why Elaine's treasured marble, symbolizing the power that enables her to produce her art, is found not on a mountain top close to heaven but in a cellar. It also makes clear why her art is hung in a gallery with similar subterranean qualities. "Sub-Versions Gallery" has clear metaphorical links with a lower domain and the place itself has certain cave-like features: a black wall, boiler pipes, track lighting, and no mention of windows (89–90). What the reader sees in Sub-Versions are not the pictures themselves but Elaine's cryptic descriptions of them. These accounts have something of an oracular quality, for they include mysterious subject matter, strange dislocations, and implausible relations, all challenging the reader to interpret them. Even the ravine where Elaine dismisses Cordelia's ghost has special sea-like properties reminiscent of a lower world. At its bottom, there is "another, wilder and more tangled landscape rising up, from beneath the surface," and this ground still covers a "treasure" hidden by her dead brother. The traffic in the distance has a "sea-sound," and the bare branches at the tops of the trees are like "dry coral." Elaine muses that jumping from the ravine's bridge would be like "diving" and that if she "died that way it would be soft, like drowning" (442). In other words, she confirms her power by descending psychologically to a place that is like an oceanic underworld.

Frye reminded his readers that descent myths are essentially about fertility, especially the regeneration of life in the spring, and that all such stories, even in their satirically comic form, are an expression of a human concern about the production of food and drink.[29] In the *Cat's Eye* story, there are, in fact, hundreds of references to food. On some occasions, allusions to what characters are imbibing—Elaine's drinks, for example, at her Retrospective—help to sustain the comic mood. More often, food and drink, and what is done to them by human beings, are satiric targets. Elaine's "prophetic" father warns against turning the water supply in the lower Great Lakes into a sewer (350). He also counsels against polluting the food chain with insecticides and criticizes genetic engineering, mercury poisoning, and nitrogen fertilizers (70, 139, 307). He suggests that the production of too much methane gas will produce a green-house effect with global warming, and further warns of poisoned trees, foul air, and the loss of whole species (231, 418). Elaine, who learns a lot from her father, refers caustically at her Retrospective to "unadulterated chlorine from the tap" and "sulfur-drenched grapes" and, when she visits the ravine the following day, remarks that the creek is "running with clear water unsafe to drink" (442). While food and drink are not the main theme of the novel, they are certainly a recurring motif and not unrelated to the main point of the satire.

In *Cat's Eye*, Elaine seeks to criticize faults in her society (including, of course, Cordelia's) by justifying her work as an artist. In response to Cordelia's glib question, "What have you got to say for yourself?" she delves deeply into her memory in order to explain the origins of her attitude and perspective. What she learns is expressed through her satiric accounts of events in her life and through her parodies, especially her semi-oracular descriptions of her paintings. She suggests, among many other things, that people—even children—should treat each other humanely and that men and women should work with each other in a spirit of equality. She upholds the value of creative energy and of the fruits of her labour as a professional artist, and implies that a painter who is independent and intelligent yet married and female can be productive. In a complex, modern economy, such values are related directly to the shaping of human taste and indirectly to the social and economic conditions that can ensure a secure supply of food and drink. The ironically comic narrative and the satiric wit that shape this autobiography thus indicate that the novel is less a new kind of portrayal of a gendered self than a criticism, expressed through an ancient literary form, of a society in need of mending its unkind, hypocritical, and unenlightened ways.

ACKNOWLEDGMENT

I am most grateful to the University of Toronto Press's anonymous reader of an earlier version of this essay for delightfully challenging comments and useful suggestions.

NOTES

1 For Frye's analysis of the relation of the quest myth to both comedy and irony, see *AC*, 192–203.

2 Molly Hite, "An Eye for an I: The Disciplinary Society in *Cat's Eye*," in *Various Atwoods: Essays on the Later Poems, Short Fiction, and Novels*, ed. Lorraine M. York (Toronto: Anansi, 1995), 191–206.

3 Jessie Givner, "Names, Faces and Signatures in Margaret Atwood's *Cat's Eye* and *The Handmaid's Tale*," *Canadian Literature* 133 (1992): 56–75; Julie Brown, "Our Ladies of Perpetual Hell: Witches and Fantastic Virgins in Margaret Atwood's *Cat's Eye*," *Journal of the Fantastic in the Arts* 4, 3 (1991): 40–52.

4 David Cowart, "Bridge and Mirror: Replicating Selves in *Cat's Eye*," in *Postmodern Fiction in Canada*, ed. Theo D'haen and Hans Bertens (Amsterdam: Rodopi, 1992); Carol Osborne, "Constructing the Self through Memory: *Cat's Eye* as Novel of Female Development," *Frontiers: A Journal of Women's Studies* 14, 3 (1994): 95–112; Jacques Leclaire, "Margaret Atwood's *Cat's Eye* as a Portrait of the Artist," *Commonwealth Essays and Studies* 13, 1 (1990): 73–80; and Judith McCombs, "Contrary Re-memberings: The Creating Self and Feminism in *Cat's Eye*," *Canadian Literaure* 129 (1991): 9–23.

5 Osborne, "Constructing the Self through Memory," 95.

6 Margaret Atwood, *Cat's Eye* (Toronto: McClelland-Bantam, 1988), 13. Future references in the text are to this edition.

7 Rosemary Sullivan, *The Red Shoes: Margaret Atwood Starting Out* (Toronto: HarperCollins Canada, 1998), 35–6. Sullivan reports that the unexpurgated *Complete Grimm's Fairy Tales* was one of young Atwood's favourite books.

8 The Virgin Mary is a kind helper in several of Grimm's fairy tales. For discussions of some of the Virgin images in *Cat's Eye*, see Sonia Gernes, "Transcendent Women: Uses of the Mystical in Margaret Atwood's *Cat's Eye* and Marilynne Robinson's *Housekeeping*," *Religion and Literature* 23 (1991): 143–65, and Brown, "Our Ladies of Perpetual Hell." References to the Virgin in this novel include the following: 50, 79, 127, 163, 195, 196–7, 203–5, 211–12, 302, 345, 365, 368, and 442.

9 *WP*, 266–7; Jean Chevalier and Alain Gheerbrant, *Dictionary of Symbols*, trans. John Buchanan-Brown (Oxford: Blackwell, 1994), 306.

10 225, 235, 243, 249, 260, 266, 268, 273, 278, 322, 343, 358, 372, 395, 408, 412, 414, 421–2, 431, 434.

11 80, 113–14, 155, 166, 272, 351.

12 193, 322, 442. For a discussion of the perilous cemetery motif in quest literature, see Jessie L. Weston, *From Ritual to Romance* (New York: Doubleday, 1957), 177–80.

13 5, 19, 34, 36, 97, 132, 156, 169, 182, 194, 225, 227, 229, 234, 244, 268, 278, 287, 305, 322–3, 347, 372, 389, 395, 424, 432, and 434. See *Dictionary of Symbols*, 657–61.

14 13, 65, 79, 166, 169, 193, 248, 286, 354, 431, 435, and 441–3. See *Dictionary of Symbols*, 122–4, and Cowart, "Bridge and Mirror," 132–3.

15 166, 241, 249, 334, 336, and 365.

16 For a discussion of Atwood's parodic use of odalisques, see Michelle Gadpaille, "Odalisques in Margaret Atwood's *Cat's Eye*," *Metaphor and Symbolic Activity* 8 (1993): 221–6.

17 155, 178–9, 206, 268–9, 343, 357, 381–2, and passim.

18 For the marble, see 66–7, 151, 155, 166, 217, 354, 358, 388, 420, and 430. On the cat symbol, see *Dictionary of Symbols*, 162–3.

19 *Dictionary of Symbols*, 372, 677–9.

20 See V. Propp, *Morphology of the Folktale*, 2nd ed. (Austin: University of Texas Press, 1968), 50–1.

21 The archetypal significance of this type of inversion is discussed by Frye, *WP*, 241–51. See also below.

22 5, 12, 149, 161, 165, 183, 189, 200, 215, 235, 237, 243, 254, 309, 322, 358, 389, 408, 414, 421, 431, and 445.

23 13, 40, 234, 352, 374, and 388.

24 3, 5, 9, 19, 27, 32, 34, 59, 62, 67, 73, 90, 96, 102–3, 110, 132, 147, 196, 202, 227, 232, 235, 257–8, 260, 346–7, 352–3, 389, 395, 412, 422, 428, 442, and 445.

25 166, 191, 235, 258, 285, 317, 336, 347, 352–3, 400, 431, and 441.

26 E.G. Withycombe, *The Oxford Dictionary of English Christian Names*, 3rd ed. (Oxford: Clarendon, 1977), 148.

27 Elaine's mood of exasperation here is similar to that expressed by Frank Scott at the end of his satirical poem "Lakeshore." The poet, perceiving a world incapable of reform, imagines the "whole creation" drowning in a second flood.

28 24, 27, 72, 106, 109–10, 177, 212, 352, 354, 414, 430–1, and 445.

29 *WP*, 253. For a sociobiologist's recent appreciation of Frye's insight that myths are ultimately related to the basic needs for survival, see Edward O. Wilson, *Consilience: The Unity of Knowledge* (New York: Knopf, 1998), 210–37.

Frye and China

YE SHUXIAN

Myth-Archetypal Criticism in China

As one of the many contemporary Western critical schools introduced into China in the twentieth century, myth-archetypal criticism has played an active role in transforming China's literary research. This important critical school, prevalent in the West in the 1950s and '60s, originated in the Ritual School (also called the Cambridge School) which arose in Britain at the beginning of the twentieth century, and culminated in Northrop Frye's *Anatomy of Criticism* (1957). Myth-archetypal criticism consciously makes use of the insights of cultural anthropology; its emergence is also closely associated with the developing use of myth and of Jung's archetypal theory in Western literature. It attempts to identify the various images, narrative structures, and characters which repeatedly occur in literary works, to locate the fundamental forms (especially myth archetypes) underlying them, and to apply these archetypes to the analysis, interpretation, and evaluation of literary works.

While Western myth-archetypal criticism was formally introduced into China rather late, the process of digestion, assimilation, and application was completed in a short time and fruitful results were achieved. The speed of absorption is explained partly by an enthusiastic desire to engage with Western scholarship after a period of isolation, and partly by the fact that the cultural soil had already been cultivated through the dissemination of mythology and folklore before the founding of the People's Republic of China: in the first half of the twentieth century a number of prominent scholars, such as Lu Xun, Mao Dun, Zheng Zhenduo, Wen Yiduo, and Ling Chunsheng, tried to apply mythology, folklore, and anthropology to literary research.

Investigation of the translation, introduction, and dissemination of myth criticism in China thus contributes to a better understanding of the phenomena of cultural absorption and transmission.

Archetypal criticism was introduced into China's critical circles in a limited way in the early 1960s. In 1962 the Institute of Literature of the Chinese Academy of Social Sciences published *Selected Essays on Literary Theory by Modern American and English Bourgeois Critics* (1st volume). The book provided a negative example; it offered only a limited sample of Western literary theory, which was criticized and castigated in the abnormal cultural atmosphere of that time. However, *Selected Essays* revealed to some extent the tendency of Western academic developments and transformations. The book contained articles by scholars associated with the School of Myth and Ritual—selections from Jane Harrison's *Ancient Art and Ritual* and Maud Bodkin's *Archetypal Patterns in Poetry*, and Gilbert Murray's "Hamlet and Orestes," for instance—which more or less reflect the work of this school before the 1950s. It did not touch upon Frye's establishment of archetypal critical theory.

In Taiwan, students of comparative literature were well acquainted with the concept of archetypal criticism by the 1970s. Xu Jinfu's translation of W.L. Guerin's *A Handbook of Critical Approaches to Literature* was published in Taiwan in 1975. Its English original was published in 1966, when archetypal criticism was still popular in Western critical circles, and the book juxtaposes archetypal criticism with traditional, formal, psychological, and expressive criticism. Yan Yuanshu's translation of *Literary Criticism: A Short History* (1957; trans. 1977, Taiwan; 2nd ed. 1982), by New Critics William Wimsatt and Cleanth Brooks, further contributed to Chinese awareness of archetypal criticism. The thirty-first chapter of the book is devoted to "Myth and Archetype." Among the subjects discussed in this chapter are the attention paid to myth since the eighteenth century (the time when Vico lived), Cassirer's theory of myth and thought, his American disseminator Susanne Langer's view of symbolic art, and the archetypal theory of Frye and Jung. However, as their book was published in 1957, the two authors were unable to discuss *Anatomy of Criticism*; their comments on Frye were chiefly confined to his article "The Archetypes of Literature," published as part of the collection, "My Credo: A Symposium of Critics," in the *Kenyon Review* in 1951. It is a pity that Yan Yuanshu's translation omitted footnotes, so that readers find it difficult to determine the specific source of the views evaluated in the book. In 1978, the same article, regarded as an abridged *Anatomy of Criticism*, was translated into Chinese by Gao Xuejin. It provides readers with a comparatively clear explanation of archetypal theory.

Since the 1970s, some scholars in Taiwan have been employing archetypal theory in the analysis of Chinese literary works. Shui Jing's *The Art of Zhang Ailing's Novels* (1973), Yan Yuanshu's *On National Literature* (1975), Miu Wenjie's *An Attempt at an Exposition of Frontier Poetry in the Tang Dynasty from the Perspective of Archetypal Criticism* (1975), for example, all reveal attempts to borrow the method of anthropology and apply the myth-archetypal perspective to the novel, poetry, and drama. *The Development of Comparative Literature in Taiwan*, edited by Gu Tianhong, contains two papers which likewise adopt the archetypal approach: Zhang Hanliang's "The Archetypal Structure of the Story Series by Yanglin" and Hou Jian's "The Popular Romance of the Westward Voyage made by Zheng He."[1] This work shows that Chinese scholars have skilfully mastered critical methods from the West and to a great extent changed the old pattern of research in ancient literature. Archetypal criticism was little known in academic circles in mainland China, however, before the reform period of the late 1970s, although a number of translations of foreign Sinologists' works had indirectly mentioned or applied the method. For instance, British Sinologist David Hawkes used the archetypal approach in his article "The Quest of the Goddess" (1967). And scholars from the United States, Russia, and Japan employed the same method to analyse such Chinese classics as *The Dream of the Red Mansion* and other works, or to reinterpret the legend of Emperors Yao and Shun and their abdication from the perspective of a ritual trial.

The introduction of archetypal criticism into Chinese critical circles in the 1960s and '70s had two effects: it weakened the dominant position of the sociological critical mode and changed the rigid mindset of scholars in the country. The subsequent process of dissemination shows that in most cases disciplines adhering to rigid dogmas naturally adopted an exclusive attitude to new theories, whereas researchers in the field of foreign languages and literature undertook the pioneering task of introducing new theories and innovative methods. The same phenomenon may be seen in the English departments of some Euro-American universities, which also take the lead in accepting new theories.

In the 1980s, further Anglo-American theoretical texts were translated into Chinese. The journal *Research on Literary Theory*, sponsored by East China Normal University, published in its third issue in 1982 a translation of American critic Wilbur Scott's essay on the five approaches in contemporary Anglo-American literary criticism; in the following year his book, *Five Approaches of Literary Criticism* (1962), was translated by Lan Renzhe and published. The book contributed helpful information to the growing discussion of the new method. Scott introduces a number of archetypal critics, including Frazer, Jung, D.H. Lawrence, Kenneth Burke, Wilson Knight, Leslie Fiedler, and Richard Chase, although he says nothing about the already well-known Canadian critic, Northrop Frye. After quoting both appreciative and adverse assessments, Scott gives his own opinion on this critical mode: "But whether done well or ill, the totemic approach obviously reflects the contemporary dissatisfaction with the scientific concept of man as, at his highest, rational. Anthropological literature seeks to restore to us our entire humanity, a humanity which values the primitive elements in human nature. In contrast to the splitting of the human mind by emphasizing the warfare between the conscious and subconscious processes, anthropological literature reestablishes us as members of the ancient race of man. And archetypal criticism seeks to discover in literature the dramatizations of this membership."[2] Later Chinese critics in literary anthropology similarly insist that the communication among myth, rite, and reality, and the reconstruction of the relationship between the primitive and the civilized, the rational and the irrational, should remain the key concern for this school of criticism.

Also published in 1983 were two anthologies introducing Jung's archetypal psychology and Frye's archetypal criticism, respectively, which served as the prelude to the dissemination of two different schools of critical theory. The collections in question are the first issue of the *Translation Series on Literary Theory*, edited by the Institute of Foreign Literature of the Chinese Academy of Social Sciences, and *Selected Essays of Modern Western Literary Theory*, edited by Wu Lifu. *Translation Series* collects under the title "Literary Information on Western Modernism" theoretical materials concerning the stream of consciousness, translated by Ma Shiyi. From his broad reading of Jung's writings, the translator chose extracts from such works and essays as *Modern Man in Search of a Soul*, *Archetypes of the Collective Unconscious*, "The Psychology of the Child Archetype," and "Psychological Aspects of the Mother Archetype." Wu Lifu's *Selected Essays* includes under the heading "Structuralism" a partial translation of Frye's *Fables of Identity*. The translator introduces Frye as "a key representative of structuralism, famous for his analysis of myth,"[3] an evaluation which seems more appropriate for French anthropologist Lévi-Strauss than for Frye, and it can be concluded that the complete panorama of contemporary Western criticism remained obscure during the process of initial introduction into China. Translators were unable to grasp correctly the distinction between structuralism and archetypal criticism, although the two schools were already at the point of decline.

Jung and Freud, disciple and teacher, were both masters of thought unknown in China for many years. Of the two, Jung harmonizes more closely with the Chinese socialist outlook because he emphasizes "collectivism," while Freud, with his stress on individuality and sex, always looks like an iconoclast or heretic. The domestic mechanism of selection in cultural transmission also explains why archetypal criticism, transmitted into China over fifty years later than psychoanalysis, was more readily accepted.

Zhang Longxi's "Resurgence of Deities," which celebrates archetypal criticism, is typically receptive where Jung is concerned. Zhang is critical of Frye, claiming that "Frye's theory remains an examination of artistic form and never considers the social and historical conditions of literature,"[4] but he introduces Jung and Frazer in an objective and uncritical manner. What is more valuable, Zhang attempts to find in the indigenous academic tradition some root or developing point with a similarity to Western critical approaches. He thus cites Wen Yiduo's article "Myth and Poetry," which employs an anthropological method to investigate the relationship between Chinese classical poetry and myth, and declares it to be "a promising field." Zhang's essay not only helps to lessen the distance between Western and Chinese literary theory, it also transforms a simple introduction into a suggestive proposal. The poetic title "Resurgence of Deities" is prophetic: in May 1984, the Chinese Association of Mythological Studies was established and the periodical *Information in the Studies of Mythology* was sponsored to introduce new developments in the research into myth in Hong Kong, Taiwan, and foreign countries. Another periodical, *Chinese Myth*, edited by Yuan Ke, began publication in the same year. It focuses on publishing domestic research in this field. In October 1985, the first triennial congress of the Chinese Comparative Literature Association meeting in Shenzhen held a special session on "comparative mythology," so that the rising field of comparative literature in China was closely connected with mythology from its start. All of these phenomena indicated that China, a country with a tradition of "Don't talk about mysterious forces or worship weird gods," was experiencing an unprecedented revival of myth. This gave archetypal criticism the chance to flourish in the cultural soil of China.

Yuan Ke says in the preface to the first issue of *Chinese Myth*: "We are Marxists. We will use as much as possible the viewpoints and methods of dialectical materialism and historical materialism to study, ponder and solve problems of Chinese myth. However, we don't exclude foreign influence. We will adopt a 'grabbist' attitude toward anything good or partially useful to us."[5] Xiao Bing, in "The Myth Fad on China's Mainland," points out:

> Several years ago, when the Chinese academia woke up and opened its eyes to the world, it was so hungry that it devoured ravenously (and thus translated without selection) all kinds of foreign theories, including mythology. In this period, Lévi-Strauss's structuralism was still in the ascendant whereas Malinowski's functionalism was still popular; the theory of the collective unconscious favored by the followers of Freud and Jung began to revive while Frazer and Harrison's Cambridge-Ritual School experienced a resurgence. The "new generation" in the history of Chinese culture suddenly found that Chinese myth was in fact a virgin land and that mythology was a leading subject associated with a lot of heated topics; it is well known that with myth as its resource the investigation of primitive thought will lead to breakthroughs in psychology and cultural anthropology. The resurrection of the antique soul of the nation not only wakes up moderners' withering hearts, but also provides generic foundations for cultural study and cultural history.[6]

It can be concluded that the intellectual bedrock of Chinese myth-archetype criticism has several components: research into myth, folk literature, and the gods and ghosts of China; the interdisciplinary study of comparative literature; and the attempt to find the roots of Chinese culture. It cannot be regarded solely as a product of new critical methods.

The translation of and introduction to Western literary theory reached a climax after the mid-1980s. Scholars in various fields, such as philosophy, aesthetics, literature, and history, demonstrated a keen interest in archetypal theory. Liu Zaifu says, "If we can make some alterations to archetypal criticism, then our contemporary literary criticism is sure to become more colorful and profound."[7] Aware of the aspiration for variety and depth, I published a lengthy commentary, "The Theory and Practice of Myth-Archetypal Criticism," in 1986. The essay systematically illustrated the production and development of this critical school, with its different branches and applications, and pointed out its characteristics and limitations by referring to Chinese critical practice.[8] In the following year I published *Myth-Archetypal Criticism*, a collection of twenty articles by Western scholars divided into two parts: basic theory and critical practice. It contains selected works of Frazer, Frye, and Philip Wheelwright, all of which were translated into Chinese for the first time. The book focuses on Frye, the master of archetypal theory, and thus reflects the cause and the effect of the theory. Two extracts from *Anatomy of Criticism*—"Mythical Phase: Symbol as Archetype" from the Second Essay, and "Archetypal Criticism: Theory of Myths" (Third Essay)—were chosen, for the following reasons. First, they are concentrated illustrations of the methodology of archetypal theory. Second, they reveal the course of Western literature derived from myth and dependent on the displacement and reconstruction of myth-archetypes. Third, they exemplify Frye's critical style and unique perspective, a perfect combination of historical facts and theoretical exposition. The collection also contains a partial translation of "Literature as Context" and part of *The Great Code*. The former employs archetypal method to interpret Milton's "Lycidas"; the latter is Frye's famous study of the Bible. The translation became a catalyst promoting archetypal criticism in China and has been cited and quoted by many scholars.

Meanwhile, several other translated versions of Jung were published, including *Modern Man in Search of a Soul* by Huang Qiming, "Psychology and Literature" first by Wang Ning, and then by Feng Chuan and Su Ke, and Calvin S. Hall's *A Primer of Jungian Psychology*, translated by Zhang Yue, to name just a few. The theoretical connection between the collective unconscious, archetypal criticism, and literary creation thus became a long-lasting point of departure in the Chinese academic field. A number of interdisciplinary studies owe much to this elucidation of Jung's theory, including Tao Dongfeng's *Six Points on the Psycho-Aesthetics of Ancient China* and Wang Yichuan's *On Aesthetic Experience*.

Fang Keqiang, who advocated literary anthropology in the Chinese context, has also published a series of articles on archetypal criticism. He divides literary anthropology into two camps, criticism of primitivism and myth-archetypal criticism, and describes the theoretical characteristics of each. The literature of primitivism in the West compares and reflects on the primordial and the civilized in the manner of cultural anthropology. Criticism of primitivism facilitates the comparison and differentiation of Chinese and Western literature. Moreover, criticism of primitivism can to some extent make up the deficiencies of archetypal criticism. Fang attributes the vigour of literary anthropology to its tolerance and openness:

There are two reasons why it can freely use other critical methods (such as cultural anthropology, psychology, linguistics, comparative literature, structuralism, feminism, history, philosophy, religion, and art) to serve its own critical object. Firstly, literary anthropology believes that human literature is itself united and intact, pursuing an integration of human literary experience. This belief and object enable it not only to treat other critical approaches without prejudice but also to take the combination and application for granted. Secondly, literary anthropology has formulated only one methodological principle, namely, connecting the primordial with the modern and comparing different nationalities in China and abroad.[9]

It is true that literary anthropology tends to eliminate sectarian bias in accordance with the wide cultural scope of the subject of anthropology. Except for referential significance in terms of theory and method, anthropology even teaches us how to eliminate the self-conceit caused by ingrained ethnocentrism and subject-centrism, and how to prepare psychologically for the imminent globalization of knowledge.

Translations of Cassirer and Frazer have also proved influential in China. Ernst Cassirer's *An Essay on Man*, translated by Gan Yang (1985), provides a profound exposition of the philosophical and epistemological significance of myth and symbol. One hundred thousand copies of the first translated edition of this book were printed. Another book of Cassirer's, *Symbol, Myth and Culture*, translated by Li Xiaobing (1988), contains a section on the political use of myth. These works supply a higher theoretical starting-point for scholars to research mythological literature. An abridged edition of Frazer's *The Golden Bough*, regarded by Frye as a classic of literary criticism, was translated into Chinese at the end of the 1960s, but not published; the book made a great impression in China when finally published in 1987. Various local publishing houses subsequently competed to publish translated series on anthropology, comparative literature, folk culture, religion, and mythology. Moreover, scholars hungry for knowledge were enlightened by the visual field of anthropology, and their horizon became wider when they referred back to literary phenomena.

Translators recognized at the outset the problem of reconciling anthropological theory and the status quo of China's literature and arts. *Sign: Language and Arts* by Yu Jianzhang and Ye Shuxian proposes the hypothesis of a generic process occurring between human thought and its symbolic system, and sees the process as a macroscopic background for the inspection of language and art. The book views archetypes as forms of signs in the age when people thought through myths, and then explores the process of archetypal aestheticization as mythical thought is replaced by artistic thought. Zhu Di's *Research on Primitive Culture* places the difficult problem of art in the vast anthropological field and discusses new achievements in Western artistic anthropology. The author writes in the postscript: "The book is primarily concerned with cultural anthropologists' theory of primitive thought, and various theories on prehistoric art, primitive art, and myth held by anthropologists and archaeologists. Such theories seem quite distant from aesthetics, even, we can say, unrelated to aesthetics. However, it is they that constitute the important precondition for us to understand prehistoric art, primitive art and myth. And if we can really understand the significance of the earliest and the most primordial art of human beings, it is no longer difficult for us to find out the secret of aesthetic occurrence."[10] In *Exploring the Irrational World: The Theory and Method of Archetypal Criticism*, I sum up the Chinese alteration of archetypal patterns, attempt to reconstruct the space-time system of ancient Chinese myths, and demonstrate for the first time that such anthropological method can be applied to solve the problems of Chinese literature. As Ji Hongzhen remarks: "[archetypal] theory tries hard to break ethnic and cultural boundaries, hoping to establish the archetypal framework of literature in the basic relationship between humans and nature; therefore so-called universal humanity is not confined to some basic life activities such as eating and sex in order to assure racial reproduction. It also contains metaphysical contents, for instance, perceptive means as to time and space in such activities. Nationality does not disappear in the huge macroscopical background, instead, it is embodied in different perceptive forms."[11] A few other Chinese scholars also deal with the problem of whether and how we can reconstruct archetypal criticism from the Marxist point of view.

In the 1990s, Chinese scholars needed on the one hand to reflect on the translation and introduction of new theories; on the other, they proposed a cross-century view which aimed at appropriating the tradition and opening up the future. Some learned journals reflected this double necessity by establishing special columns. *Debate on Literature and Art* instituted two columns in 1990: "Fang Keqiang's Criticism of Literary Anthropology" and "Conversations on Chinese Literature and Archetypal Criticism." In 1992, it initiated the column "Ye Shuxian's Research on Literary Anthropology." *Literary Criticism in Shanghai* in 1992 established a special column on "Contemporary Critical Theory and Methodological Research," and published in its first issue a collection of essays under the title "Literary Anthropology and Archetypal

Criticism." Among the essays, Fang Keqiang's "Review of Criticism of Literary Anthropology in the New Period" attempts the first summary of the critical practice of archetypal theory to that date. My own "Decoding and Reconstruction—the Developing Tendency of Archetypal Criticism" comments on the development of archetypal criticism after Frye in Europe and North America. It introduces a set of famous works, including John White's *Mythology in the Modern Novel* and "Mythological Fiction and the Reading Process," Eric Gould's *Mythical Intentions in Modern Literature*, John B. Vickery's *The Literary Impact of "The Golden Bough"* and *Myths and Texts*, and Harry Slochower's *Mythopoesis: Mythic Patterns in the Literary Classics*. The journal *Comparative Literature in China* published in 1992–5 a special column, "Research on Mythical Archetypes." These various columns with concentrated themes serve as a link between past and future, Chinese and foreign, effectively pushing forward the acceptance and study of archetypal criticism in China.

In dealing with the reception of Northrop Frye and his theory in China, I should conclude by mentioning two important events. The International Conference on Northrop Frye: China and the West was co-sponsored by Peking University and Victoria University in the University of Toronto in July 1994. More than thirty Chinese and Western scholars spoke at the meeting, which constituted the first theoretical dialogue between Chinese and Western scholars in Frye studies. A direct result of this conference, the volume *Frye Studies: China and the West*, edited by Wang Ning and Xu Yanhong and published by China Social Sciences Publishing House in 1996, initiated the ambitious project on Northrop Frye Studies, which has been supported by the Government of Canada through the Canadian Embassy in Beijing and which has got together all the eminent scholars on Frye studies in China under the directorship of Wang Ning. The Series on Frye Studies has so far published, with Peking University Press and China Social Sciences Publishing House, four works by Frye himself, including *Selected Critical Essays of Northrop Frye, The Great Code, The Critical Path*, and *Anatomy of Criticism*, all of which serve as good theoretical bases for the further development of archetypal criticism and cultural criticism. To meet the demand of Chinese and Western scholars and also by virtue of their support, a second conference, the International Symposium on Northrop Frye Studies, was held at the University of Inner Mongolia in July 1999 in order to make a complete review of the achievements and shortcomings of Frye scholarship in the past century.

NOTES

1 *Chinese and Foreign Literatures* (Taiwan: National Taiwan University) 6, no. 10 (1978) and 4, no. 3 (1975).

2 Wilbur Scott, *Five Approaches of Literary Criticism* (New York: Macmillan, 1962), 251. The translated version by Lan Renzhe was published by Chongqing Publishing House, 1983.

3 Wu Lifu, *Selected Papers of Western Modern Literary Theory* (Shanghai: Shanghai Translation Press, 1983), 339.

4 *Reading* (1983), no. 6.

5 *Chinese Myth* 1 (1987): 2. Published by the Publishing House for Chinese Folk Literature and Arts.

6 This is the preface by Xiao Bing to Xu Hualong's book *Research on Chinese Myth and Legend*.

7 *Several Developing Trends of Literary Research in Our Country in Recent Years*.

8 Ye Shuxian, "The Theory and Practice of Myth-Archetypal Criticism," *Journal of Shaanxi Normal University* (1986) 2: 112–21, and 3: 45–53.

9 Fang Keqiang, *The Critical Method of Literary Anthropology* (Shanghai: Publishing House of Shanghai Academy of Social Sciences, 1992), 210.

10 Zhu Di, *Research on Primitive Culture* (Beijing: Sanlian Publishing House, 1988), 780.

11 Ji Hongzhen, "The Decline and Resurgence of Myth—On Probing the World of Irrationality," *Literary Review* (1989) 4: 87–92.

WU CHIZHE

Reconsidering Frye's Critical Thinking: A Chinese Perspective

During the past two decades, Chinese critics and literary scholars have taken an immense interest in Northrop Frye's critical thinking, regarding it as a precious heritage not only for Canadians, but also for scholars beyond North America and in China. Frye's criticism dwells upon the most diversified aspects of human literary experience and offers discerning insights into human imagination and creation. To judge whether or not a literary theory is universally valid is to examine whether its arguments are applicable to the literature of all nations. When I read the work of Frye—an outstanding twentieth-century Western critic and thinker who enjoys a worldwide academic reputation—while admiring him for his erudition and profundity of scholarship, I pay particular attention to two aspects: the possible applicability of his statements to Chinese realities, and the comments Frye makes on Chinese literature or culture. To my mind, at least, a number of citations of, or comments on, Chinese language, literature, and philosophy in Frye's writings are significant in reconsidering his critical thinking from a Chinese perspective.

Language

As Frye points out, "the artist of today cannot think of himself as being pushed along at the end of a thin line of historical development through Greece, Rome, and Western Europe. He is now a citizen of all time and space; ... Chinese calligraphy ... may take its place in his tradition" (*RW*, 47). Frye is certainly correct in calling Chinese calligraphy an art, because roughly as early as 1500 B.C. our ancestors, in carving their inscriptions on bones, tortoise shells, and bronze vessels, were concerned with the aesthetic value as well as the practical use of each character. Frye notes that in the Chinese character, "a group of radicals are combined to produce a single verbal picture," and he even quotes Ezra Pound as saying that "the predication [i.e. 'is' in a metaphor] may often be only an unnecessary concession to a prose mind. Once we take out 'is', we move from explicit to implicit metaphor, which is produced by the juxtaposition of images only" (*GC*, 56). The Chinese developed "the ideogram or image-cluster as the basis of language" (*NFCL*, 198). Although Frye did not understand Chinese and knew little of Chinese culture, his insightful perception of the subtlety of the Chinese cultural and aesthetic spirit allowed him to grasp the major characteristics of the Chinese language.

In fact, we can cite innumerable examples of this sort in Chinese written language: to mention a few, 男 (man, symbolizing "labour force in the crop field"); 从 (to follow, indicating "one person following another"); 旦 (dawn, literally "the sun above the horizon"), and so on. Even today, one can judge the meaning of a word through its mere image; thus the word 鲜 (tasty, delicious) consists of two halves, the left being "fish" and the right "mutton," which implies that since antiquity, fish plus mutton has made what is delicious for us Chinese.

Literature

Frye says that "poets being a conservative breed [were] inclined to imitate their predecessors, and many centuries of development lie behind the brief lyrics, with the strong visual focus that writing provides, which we find ... in Chinese poetry" (*CP*, 42). That is exactly the case with Chinese poetry, which began with lyrics. All of the 305 ancient odes in the *Book of Odes* compiled by Confucius to instruct his disciples date from the sixth to the eleventh century B.C. And just as for centuries the Anglo-Saxon poets preferred native words like fall, stream, deer, tide, fare, and shield to loanwords like autumn, river, animal, hour, travel, and defend, which had had a much shorter history, so Chinese poets chose ancient words and expressions. Frye also implies that "tidiness" is one of the "Chinese standards" (*AC*, 24) in poetry. Thus, in the *Book of Odes*, all poetic lines consist of four characters; in poems of the *jueju* and *lushi* type that flourished during the Tang dynasty, each line has five or seven characters.

Mere juxtaposition of a series of images is another distinct feature of classical Chinese poetry. To Frye, this is "implicit metaphor," for here there is no predication whatever to link up these images. Out of the numerous examples suffice it to quote "Autumnal Melancholy" by Ma Zhiyang:

> A withered ivy
> Round a hollow tree,
> Crows at dusk;
>
> A small bridge,
> A running brook below,
> And a solitary cottage;
>
> An ancient postroad,
> A blast of west wind,
> A skinny horse;
>
> The sun sinking in the west,
> A traveller wandering, heartbroken.[1]

If Wordsworth regards "metre as the source of excitement in verse" (*AC*, 257), then we could well add visual images to metre to form the source of excitement in Chinese verse. In Western poetry Ezra Pound initiated an imagism precisely based on his understanding of Chinese poetry, for he "brought some exotic ... Chinese flavours not only into his own poetry but into the culture of his time" (*RW*, 394).

Frye greatly appreciates *The Chalk Circle*, a poetic play written by Li Qianfu of the Yuan Dynasty, in which "a concubine bears her master a son and is then accused of having murdered him by the wife, who has murdered him herself, and who also claims the son as her own" (*FI*, 26). A wise judge[2] performs an experiment in a chalk circle, ordering both the concubine and the wife to pull the son with force; this the concubine refuses to do lest her own son should be hurt, and so the judge concludes that the concubine is the mother. To Frye, almost all means of "discovery" or "recognition" for solving a dramatic conflict can be found in this Chinese play (ibid.).

In Western literature, Frye points out, "the masque is flanked on one side by the musically organized drama which we call opera, and on the other by a scenically organized drama, which has now settled in the movie" (*AC*, 288). That is, both opera and movie have grown out of the masque as two more modernized forms of art. He also observes that Chinese drama is accompanied with "a running musical commentary," which was later adopted by the movie, because "a continuous use of musical symbolism is in complete accord with [its] whole structure" (*RW*, 26).

Philosophy

In China there is a famous saying handed down from ancient times, "Heaven and the human are one," which embodies the important idea of "harmonious unity," 和合. This traditional idea of harmonious unity includes at least three aspects, viz., (1) unity of humankind with the natural environment; (2) harmonious relations between individuals in society; and (3) unity in each individual himself. As the founder of Taoist philosophy, Laotze, says, "The sage embraces oneness."[3] Frye comments, "Surely Laotze does not mean by 'oneness' something to be 'reconciled' to what by hypothesis is something else. He is not talking about a mode of apprehension but about total identification" (*NFCL*, 110). Laotze's conception of the self is one "in which the self becomes fully enlightened by realizing its identity with a total self, an indivisible unity of God [or Heaven], man, and the physical world" (ibid., 120). Here a very difficult question challenges us: why, even in doing scholarly research, do we Chinese tend to see the macrostructure of a matter, that is, to view things in their entirety, and prefer to synthesize and rely more on the collective, whereas Westerners tend to view things with microscospic attention, and prefer to analyse and rely more on the individual?

In my view, at least, Northrop Frye's encyclopedic system of cultural and literary criticism is an inexhaustible source of enlightenment and stimulating wisdom. If I had sufficient time, I would very much like to write a monograph comparing his critical thinking with Chinese realities. In the meantime, what I want to emphasize in this essay is my reconsideration of some issues in his critical thinking, for I believe they may be of great use in our interpretation of Chinese literary texts and other phenomena.

Myth and Archetype

That literature originated from, or grew out of, myths seems to be a universal truth; this Frye expounds at length and in detail in many of his writings. In China, too, as early as 1924, Lu Xun pointed out that "[tales of marvels] must have sprung out of myths and legends ... For myths were not only the beginning of religion and art but the fountainhead of literature." He further explains that "When these myths developed and became more human, demigods appeared—ancient heroes who achieved great deeds by means of superman attributes given them by the gods ... These tales, which show the difference between demigods and ordinary men, are today called legends. Then these stories evolved further, and truthful accounts became history while other anecdotes became fiction." [4] This development confirms exactly Frye's explanation of realism as "a growth in the humanization of the projected myths" (*MC*, 58).

For years people believed that in China few myths have been handed down to the present day. According to Lu Xun, "It seems likely that Chinese myths remained separate fragments for the following reasons: First, the early dwellers in the Yellow River Valley were not an imaginative people; and since their life was hard and they devoted most of their energy to practical matters without indulging in flights of fancy, they did not combine all the old legends into one great epic. Secondly, Confucius appeared with his teaching about the way to cultivate morality, regulate the family, rule the state and bring peace to the world. Since he disapproved of talk of the supernatural, the old myths were not quoted by Confucian scholars, and instead of undergoing further development many of them were lost" (17–18).

It is true that China has had an abundance of myths in its cultural and literary history. The problem is that though they were produced in clan society, what written records we can find today were made much later, in feudal society. Yuan Ke devoted some fifty years to research on this subject and succeeded in reorganizing into a complete system the rich myths found in such classics as *The Book of Mountains and Seas, Huainantze, Elegies of Chu, Lü's Almanac, Zhuangtze, Laotze,* and so forth. In so doing, Yuan Ke discovered that Confucius and his later followers were the main force in turning myths into history. "They took great pains either to humanize the gods or to interpret myths and legends in a rational way so as to make them conform to their own doctrine ... Once written in books, the original content of the myths changed beyond recognition; and in course of time, people came to believe what was recorded in books as history and the myths themselves gradually disappeared."[5] Just as in ancient Europe, in ancient China what we call "literature" today was not differentiated as a genre from other written documents. So literature was mixed up with the writing of history and philosophy, and history and story are the same thing; if the ancient Hebrews turned much of their own history into myths which no longer embodied their true history, then what the Confucian scholars in China rewrote from myths is not credible history either.

Although Chinese literature has a long tradition of mythology, myth-archetypal criticism as initiated by Frye was first introduced into China in 1987, when Ye Shuxian published his collection of translated essays by Frye and other Western scholars.[6] It was continued on a larger scale in 1994, when Wang Ning and Wu Chizhe began to publish their co-edited Series on Northrop Frye Studies, which has allowed Chinese literary scholars and critics to gain a better understanding of Frye and his works. Between 1985 and 1997, more than 330 articles from the myth-archetypal perspective were published in China.[7] Myth-archetypal criticism has since been widely accepted, as it offers new perspectives enabling Chinese critics to interpret literary texts or cultural phenomena with a much broader field of vision and to reveal hidden and often more profound meanings in the texts. Chinese critics not only reinterpret such literary masterpieces as *The Dream of the Red Mansion*, *Pilgrimages to the West*, and the *Book of Odes*, but even decipher, so to speak, philosophical classics such as *Zhuangtze* and *Laotze*. Our critics also manage to find numerous archetypes in ancient Chinese literature, including themes, characters, images, and symbols.

At the International Symposium on Northrop Frye Studies held in Hoh-Hot in mid-July, 1999, A.C. Hamilton asked me why the archetypal aspect alone is emphasized in China, while other major aspects of Frye's critical thinking, such as the linguistic, generic, and rhetorical aspects, are seldom mentioned. The reason, as I see it, is perhaps that the archetype is more easily applicable to our new interpretation of Chinese literary texts. Frye's discussion of metre, rhyme, rhythm, syntax, and metaphor in English literature can serve as a reference, but, being language-restricted, it cannot be used immediately in the Chinese context, while rhetorical criticism requires considerable adaptation for the interpretation of Chinese literature.

However, this by no means implies that we should neglect the importance of literary genres. In fact Chu Binjie discusses this problem in detail in his *Outline of Ancient Literary Genres in China* (Beijing, 1989). Genre is also an archetype in that it is a recurrent literary structure. Though Frye admits that the theory of genres is an undeveloped subject in criticism, we learn much from his meticulous analysis in *Anatomy of Criticism* (246–326), in which, just like a taxonomist well versed in Darwin's evolution of species, he manages to trace the origin and evolution of dozens of literary genres. According to Darwin, natural selection will result in the gradual adaptation of every species to its environmental conditions: the same species living in different external conditions may develop into a new variety.[8] Similarly, Frye explains that "social conditions and cultural demands" produce the genre (*FI*, 11), yet he goes on to analyse how each new genre evolves from an old one according to its own inner and seemingly hereditary structural principles. Thus drama has its music and scenery; as noted before, the former develops into opera and the latter has settled in the movie (*AC*, 288). In China, too, the poems in five- or seven-word lines of the Tang Dynasty gave rise, if not place, to the *ci*-poems of the Song Dynasty, which use a variety of rhymes and different sentence patterns and consist of lines with an irregular number of words. This change of genre is partly influenced by the music of Western China or even foreign music, and is partly "a concession to a prose mind," as Frye says. The Song *ci*-poems were followed in turn by the verse drama of the Yuan Dynasty, when another form of verse *qu* began to flourish, as the Mongol ruling class, who were fond of verse drama, promoted it. This new form of verse *qu* is composed to various tunes and easily adapted for recounting stories in verse, hence giving rise to *zaju*, a verse drama which marks the maturity of dramatic literature in China.

Tragedy and Comedy

Frye is right in replacing traditional historical criticism, a mere chronological arrangement of authors and works, with his theory of modes, asserting that since ancient times modes have gone through five stages: mythic, romantic, high mimetic, low mimetic, and ironic. Chinese literature has evolved in roughly the same direction, though some differences can be identified.

Unlike the Europeans, in China we do not have the literary categories "tragedy" and "comedy" in the Aristotelian sense. They are not even found as entries in the volume *Chinese Literature* of *The Chinese Encyclopedia*, published in Beijing in 1986. To my knowledge, it was not until the turn of the twentieth century that the term "tragedy" was first used, by Wang Guowei (1877–1927), a man obviously influenced by Schopenhauer and who evidently introduced it from Europe because he was versed in European literary theories. In China, tragedy as a dramatic form (though not so called) emerged with the rise of the bourgeoisie in about the thirteenth and fourteenth centuries. Among these plays special mention should be made of Ji Junxiang's *The Orphan of the Zhao Family* and Guan Hanqing's *The Death of Dou E under a False Charge*. Frye would have called the former a high mimetic tragedy and the latter a low mimetic tragedy. The former tells how two upright courtiers in the Jin state in the seventh century B.C. risk their own lives to protect and rear the orphan of a courtier named Zhao, after his entire family were killed by General Du; the orphan grows up and finally revenges himself upon the treacherous general. The latter tells how the pretty young widow Dou E dies in untold misery because she can appeal to no one for redress of an unjust accusation against her.

There seem to be three reasons for the late emergence of tragedy and the lack of categories of "tragedy" or "comedy" in Chinese aesthetics. First, the ancients in China meditated on survival rather than on death or fate, and longed for longevity. The ancient Greeks, in contrast, tended to meditate on death, for according to Plato, philosophy is the training for death.[9] No wonder then that in a tragedy by Seneca or Shakespeare there should be as many as a dozen deaths on the stage. The Chinese philosopher Zhuangtze (369–286 B.C.) says, "Life and death are both inevitable, a natural law just like the eternal succession of day and night." When Zhuangtze's wife died, a friend of his came to condole with him only to find that Zhuangtze, seated on the floor, was beating a musical instrument and singing merrily. When asked why, he answered, "She originally had no life, no body, not even her breath. Now that she has gone back to nothing, what is the good of weeping and wailing by her side while she is so peacefully sleeping?"[10] Second, for many centuries, the Chinese critic believed that a character's tragic or comic end pertains rather to the content of a play than to its form. So far as a play is concerned, four or five acts plus a prelude is sufficient to represent everything for the story, including its climax and denouement. Finally, the this-worldliness and moral teaching of Confucianism that prevailed in China for centuries left no room, or at least little room, for any belief in the supernatural. So there could have been no tragedy of fate like that of Oedipus, whose tragic fate seems to be caused by an invisible supernatural power. Nor could there be tragedies of character like those by Shakespeare, in which a mere flaw in the otherwise virtuous character of a hero—Lear's fondness for flattery, Hamlet's hesitation to revenge, or Othello's jealousy—eventually leads to his own destruction. Instead, we have comedy in which the alazon character eventually becomes a laughing-stock in the eyes of the audience. What has been and is widely accepted is the social tragedy, like *The Orphan* and *The Young Widow Dou E* mentioned above.

Comedy in China, as is often the case, contains irony or satire. Characters described by a playwright in irony are usually those who, as Frye puts it, are eventually accepted back into society, whereas characters on whom the playwright's bitter satire is focused are excluded from society at the end of the play.

Two-way Exchange

One can never overestimate Confucius's influence on traditional Chinese literary criticism, for the principle of "making Tao [logos] manifest in writing" and "writings as the vehicle of Tao" has permeated Chinese literary history. However, his didacticism and utilitarianism have for a long period of time overshadowed and to a certain extent checked the further development of literary criticism. It was not until some nine hundred years after his death, in 501–2 A.D., that Liu Hsieh (*ca.* 465–532) published the first systematic critical work, entitled *Wenxin diaolong* (*The Literary Mind and the Carving of Dragons*). Although he follows Confucius's tradition in saying "Tao is handed down in writing through sages, and sages make Tao manifest in their writings," and "Poetry means discipline, disciplined human emotion,"[11] Liu Hsieh manages to interweave literary history, literary theory, literary appreciation, and evaluation into his own system of criticism. He makes a thorough study of the literary genres in ancient Chinese writings and concludes, "One's emotion has a number of different moods, and each must be expressed in a particular style. All writers choose the genres which accord with their emotional moods, and adopt the styles proper to these genres."[12] Liu Hsieh formulates eight possible styles: (1) elegant and graceful; (2) far-ranging and profound; (3) polished and concise; (4) lucid and logical; (5) profuse and flowery; (6) vigorous and beautiful; (7) fresh and extraordinary; and (8) light and ethereal. Moreover, Liu points out, "The genres, because of the definite correspondence between their names and content, have to base themselves on established principles; but because the style must maintain its flexible adaptability to varying situations, its very essence is its sensitivity to new modes and cadences."[13] So, of the twenty-two genres that existed in Liu's time, quite a few have since been either utterly lost or developed into new ones to meet ever-changing social and cultural demands. We experience the same delight in reading these profound insights as we do when appreciating Frye's brilliant analysis of literary genres in his *Anatomy of Criticism*.

Another feature of Liu's criticism that deserves our careful attention and suggests an interesting comparison with Frye or Spengler is that Liu traces a close analogy between literary creation and nature. He comments, for instance, "When we extend our observations, we find that all things, both animals and plants, have patterns of their own ... Now if things which are devoid of consciousness express themselves so extremely decoratively, can that which is endowed with mind lack a pattern proper to itself?"; "Words with pattern indeed express the mind of the universe"; and, "Poetry is the mind of music and sound is its body."[14] And in his criticism Liu uses such terms as bone, marrow, skeleton, body, muscle, flesh, breath, spirit, heart, appearance, wind, sound, root, branch, foliage, and so forth, which are all taken directly either from nature or from the human body.[15]

Having just stepped over the threshold of the twenty-first century, let us look forward to a two-way cultural exhange, introducing Chinese literary criticism to the world at the same time as we continue to study Western criticism in our country. I am sure that in years to come, say in a few generations, Eastern and Western thought will eventually be fused on the basis of what is common, with each side preserving its own distinct features.

Criticism as a Science

Viewing literary study as branch of science, at least as a branch of social science, has been a common goal of all the formalism-oriented theorists and scholars. Working in this tradition, Frye devoted his lifetime to formulating literary criticism as a social science. He locates it as an independent science, focused on literature but not subordinate to it, and maintains that criticism should enter into relations with a variety of its neighbours in any way that will guarantee its own independence (*AC*, 19). In other words, literary criticism requires total coherence, or a coordinating, integrating principle, such as is found in Darwin's theory of evolution, which sees the phenomena it deals with as parts of a whole (*FI*, 9). Frye's methodology in building his edifice of criticism combines induction with deduction; hence it is fully scientific. Nobody would argue that Darwin's theory is unscientific, though a number of his hypotheses remain to be verified. I tend to believe that Frye's critical theory is already a scientific system, even if many of his statements or arguments require further research and testimony. Some of the problems raised by Frye will probably require the successive interdisciplinary efforts of several generations for perfect solution. Future critics may knock away the scaffolding of Frye's theoretic edifice, repair it, or rebuild part of it, but whenever they look back to *Anatomy of Criticism*, a monument that figures so prominently in literary history, they will surely feel deeply indebted to Northrop Frye and acknowledge his brilliant achievements.

NOTES

1 "Autumnal Melancholy" by Ma Zhiyang (1250?–1321?) is one of his *qu*-poems, a form of verse for singing which flourished during the Yuan Dynasty. Translations are mine.

2 The wise judge here refers to Bao Zheng (999–1062), magistrate of Kai Feng Prefecture during the Song Dynasty. An honest and upright official, he enforced the law strictly and tried every case impartially. In China many novels and plays eulogize him.

3 "The sage embraces oneness [the Tao] in his behaviour, thus setting an example for the world." See chap. 22 of Laotze [Lao Tze]. *Tao Te Ching*.

4 Lu Xun, *A Brief History of Chinese Fiction* (Beijing: Foreign Languages Press, 1979), 9, 375. The reference in the next paragraph is also to this edition.

5 Yuan Ke, *Zhongguo gudai shenhua* (*Ancient Mythology in China*) (Shanghai: Commercial Press, 1957), 17.

6 Ye Shuxian, ed., *Shenhua yuanxing piping* (*Myth-Archetypal Criticism*) (Xi'an: Shaanxi Normal University Press, 1987). See also the essay by Ye in this volume.

7 Lu Tan, "Shenhua yuanxing piping zai zhongguo" (Myth-Archetypal Criticism in China), *Wenyi bao* (*Literature and Art Gazette*), 21 Sept. 1999.

8 Charles Darwin, *The Origin of Species*, 6th ed. (London: Murray, 1911), chaps. 4 and 5.

9 Quoted in Liu Shilin, *Culture of Poetic Quality in China* (Nanjing: Jiangsu People's Press, 1998).

10 *Zhuangtze*, annotated by Lei Zhongkang (Wuhan: Wuhan Press, 1997), 54, 152–3.

11 My quotations from Liu Hsieh's important book are based on *Wenxin diaolong*, ed. and trans. into modern Chinese by Zhou Zhengfu (Beijing: Zhong Hua Book Co., 1995); the English translation of Liu's passages is taken from Vincent Yu-chung Shih's *Liu Hsieh, The Literary Mind and the Carving of Dragons: A Study of Thought and Pattern in Chinese Literature* (Hong Kong: Chinese University Press, 1983). For these sentences see chap. 1, "On Tao, the Source," and chap. 5.

12 Ibid., chap. 30

13 Ibid., chap. 29.

14 Ibid., chaps. 1 and 7.

15 It is not easy to translate Liu's literary categories into English correctly, especially when the meaning varies with different contexts. For Liu Hsieh, for example, the "correct organization" of writing "consists of feeling and ideas as the soul, of facts and meaning as the bone and marrow, of linguistic

patterns as the musculature and integument" (chap. 23). Even in introducing Western criticism, there is endless disagreement among translators in China as to how to make Western terms known to the Chinese reader, for in many cases the denotation and connotation of each concept in English are not the same as that in Chinese.

GU MINGDONG

The Universal Significance of Frye's Theory of Fictional Modes

In his *Anatomy of Criticism*, Northrop Frye proposes an influential theory of historical criticism in terms of fictional modes underlying the development of the Western literary tradition. Based on a modification of Aristotle's scheme of the relative elevation of character in the *Poetics* and an observation of Western fiction, this theory conceptualizes European fiction into five modes characterized by "the hero's relative power of action": (1) myth; (2) romance; (3) the high mimetic mode; (4) the low mimetic mode; and (5) the ironic mode.

In an attempt to refute the "conception of the critic as a parasite or jackal," and to emancipate literary criticism from the servile state of appending itself to other domains of learning, Frye criticizes what he calls "determinisms" in literary criticism: "It would be easy to compile a long list of such determinisms in criticism, all of them, whether Marxist, Thomist, liberal-humanist, neo-Classical, Freudian, Jungian, or existentialist, substituting a critical attitude for criticism, all proposing, not to find a conceptual framework for criticism within literature, but to attach criticism to one of a miscellany of frameworks outside it." He deems it necessary for theories of criticism to grow out of literature itself: "If criticism exists, it must be an examination of literature in terms of a conceptual framework derivable from an inductive survey of the literary field" (*AC*, 6–7). In the *Anatomy of Criticism*, Frye conducts his theoretical inquiries through an inductive survey of the Western literary tradition and arrives at his critical principles as if independent of other fields of learning.

Given the well-established theory of overdetermination, I wonder whether Frye's theory, or any other theorist's theory, could totally escape the influence of other fields of learning. Since Frye was a conscientious reader of Freud, Jung, and other psychoanalytic thinkers of his day, my question is: even though Frye consciously bases his theory of historical modes on an inductive observation of Western literary history, could his conceptualization have been unconsciously influenced by his knowledge of psychoanalytic theory? In this paper, I do not intend to argue, as one scholar suggests,[1] that Frye's theory was at least partially derived from psychoanalysis; nor do I wish to suggest that Frye incorporated psychoanalytic theory in the formulation of his theory without acknowledging it. I want only to point out a parallel between Frye's theory and psychoanalytic theory, and to explore its potential significance for literary studies in cross-cultural contexts.

I shall demonstrate that Frye's division of epochs coincides with the major stages of human development in psychoanalytic psychology as first proposed by Freud and then modified by other psychoanalytic theorists—stages that chart the ego's movement from pleasure principle to reality principle. Instead of describing an individual's mental development, however, Frye has charted the course of a macroperson: Western literary tradition. In a way, the correspondence may be an archetypal one that underlies the relationship between the hero in fiction, whose historical position undergoes a steady fall, and the phylogenesis of the reality sense of the human race. My suggestion does not in any way diminish the importance of Frye's theory. On the contrary, if Frye's theory is found to parallel certain principles of psychoanalysis, it is reasonable to assume that he has located a pattern of literary development that has significance not only for the Western literary tradition but for non-Western literature as well.

The development of the forms of mental activity in the individual consists, as Freud has shown, in the resolution of the originally prevailing pleasure principle, and the repression mechanism peculiar to it, by the individual's adjustment to reality, as he or she grows from infancy (in which the mental activity is dominated by the seething cauldron of the id) to the formation of a realistic ego and a repressive superego. Freud describes the process of reality sense formation thus:

> the sexual instincts, from beginning to end of their development, work towards obtaining pleasure; they retain their original function unaltered.
> The other instincts, the ego-instincts, have the same aim to start with. But under the influence of the instructress Necessity, they soon learn to replace the pleasure principle by a modification of it. For them the task of avoiding unpleasure turns out to be almost as important as that of obtaining pleasure.

The ego discovers that it is inevitable for it to renounce immediate satisfaction ... and to abandon certain sources of pleasure altogether. An ego thus educated has become "reasonable"; it no longer lets itself be governed by the pleasure principle, but obeys the *reality principle*, which also at bottom seeks to obtain pleasure, but pleasure which is assured through taking account of reality, even though it is pleasure postponed and diminished.[2]

Thus the secondary process of the normal person in waking thought—the ability to make judgments in accordance with the reality principle—grows out of the primary psychical process, a process to be found in the mental activities of primitive beings (animals, savages, children), and in primitive mental states (dreams, neurosis, fantasy).

Freud, who believes that racial character is the precipitate of racial history, leaves unanswered the question of whether the movement from pleasure principle to reality principle can be studied in the development of the mind of a literary tradition. But he does point to a correspondence between the hero in fiction and the author's ego. In his "Creative Writers and Daydreaming" he says:

One feature above all cannot fail to strike us about the creations of these story-writers: each of them has a hero who is the centre of interest, for whom the writer tries to win our sympathy by every possible means and whom he seems to place under the protection of a special Providence ... The feeling of security with which I follow the hero through his perilous adventures is the same as the feeling with which a hero in real life throws himself into the water to save a drowning man or exposes himself to the enemy's fire in order to storm a battery. It is the true heroic feeling, which one of our best writers has expressed in an inimitable phrase: "Nothing can happen to *me!*" It seems to me, however, that through this revealing characteristic of invulnerability we can immediately recognize His Majesty the Ego, the hero alike of every day-dream and of every story.[3]

Freud's notion of correspondence was articulated to illustrate his theory of the resemblance of literary creation to daydream. He did not relate the power of action of the hero to the formation and developmental stages of the ego in the child. His generalization is too sweeping and inclusive to divide the correspondence into various stages. It is precisely in this area, however, that we find an amazingly similar phenomenon in the historical development of fiction in different cultures and civilizations.

In our study of this subject, Freud's classical developmental model of the ego is inadequate for several reasons. First, Freud does not believe that the ego exists at the child's birth. By comparison, Object Relations theorists not only affirm that the ego exists at the birth of a child,[4] but a few of them, including Kernberg, have radically reversed the classical psychoanalytic sequence of the id's existing prior to the ego and suggested that the structure of the ego seems to precede the structure of the id.[5] Second, Freud's model is an instinctual model built upon the nature of the libidinal aim: that is, how a child gets satisfaction and how libido is manifested in an erogenous zone of the body. It does not lay sufficient emphasis on the relationship between the child and his or her environment. Given this inadequacy, we need the developmental models of later psychoanalytic theories. In other words, we need a synthesized model of development based on Erik Erikson's revised version of the classical Freudian model, the models of Object Relations theorists like Klein, Winnicott, and Kernberg, and Lacan's theory of the imaginary, symbolic, and real orders.

Frye's theory of fictional modes has a central premise: the historical development of fictional modes illustrates decreasing powers of action in the protagonists in literary works. This idea corresponds with the development of the child through the five stages of the oral, anal, urethral, phallic (intrusive), and Oedipal. In the oral stage, the child feels he or she is the centre of the world; a decrease in superiority and omnipotence then follows, until at the end of the Oedipal stage, the child is fully aware of having fallen from the exalted position of a monarch to the lowly position of a servant at the beck and call of the civilization within which his or her freedom is impinged upon from every direction and his or her movement curtailed by the familial, social, moral, and legal rules and restrictions of society. Frye sums up the core of his theory in these words: "Fictions, therefore, may be classified, not morally, but by the hero's power of action, which may be greater than ours, less, or roughly the same" (AC, 33). The three terms "greater than," "roughly the same," and "less than" correspond pretty well with the landmarks for the ego on its march from pleasure principle to reality principle.

Freud's oral period is one of unconditional omnipotence, a period of human life immediately after birth. This "is a stage in human development that realizes this ideal of a being subservient only to pleasure, and that does so not only in imagination and approximately, but in actual fact and completely." Frye's first epoch or mythic mode corresponds with this phase. In this mode, the hero is "superior in *kind* both to other men and to the environment of other men" and is "a divine being" (AC, 33). This is another way of stating Freud's "His Majesty the Ego." In the period from birth to the anal phase, the infant is totally dependent on the mother, who provides all the necessary conditions for his survival. In a symbiotic state with the mother, the infant is unable to distinguish between self and other, illusion and reality. In order for the infant to survive, at the first stage, a good-enough mother (Winnicott's famous coinage) must devote 100 per cent of herself to the baby. A good-enough mother, according to Winnicott, will make adaptive moves so as to satisfy all of the infant's needs. As a result of this total devotion on the part of the mother and 100 per cent satisfaction on the part of the baby, the baby fosters an illusion of omnipotence and superiority.[6] At this stage, the infant gradually develops the capacity to conjure up what is actually available, for instance, by crying, facial expressions, and other gestures, and the good-enough mother, without fail, continues to meet the infant's demands and needs. As the mother successfully and repeatedly meets the infant's spontaneous and intentional gestures, she makes real the infant's sensory hallucination.[7] This fosters in the infant a sense of omnipotence and the infant begins to believe in an external reality that appears as if by magic and behaves as if under his or her control. This illusion makes the infant feel like a god or divine being. This sense of omnipotence and superiority never evaporates but is repressed into the unconscious and re-emerges from time to time in the arts and creative writing.

Literary productions of the human race in its beginning are mostly myths which reflect the unconscious longings for "the return of a state that once existed," those "good old days" in which the new-born was the centre of the family and in which it mistakenly assumed an unconditional omnipotence. In the writings of early humanity, especially in mythologies of different nations and cultures, the hero or heroine is always depicted as a divine being, superior to others in kind and omnipotent in many spectacular ways. Like the infant at the oral stage, the hero is always in the position to conjure up miraculous happenings and perform superhuman actions beyond credulity. It is for this reason that scholars in East and West alike recognize the essential nature of mythology as the fantasies that reflect the primordial mentality of humanity in its remote childhood. In the West, as Frye points out, "In the pre-medieval period literature is closely attached to Christian, late Classical, Celtic, or Teutonic myths" (AC, 34). In the Chinese tradition of the Far East, although mythology is short and fragmented and does not form as well organized a system as that of the Western tradition, there is no lack of collections of myths. A random list would include *Shanhai jing* (*The Book of Mountains and Seas*), *Huainan zi* (*Scholars at the*

Court of King Huainan), and *Duyi ji* (*Records of the Unique and Extraordinary*). In these mythic tales, protagonists, whether male or female, are all endowed with supernatural or superhuman power.[8]

The sense of superiority and omnipotence persists in the whole oral phase but begins to decrease as the child enters the second or anal phase. At this stage, a good-enough mother needs to adapt less and less to the needs of the infant and at times she must deliberately frustrate her child so as to make the infant realize that he or she is a separate being.[9] The child's sense of superiority and omnipotence begins to wane during the process of toilet training. All cultures place restrictions on defecation. Toilet training interferes with the infant's indulgence in anal pleasure, and such interference enables the infant to realize that he or she is subject to an external authority. At this stage, the infant retains a strong sense of omnipotence, particularly when he or she does certain things, such as obeying the caretaker's order for excreting. Also in this period, the infant is able to utter certain words, which brings satisfaction to its need for food, drink, or care, and thus derives a sense of magically hallucinatory omnipotence.

When we correlate this sense of circumscribed superiority with the development of fictional modes, we may find it to correspond with what Frye calls the romantic mode, in which the hero is a character who is only "superior in degree to other men and to his environment" and "whose actions are marvellous but who is himself identified as a human being" (*AC*, 33). In romance of any culture, the hero lives in a world in which the ordinary laws of nature are slightly suspended. He is still capable of performing some extraordinary actions. What is more, he can always escape unharmed from perilous situations. As Freud puts it, "If, at the end of one chapter of my story, I leave the hero unconscious and bleeding from severe wounds, I am sure to find him at the beginning of the next being carefully nursed and on the way to recovery; and if the first volume closes with the ship he is in going down in a storm at sea, I am certain, at the opening of the second volume, to read of his miraculous rescue—a rescue without which the story could not proceed."[10] This pattern is true not only of romance of ancient times but also of modern romance. Just as the child at the anal stage is required to abide by rules stipulated by his or her caretaker with regard to defecation, so in romance, the hero must obey laws laid out by a sage, prophet, or divine being. Very often, his perilous experiences are the consequences of a deliberate or unwitting breach of the stipulated rules of conduct or restrictions. In romance, the hero has transformed from a divine being to a favourite of a divine being.

In the Western tradition, both major forms of romance, whether "dealing with chivalry and knight-errantry, or "devoted to legends of saints," "lean heavily on miraculous violations of natural law for their interest as stories" (*AC*, 34). In the Far East, certain ancient Chinese historical texts, such as *Shu jing* or *Book of Documents*, *Zuo zhuan* or *Zuo's Commentaries*, and *Guo yu* or *Conversations of the States*, are regarded as part of the Chinese literary tradition. These so-called historical texts often contain episodes that show historical figures possessing some extraordinary power or able to overcome humanly insurmountable obstacles with the aid of a supernatural force or the metaphysical concept of *Tian* or Heaven. These texts, which have been read as enthralling stories, may be classified as fiction of the romantic mode. The concept of the "mandate of Heaven" in *Shu jing*, as expounded by the Duke of Zhou, which explains how a ruler gains sovereignty from Heaven, may be viewed as an anal concept in terms of psychoanalytic analysis. Just as a child who behaves well in his or her toilet habits is rewarded with good things, a would-be founder of a dynasty is favoured by the half-personalized spiritual power called Heaven and granted the mandate to establish a dynasty.[11] In some accounts of legendary and historical figures in *Shi ji* or the *Grand Scribe's Records* by Sima Qian (145–85 B.C.), legendary rulers like Xun, Yu, and Hou Ji were able to accomplish extraordinary feats with the aid of supernatural forces and were given the power to rule. Heroes in *Chuanqi* tales of the Tang dynasty (618–907) likewise belong to this category.

The hero's power of action described by Frye in the high mimetic mode corresponds roughly to the conditions of the infant's ego response to his or her environment in the urethral phase. At this stage, the most significant features of the child are impulsiveness and an ability to plan. Holland sums up the psychoanalytic findings of this stage thus: "If we state the issues of the urethral stage in their largest terms, the child who has reached the end of the stage must be able to say, 'I can plan my urination so they [parents] will give me admiration, not shame.' The basic question the phase poses must be, then, Can you relate your impulses to your long-term wishes? Can you *plan*?"[12] Impulsiveness and the ability to envision a long-term plan belong to a leader. These two basic characteristic features of the urethral period fit Frye's analysis of the hero's power of action in the high mimetic mode: "The hero is a leader. He has authority, passion, and power of expression far greater than ours, but what he does is subject both to social criticism and to the order of nature" (*AC*, 34). At this stage, the child is already aware of being separate from his or her environment; he or she is able to recognize siblings and other related persons; the child is able to talk; his or her babbling sometimes results in the satisfaction of desires but most of the time occasions frustration. The child enjoys more privileges than people around him or her, but also becomes aware that he or she is constantly subject to a curtailment of freedom. He or she is always raising demands for satisfaction, but the outcome depends very much on the environment. In a word, the child finds himself like the hero in Frye's analysis, "superior in degree to other men but not to his natural environment" (*AC*, 33–4).

In the Chinese tradition, historical personages in Sima Qian's *Grand Scribe's Records*, and heroes in stories of the Tang, Song, Yuan, and Ming dynasties are superior in degree to other men but not to their social environments. I will cite a single example to illustrate my point. In the *Grand Scribe's Records*, there is a biographical account of Xiang Yu, whose heroic story has been dramatized again and again in Chinese history. Xiang Yu is a man with almost superhuman power. In Sima Qian's account, the hero is endowed with a strength that "plucked up the hills" and a might that "shadowed the world." He rises in rebellion against the tyrannical rule of the Qin and with other rebellious forces topples the empire built by Qin Shihuang, the first emperor of China. In the ensuing struggle for the dominance of China, in spite of all his victorious battles, he loses the war to Liu Bang, a man of mediocre talent. Sima Qian makes his hero utter these words of impotent rage against an implacable fate before he commits suicide: "It has been eight years since I first led my army forth. In that time I have fought over seventy battles. Every enemy I faced was destroyed, every one I attacked submitted. Never once did I suffer defeat, until at last I became dictator of the world. But now suddenly I am driven to this desperate position! It is because Heaven would destroy me, not because I have committed any fault in battle."[13]

As the child grows, his or her needs multiply and the environment becomes more demanding. "With the increase in the extent and complexity of the wants goes naturally an increase, not only of the 'conditions' that the individual has to submit to if he wishes to see his wants satisfied, but also of the number of cases in which his ever more audacious wishes remain unfulfilled even when the once efficacious conditions are strictly observed. The out-stretched hand must often be drawn back empty; the longed-for object does not follow the magic gesture. Indeed, an invincible, hostile power may forcibly oppose itself to this gesture and compel the hand to resume its former position."[14] In this period, the child develops a sense of reality. This is traditionally referred to as the "phallic" stage in child development, but to avoid

using a "phallocentric" view of development, which takes the male
child as the norm and the female as a deviation, we may borrow a term
used by Erikson and call it the "intrusive" stage.[15]

The intrusive stage roughly corresponds to the characteristic of the
hero described in Frye's fourth mode, the low mimetic. At this stage,
the child comes into closer contact with his or her environment
because of an increased ability to move about. As Holland sums it up,
"the two- and three-year old, standing, toddling, walk[s] out into the
world and adventurously crash[es] about in it. Parents will recognize
the stage as one of loud noises, physical banging on either parents or
playmates, persistent talking, and a charming, if tiresome, curiosity.
The child seems to be trying out different ways of getting into the
world, both the world of grown-ups and the world of children."[16]
Object Relations theorist Margaret Mahler calls this stage "rapproche-
ment."[17] During this stage, the child develops two conflicting tenden-
cies (ambitendency, as Mahler puts it): "I am not weak and dependent.
I can do all these things. I am superior to the child I was." At the same
time, he or she would call out, "Help me! I can't manage, and I am
worthless because I can't." Holland puts it in another way: "during
this crisis the child goes to and fro, sometimes proclaiming a grandiose
self, sometimes wailing about the exact opposite, a self mortified by
feelings of dependency, helplessness, failure, humiliation, and fear."[18]
As a result of ambition and frustration, the child feels like the protagonist in Frye's low mimetic mode: he is "superior neither to other men
nor to his environment." In literature, Frye observes, "the hero is one
of us: we respond to a sense of his common humanity, and demand
from the poet the same canons of probability that we find in our own
experience" (AC, 34). In the low mimetic mode, "the characters exhibit
a power of action which is roughly on our own level, as in most comedy and realistic fiction" (AC, 366).

At this stage, the child enjoys "head-on attack, competition, conquest, winning the goal or (most often in girls) teasing, provoking, or
otherwise 'snaring.'"[19] But the more he participates in head-on competition, the more clearly he realizes his limited power and capability,
until at the end of the stage, he becomes fully aware of the fact that the
mysterious power of the penis to rise (a persisting metaphor for
achievement and power) eventually ends with a fall. The rise of the
hero is invariably followed by his fall in realistic fiction. Frye's observation on the difficulty of retaining the word "hero" applies to both
literature and psychoanalysis. Thackeray's obligation to call *Vanity Fair*
a novel without a hero is entertained by writers of fiction both in the

East and West. Becky Sharp in Thackeray's *Vanity Fair*, Julien Sorel in Stendhal's *The Red and the Black*, Ximen Qing in the *Jin Ping Mei* or *A Plum in the Golden Vase*, and Jia Bao-yu in *The Dream of the Red Mansion* typify female and male protagonists in Western and Eastern literature who either rise to glory only to meet their fall or appear to be non-heroes or anti-heroes.

If, in the low mimetic mode, the protagonist can control his or her fate to a certain extent, in the ironic mode, the protagonist feels helpless in the face of stark and harsh social realities. Just like the child who reaches the Oedipal stage, he or she is thoroughly disillusioned as to any superiority and omnipotence. At the Oedipal stage, Lacan observes, "genital libido operates as a supersession, indeed a blind supersession, of the individual in favour of the species," and "its sublimating effects in the Oedipal crisis lie at the origin of the whole process of the cultural subordination of man."[20] A child's relationship with the other has evolved from a dyad between child and mother to a triangle among child, mother, and father. If at the earlier stages the child can split the mother into part-self and part-other, and tries to harmonize the dichotomy, now the father (or father-figure) is entirely an other, an alien force representing society that controls and restricts the child's power of action. With the dissolution of the Oedipus complex, the child enters what Lacan calls the Symbolic Order. The most salient feature of the Symbolic Order is the law on which the order is based. The law is, in Lacan's words, *le nom du père* (the name of the Father). It is also *le non du père* (the No of the Father), which is the "agency" that promulgates the law. Instead of enjoying the freedom of earlier stages, the child is constantly subject to a series of "Thou Shalt Not" which emanates from the law.[21] The law is related to *le phallus*, which is the symbolic value of the father, culture, and language. It is also the signifier of signifiers.[22] *Le phallus* propels us through the network which is the symbolic fear of castration (for boys) and the illusion of castration as a fact (for girls) and compels the child to recognize the authority of the father, and to obey the commandments of society. In a way, Lacan's *le phallus* resembles Freud's concept of the superego. The formation of the superego in the child's psyche signifies an internalization of the authority of the father, society, and culture. The ego may repress the demands of the id, but it is at the command of the superego, like a servant. The Symbolic Order is the reality conceived of by the child as "other," which is in no way derived from or related to the self. In the face of this reality, the child feels inferior, impotent, and frustrated. The ego condition of the child at the end of the Oedipal stage corresponds to what Frye describes as the ironic mode: the hero is "inferior in power or intelligence to ourselves, so that we have the sense of looking down on a scene of bondage, frustration, or absurdity" (*AC*, 34). Protagonists in fictions across cultural boundaries—James Joyce's *Ulysses* and *Finnegans Wake*, D.H. Lawrence's *Sons and Lovers* and *Women in Love*, Virginia Woolf's *Mrs Dalloway* and *To the Lighthouse*, Thomas Mann's *Magic Mountain*, Franz Kafka's *The Judgement* and *The Metamorphosis*, Marcel Proust's *Remembrance of Things Past*, William Faulkner's *As I Lay Dying* and *The Sound and The Fury*, Lu Xun's *The True Story of Ah Q*, Mao Dun's *The Midnight*, and Yu Da-fu's *Sinking*—are all characterized by helplessness and impotent rage.

To sum up, in the five stages of the ego's development, the child becomes increasingly aware of the harsh fact that he or she is not the centre of the world, nor is his or her ego "His Majesty"; the child's power is increasingly limited by the world with which he or she comes into closer and closer contact, until at the post-Oedipal stage, when the child's ego has fully developed, he or she feels ensnared within a social web woven with myriad restrictions. This maturational process of the ego corresponds in literary history with what Frye calls the downward movement of the fictive centre of gravity from the mythic mode through the romantic, high mimetic, and low mimetic modes to the ironic mode. It is testimony to the validity of the psychoanalytic theory that infantile development has left an indelible impact not only on the later development of the mature person, but also on the development of human endeavours like literature and arts.

Frye has observed a cyclic movement in Western literature: "Irony descends from the low mimetic: it begins in realism and dispassionate observation. But as it does so, it moves steadily towards myth, and dim outlines of sacrificial rituals and dying gods begin to reappear in it. Our five modes evidently go around in a circle. This reappearance of myth in the ironic is particularly clear in Kafka and in Joyce" (*AC*, 42). What is the motivating force behind such a movement? This is a subject beyond the reach of this paper, but I venture to suggest a possible answer: it may be an unconscious human wish for a return to the origin, where the child enjoys not just unconditional omnipotence, but a sense of serenity, of desirelessness: "The feeling that one has all that one wants, and that one has nothing left to wish for. [In the womb,] The fetus ... could maintain this of itself, for it always has what is necessary for the satisfaction of its instincts, and so has nothing to wish for; it is without wants."[23]

I have demonstrated that there is a parallel not only between Frye's theory of fictional modes and the phylogenesis of the reality sense in psychoanalysis but also between the ego's movement from pleasure principle to reality principle and the movement of literature. This parallel may have a universal significance because, as I have briefly indicated, Chinese literature, unrelated to Western literature, falls within the same pattern of development. Frye himself mentions only the first two epochs of Oriental literature, remarking, "Oriental fiction does not, so far as I know, get very far away from mythical and romantic formulas" (*AC*, 35). Nor, given his unfamiliarity with Oriental literatures, does he offer any elaboration of Oriental examples. In the remainder of this essay, I intend to explore this point further and to inquire into the universality of Frye's theory of fictional modes against the background of Chinese literature.

Chinese critics and readers since ancient times have, like Frye, liked to view a given literary work in terms of the hero's power of action. Sima Qian, the aforementioned Grand Scribe of the Han dynasty, who set the pattern of history writing for subsequent historians and who unconsciously pioneered Chinese historical fiction and traditional ways of characterization, organized his monumental work *Shi ji*, or the *Grand Scribe's Records*, around the life stories of important historical personages before and in his times. Chinese fiction continued to followed the same pattern of narration, centring on the personal history of a hero or anti-hero. The story of a hero was accorded so much prominence that we scarcely encounter a pre-modern Chinese novel in the Western sense of the word. Most are but a series of episodes strung together by the actions of a hero or heroine.

Scholars of Chinese fiction have, since Lu Xun's pioneering work, *A Brief History of Chinese Fiction*, adopted an historical and chronological approach to the division of fictional epochs. While simple, it is at the same time a "lazy" approach, as Lu Hsun himself called it. The division of Chinese fiction in accordance with the rise and fall of dynasties cannot adequately account for the inner mechanism of Chinese fictional development. Frye's theory of epochs may assist us in providing a new approach.

A collation of Chinese literary tradition with Frye's theory of historical modes and with the phylogenesis of the reality-sense informs us that Chinese literature, especially Chinese fiction, essentially follows the same pattern of development, with its major stages: (1) myths and legends; (2) tales of the supernatural, and prose romance; (3) historical romance; (4) fiction of manners and social satire; (5) modern fiction. Using Frye's theory of fictional modes, I venture to divide the history of Chinese fiction into five periods: the mythic mode, which includes early Chinese mythology and legends (1027 B.C.–220 A.D.) and the tales of the supernatural of the Six dynasties (222–589); romance, which includes the prose romance of the Tang (618–907) and Song (960–1279) dynasties; the high mimetic mode, which covers the historical romances of the Yuan (1260–1368) and Ming (1368–1644) dynasties; the low mimetic mode, which includes novels of manners and imitations of Song stories in the Ming dynasty; the ironic mode, which includes novels of social satire, novels of manners, novels of exposure, and imitation of classical tales in the Qing (1644–1911) dynasty.

Having divided the history of Chinese fiction into these five modes or stages, I have come to a better understanding of why previous scholars have been reluctant to adopt approaches other than the historical and chronological. The difficulty lies in the overlapping of fictional modes that has been succinctly summed up by Lu Xun in his pioneering study: "Many historians have told us that the history of mankind is evolutionary, and China naturally should be no exception. But when we look at the evolution of China we are struck by two peculiarities. One is that the old makes a comeback long after the new has appeared—in other words, retrogression. The other is that the old remains long after the new has appeared—in other words, amalgamation ... The same applies to literature, including fiction. For instance, today we still find dregs of the Tang and Sung dynasties in modern writing, or even the ideas and behaviour of primitive man."[24] This difficulty makes me feel more convinced of the circular pattern of literary movement. I agree that the return to an earlier mode will take place, but the recurrence depends largely on a psychologically circular mode. This is mainly because modern writers become more and more self-conscious in turning against the older modes and trends. Also, as the literary history of each nation reaches maturity, it will try to seek something new. "The New is not a fashion," says Roland Barthes, "it is a value, the basis of all criticism."[25] The search for something new may dislocate the orderly, circular recurrence of fictional modes, but psychologically the circular pattern remains. Science fiction in modern times is undoubtedly a modern form of ancient myths. *Star Trek*, the American TV series, has captivated viewers all over the world, partly because it provides a means to satisfy modern people's (un)conscious longing for the long-lost infantile hallucinatory sense of omnipotence.

Different nations and cultures have mental fixations on certain periods in their development. The writers of one nation may thus consciously or otherwise prefer one of the five modes, while the writers of another nation may prefer another of the fictional modes. According to my own observation, in Chinese literature up to modern times the most prestigious form was the lyric (one of Frye's thematic modes), while in the less esteemed genre of fiction the romantic mode was favoured. After the stage of the ironic mode was reached at the turn of the twentieth century, Chinese literature did not revert to the mythic mode; instead, the romantic mode seems to have dominated. In the period 1919–49, although realistic fiction in the high mimetic and low mimetic modes flourished for a considerable time, fiction of the romantic mode gradually gained the upper hand. This can be seen from the prevalence of popular romance and the so-called Mandarin Ducks and Butterfly fiction of the 1920s and '30s, the proletarian romance of the 1930s and '40s, Communist romance in the 1950s through the 1970s, and the modern romance in TV series and fiction of martial knights from the late 1970s to the present day.

Although Frye's theory of historical modes does not entirely fit Chinese literature, its universal significance is not to be doubted, as I have briefly illustrated with examples from Chinese literary history. The corresponding situation in Chinese literature seems to affirm that the developmental model in Frye's theory of fictional modes may perhaps be viewed as a hidden structural pattern in long-term human endeavours such as the movements of history, literature, art, civilization, and culture.[26]

NOTES

1 Bernard Paris, an American psychoanalytic critic, briefly suggests in his study of Jane Austen's novels that "The devices which a realistic writer uses to make his plots seem plausible and morally acceptable Frye calls 'displacement.' It is displacement also which accounts for the movement from mode to mode. This concept is taken from Freud, and Frye's reliance on it indicates that his system is not derived purely from an inductive survey of literature, as he claims. The conflict between the mythic and the mimetic impulses corresponds to the struggle between the pleasure principle and the reality principle, and the evolution of Western literature represents a series of stages in the development of the sense of reality." See *Character and Conflict in Jane Austen's Novels: A Psychological Approach* (Detroit: Wayne State University Press, 1978), 14.

2 Sigmund Freud, *Introductory Lectures on Psycho-analysis*, trans. and ed. James Strachey (New York: W.W. Norton, 1966), 357.

3 *The Freud Reader*, ed. Peter Gay (New York: W. W. Norton, 1989), 440–1.

4 For example, Melanie Klein affirms that the ego is present from birth. See Michael St Clair, *Object Relations and Self Psychology* (Monterey, Cal.: Brooks/Cole, 1986), 16 and 43.

5 St Clair, *Object Relations and Self Psychology*, 133.

6 Ibid., 70–1.

7 D.W. Winnicott, "Ego Distortion in Terms of True and False Self," in *The Maturational Processes and the Facilitating Environment* (New York: International Universities Press, 1960), 140–52.

8 For detailed information, please refer to Yuan Ke's *Ancient Chinese Mythology* (Beijing: Renmin wenxue chubanshe, 1962).

9 D.W. Winnicott, *Playing and Reality* (New York: Basic Books, 1971), 4–13.

10 *The Freud Reader*, 441.

11 In his study of early Chinese literature, Burton Watson gives a detailed account of how the Duke of Zhou justifies the overthrow of the previous dynasty with the concept of Heaven in *Shu jing*. See Watson's *Early Chinese Literature* (New York: Columbia University Press, 1962), 27–30.

12 Norman N. Holland, *The I* (New Haven: Yale University Press, 1985), 207.

13 See *Anthology of Chinese Literature*, ed. Cyril Birch (New York: Grove Press, 1965), 120.

14 Sandor Ferenczi, *Sex in Psycho-analysis*, trans. Ernest Jones (London: Hogath Press, 1963), 226.

15 Erik Erikson, *Childhood and Society* (New York: Norton, 1962), 87–8.

16 Holland, *The I*, 209.

17 Margaret S. Mahler, et al., *The Psychological Birth of the Human Infant: Symbiosis and Individuation* (New York: Basic Books, 1975), 80–95.

18 Holland, *The I*, 211.

19 Ibid., 210.

20 Jacques Lacan, *Écrits: A Selection*, trans. Alan Sheridan (New York: W.W. Norton, 1977), 24.

21 Ibid., 66–8.

22 Ibid., 286–90.

23 Ferenczi, *Sex in Psycho-analysis*, 219.

24 Lu Xun, *A Brief History of Chinese Fiction* (Beijing: Foreign Languages Press, 1979), 393.

25 Roland Barthes, *The Pleasure of the Text*, trans. Richard Miller (New York: Hill & Wang, 1975), 40.

26 Because of the limitations of space, my discussion of Chinese literature is very brief. For a detailed discussion, see Gu Mingdong, "The Genesis and Evolution of Literary Forms: An Inquiry Across Cultural Boundaries," *Tamkang Review* 27, 4 (1997): 443–76.

Frye Studies in China: A Selected Bibliography of Recent Works

All the following publications are in Chinese. In accordance with Chinese practice, inclusive page numbers are not given. The list, which was compiled by Ye Shuxian and Wang Ning, includes essays on Frye's theory and applications of it to Western and Chinese literature. For earlier essays and translations, see the paper by Ye in this volume.

Translations of Frye's Works

Frye, Northrop. *Anatomy of Criticism*. Trans. Chen Hui et al. Tianjin: Baihua Literature and Art Press, 1998. Revised by Wu Chizhe and annotated by Wu Chizhe and Robert D. Denham. Tiajin: Hundred-Flower Literary and Art Press, 2000.
- *The Critical Path*. Trans. Wang Fengzhen et al. Beijing: Peking University Press, 1998.
- *The Great Code*. Trans. Hao Zhenyi et al. Beijing: Peking University Press, 1998
- *The Modern Century.* Trans. Sheng Ning. Shenyang: Liaoning Educational Press, 1998; Hong Kong: Oxford University Press, 1998.
- *Selected Critical Essays of Northrop Frye*. Ed. Wu Chizhe. Beijing: China Social Sciences Publishing House, 1997.
Myth-Archetypal Criticism. Ed. Ye Shuxian. Xi'an: Shaanxi Normal University Press, 1987.

Critical Works

Chen Houcheng and Wang Ning, ed. *Contemporary Western Critical Theories in China*. Tianjin: Hundred-Flower Literary and Art Press, 2000.

Chen Jincheng. *Archetypal Criticism and Reinterpretation.* Beijing: Dongfang Press, 1998.

Wang Ning and Xu Yanhong, ed. *Frye Studies: China and the West.* Beijing: China Social Sciences Publishing House, 1996.

Ye Shuxian. *Exploring Literary Anthropology.* Guilin: Guangxi Normal University Press, 1998.

– *Exploring the Irrational World: The Theory and Method of Archetypal Criticism.* Chengdu: Sichuan People's Press, 1988.

Essays

Gu Hanyan. "On the Archetype in Joseph Conrad's Novels." *Journal of Yancheng Teachers' College* 1 (1992).

Ji Tong. "Three Myth Archetypes in Franz Kafka's Novels." *Journal of Hebei Normal University* 4 (1994).

Lin Xianghua. "Northrop Frye and His Myth-Archetypal Criticism." *Global Literature* 3 (1990).

Liu Jishen. "The Myth of the Grand Garden and the Archetype of the Mother." *Journal of the Humanities* 5 (1992).

Liu Lianxiang. "The Eden Myth in the Bible and the Archetype of the Mother." *Foreign Literature Review* 1 (1990).

Liu Xiaochun. "The Chinese Archetype of the Story of Cinderella and Its World Significance." *Chinese Culture Research* 1 (1997).

Li Yan. "An Archetypal Analysis of the Image of the Moon in Classical Chinese Poetry." *Journal of Shandong Education College* 5 (1996).

Lu Tan. "Myth-Archetypal Criticism in China." *Literature and Art Gazette* 21 September 1999.

Mao Yu. "The Displacement of Myth: Two Essays from an Archetypal Perspective on Folk Literature." *Journal of Henan* 1 (1991).

Ma Xiaochao. "On the Archetype." *Studies of Literature and Art* 2 (1987).

Sheng Ning. "Criticism of Criticism: On Frye's Myth-Archetypal Criticism." *Foreign Literature Review* 1 (1990).

Sun Hong. "The Archetypal Significance of Lin Daiyu and Xue Baocai." *Journal on The Dream of the Red Mansion* 3 (1997).

Tian Zuhai. "On the Archetype and Typology of the Goddess Zigu." *Journal of Hubei University* 1 (1997).

Wang Ning. "Northrop Frye as a Pioneering Figure of Contemporary Cultural Studies." *Foreign Literatures* 3 (2001).

– "On Northrop Frye." *Literature and Art Gazette,* 23 September 1993.

Wang Xiaochu. "On the Archetypal Imagery of 'Wild Grass.'" *Journal of Sichuan University* 1 (1992).

Wan Shuyuan. "On the Evil Archetype in Literature." *Foreign Literature Review* 1 (1990).

Wu Gongzheng. "The Aesthetics of Archetype: the Aesthetics of *Book of Poetry* and *Lisao*." *Jianghan Forum* 12 (1989).

Yang Rui. "The Archetype of the Mother in *Liaozai Zhiyi*." *Literature, History and Philosophy* 1 (1997).

Ye Shuxian. "The Archetype and Chinese Characters." *Journal of Peking University* 2 (1995).

– "Frye and New Historicist Cultural Studies," in *Chinese and Foreign Culture and Criticism*. Chengdu: Sichuan University Press, 1996.

– "Frye's Literary Anthropological Thinking," in *Toward a New Age of Comparative Literature*. Chengdu: Sichuan People's Press, 2000.

– "Myth-Archetypal Criticism in China." *Studies of Social Sciences* 2 (1999).

– "The Theory and Practice of Myth-Archetypal Criticism." *Journal of Shaanxi Normal University* 2–3 (1986).

Zhang Chengquan. "The Archetypal Significance of the Genre *Dunhuang Bianwen*." *Journal of Yindu* 3 (1992).

Zhang Deming. "On the Myth-Archetypal Mode of Blake's Poetry." *Foreign Literature Review* 1 (1990).

Zhang Jie. "The Hermeneutic Definition of the Archetype." *Journal of Hubei Minority College* 1 (1997).

– "The Three Levels of an Archetypal Interpretation." *Studies of Literature and Art* 5 (1996).

Zhao Linghe. "The Influence of Myth-Archetype on Chinese and Western Romanticist Literature." *Forum on Folk Literature* 2 (1997).

Zhou Jianzhong. "Xiao Bing's Studies of Chuci and Frye's Archetypal Criticism." *Journal of Huaiyin Teachers' College* 4 (1996).

Zhu Diguang. "The Archetype and Three Ancient Chinese Classics." *Journal of Hengyang Teachers' College* 5 (1996).

JEAN O'GRADY

Epilogue

This volume, based largely on the Chinese reception of Frye, provides a double mirror: the West and its critical theory is reflected in China, and China reflects back to the West the use it has made of it. We have preserved this shape by opening with an introduction from the Chinese perspective by Wang Ning, and closing with some reflections from my point of view as a Western scholar. If the Eastern scholars are in one sense the recipients as they learn more about Frye, in another sense the little band of Canadian scholars who arrived in Hoh-Hot were the learners. The sights and sounds of China, the intellectual excitement, the overwhelming hospitality—the whole strange and unlikely phenomenon of coming to Inner Mongolia to confer about Northrop Frye—these are with us still, and are still being assimilated.

A Canadian student of Frye, accustomed to a certain lack of enthusiasm for her specialty on the part of academics (though not among the general population) at home, cannot but be delighted at the interest taken in Frye at the present time in China. Delighted, but at the same time bemused: what is it about Frye that particularly appeals to such a different culture? Conference host Wu Chizhe, when questioned about this, pointed out that the interest in Frye was but part of a desire to investigate a broad range of Western thinkers—deconstructionists, cultural theorists, reception theorists, new historicists, and so on—in the new climate of openness. Undoubtedly this is true, yet Frye nonetheless seems to have an influence disproportionate to his place in the current literary scene, where his admirers are fervent but few. No other Western theorist, I believe, has been the subject of two conferences in China.

One aspect of Frye (mentioned first merely to dispose of it) that seems relevant is his predilection for numbered lists and schematic diagrams. Not only does this method give his thought a particular clarity and "graspability" missing from that of his more amorphous colleagues, but it seems to answer to something in the Eastern mind: examples could be found from Buddha's Four Noble Truths to the Four Modernizations of recent campaigns. The primary concerns of *Words with Power*, divided neatly into four groups, each with its material and spiritual aspect (as discussed in Glen Gill's essay) illustrate this kind of schematization. Obviously such pattern-making does not pretend to mirror the actual number of our needs, but must be judged by its utility in the widest sense, mnemonic, aesthetic, or symbolic. One can imagine the "four spiritual concerns" becoming more widely cited in China than in the West. Certainly it is notable that no aspect of Frye's theory, apart from the archetypes themselves, has been more accepted and applied by Chinese students than the five descending stages of the hero at the opening of the *Anatomy*.

There is also the fact that there are some thirty centres of Canadian studies in China. China and Canada share many aspects, such as geographical extent (though not a range of time zones, which we were surprised to learn do not exist in China), proximity to another large power, and the presence of cultural minorities. What then could be more natural than the Chinese interest in Canada's premier literary critic and cultural theorist, the advocate of cultural diversity within a larger political unit?

Archetypal theory has a more complex relationship with Chinese culture. Both Wu and Ye note that its aspirations of universality harmonize with the Chinese tendency to favour the collective over the individual. Classical Chinese literature, as Wang Ning points out, is in one sense well suited to this approach, because of its strongly formalist nature and respect for ancestral stories. It exemplifies, more clearly than many literatures do, Frye's contention that poems are made out of other poems. But in another sense, what is notable about Chinese culture is the apparent absence of myth. Wu argues that Confucius and Confucian scholars historicized and rationalized myths; Ye suggests that the traditional attitude was one of "Don't talk about mysterious forces or worship weird gods"; graduate students at the conference, to the amazement of the Western participants, maintained that China had no "earth mother" myth. But Ye's paper also testifies to the sense of liberation with which, in scholarly circles at least, the mythical roots of Chinese culture are being rediscovered. This phenomenon helps to explain the eager reception of Frye's early work, especially the *Anatomy*, and the embracing of "myth-archetypal criticism," to use the usual Chinese term.

It may be, in fact, that Frye's theory has entered China in too close conjunction with the work of other myth theorists, such as anthropologists and Jungians, for its distinctiveness to be truly appreciated: Ye's paper certainly leaves this impression. Frye, always sensitive to accusations of taking the term "archetype" from Jung, insisted on the independence of criticism from these other disciplines. He stressed that his myths and archetypes depend neither on a collective unconscious nor on a pre-literary past; rather, they are found in the structure of literature itself, and are disseminated through culture. To put it another way, the meaning of a myth for Frye resides not in some hypothetical original version but rather in what the poets have made of it.

This being so, the extent of the literature surveyed becomes a crucial factor. It remains to be seen to what extent Frye's findings will be able to illuminate a literature as different as the Chinese. The question is particularly interesting in regard to the great structures he discerned: both the "circle of mythoi" or pre-generic types of comedy, romance, tragedy, and irony, and the specific genres. According to Wu, comedy and tragedy are not generally recognized literary genres in China, while a conference paper read by graduate student Liu Yongnan highlighted the lack of an epic in Chinese literature proper. So far, this generic aspect of Frye's theory has not been widely investigated in China. Even the absence of four distinct seasons in some parts of the world might call into question the universality of his schema. As the work proceeds, perhaps what will emerge is a taxonomy of Chinese literature inspired by Frye but conscious of divergences.

Another aspect of Frye's thought that is sure to be more widely studied in the East as texts become available is his social and cultural criticism. As Wang suggests, aspects of Frye's work can be revisioned as postmodern or postcolonial. This is particularly true of his previously unpublished personal writings—diaries and notebooks—which will undoubtedly lead to a complete revaluation. As these are only now making their way into print even in Canada, however, it is too early to speak much of them. But *The Critical Path* and *The Great Code* have been translated into Chinese as part of the Northrop Frye Studies series, and *Words with Power* is soon to be included in the same series. Along with shorter works and speeches (some of which have also been translated), they offer insights into such far-reaching topics as the role of intellectuals in society, the relation of culture to human needs, the notion of human betterment, and the very nature of mankind as a civilization-building and language-using species.

As with literature, however, a cultural divide is apparent. Frye repeatedly stressed that all perceptions are shaped by an "envelope" of language and thought-systems. The imaginative universe he explores in his last books is derived from the structure and imagery of the Bible, the chief such envelope in the West. It will be interesting to see what Chinese critics, and others from non-Bible-based societies, will find germane in these works. English-speaking scholars of Frye will benefit enormously when such studies are translated into English, helping to reveal the extent to which a radically different language and mythology alters the articulation of desire and primary need.

As early as 1947, in reviewing F.S.C. Northrop's *Meeting of East and West*, Frye anticipated the current debate on globalization. He noted that while internationalism was acceptable in politics and economics, cultures were more local: "There is no earthly reason why the world should be culturally federalized" (*NFCL*, 109). Criticism and other scholarly disciplines are more portable than the cultures they study, but still retain some local specificity. Even in so mundane a sphere as scholarly editing, we have found during the course of producing this volume, there are differences of approach and assumption. But the fact that the volume has appeared, and that the editors remain colleagues at the end of the process, is itself a testimony to the possibility of cross-cultural dialogue. We hope that this book will further such dialogue and encourage Frye studies in an international arena, with the aim, as Frye might put it, not of uniformity but of a more valuable unity.